NAGAS AS A SOCIETY AGAINST VOTING

and other essays

Jelle J.P. Wouters

http://www.highlanderbooks.org

Highlander Books – Kohima
The Kohima Institute
Kohima, Nagaland 797003

Highlander Books – Thimphu
Royal Thimphu College
PO Box 1122, Ngabiphu, Bhutan

Highlander Books – Edinburgh
C/o Arkotong Longkumer
New College, Mound Place, Edinburgh
United Kingdom EH1 2LX

© 2019 Jelle J.P. Wouters
© 2019 Highlander Books

The text of this book is licensed under a Creative Commons Attribution-NonCommercial-NoDerivatives 4.0 International license (CC BY-NC-ND 4.0). This license allows you to share, copy, distribute and transmit the work for non-commercial purposes, providing attribution is made to the author (but not in any way that suggests that he/she endorses you or your use of the work). Attribution should include the following information:

Author surname, Author initial. Chapter title. In *Nagas as a society against voting: and other essays*. Kohima, Thimphu, Edinburgh: Highlander Books.

To access detailed and updated information on the license, please visit http://www.highlanderbooks.org/index.php/home/about

Further details about CC BY-NC-ND licenses are available at https://creativecommons.org/licenses/by-nc-nd/4.0/

ISBN: 978-0-578-52110-7
Library of Congress Control Number: 2019946522

Cover image by Zhoto Tunyi
Design and layout by Alina Ronghangpi
Typeset in Gaudy Old Style by Prepress Plus

To my parents

CONTENTS

List of illustrations vii
Foreword ix

Chapter 1   Nagas as a 'Society against Voting?'
Consensus-Building, Party-less Politics and a
Culturalist Critique of Elections in Northeast India   1

Chapter 2   Sovereignty, Integration or Bifurcation?
Troubled Histories, Contentious Territories,
and the Political Horizons of the Long Lingering
Naga Movement   21

Chapter 3   Polythetic Democracy: Tribal Elections,
Bogus Votes, and Political Imagination in the
Naga uplands   41

Chapter 4   The Making of Tribes: The Chang and
Chakhesang Nagas   65

Chapter 5   Performing Democracy in Nagaland:
'Past Polities' and 'Present Politics'   83

Chapter 6   Difficult Decolonization: Debates, Divisions,
and Deaths Within the Naga Uprising, 1944–1963   101

Chapter 7	Genealogies of Nagaland's 'Tribal Democracy'	133
Chapter 8	Land Tax, Reservation for Women, and Customary Law in Nagaland	149
Chapter 9	Feasts of Merit, Election Feasts, or No Feasts? On the Politics of Wining and Dining in Nagaland	159
Chapter 10	What Makes a Good Politician? Democratic Representation, 'Vote-Buying', and the MLA Handbook in Nagaland	175
Chapter 11	The Fieldworker Imagined Among the Nagas	197
Endnotes		211
References		233
Index		253

LIST OF ILLUSTRATIONS

Image 1.   Clan-meeting in Phugwumi
           (Photo by the author)

Image 2.   Frontier Nagaland banner on the façade of a shop in Noksen Town
           (Photo by the author)

Image 3.   Villagers lined up for voting in Phugwumi amidst the presence of security forces
           (Photo by Zhoto Tunyi)

Image 4.   View of Noksen village
           (Photo by the author)

Image 5.   Polling Day in Phugwumi
           (Photo by the author)

Image 6.   'Underground' and 'Overground' Politics: NNC calendar and NPF flag
           (Photo by the author)

Image 7.   View of Phugwumi village
           (Photo by the author)

Image 8.   Traditional warrior dance
           (Photo by Zhoto Tunyi)

Image 9.   Megaliths erected in honour of a feast-giver in Phugwumi
           (Photo by the author)

Image 10. Clean Election Campaign banner in Phugwumi
           (Photo by the author)

Image 11. Marriage feast in the church compound in Phugwumi
           (Photo by the author)

FOREWORD

The essays in this volume were written over the course of the last five years. They engage a range of subjects, and each can be read on its own, as an independent essay. They, however, converge on certain broad themes and together amount to a treatise on politics and society in Nagaland. I have, for the most part, left the essays in the form in which they originally appeared, although I have sought to correct any errors where appropriate. Consequently, there is some repetition in the observations, arguments, and theoretical overtures between some of the essays, but this could not be avoided without affecting the coherence and contexts of the particular arguments I pursue in each independent essay.

Besides a broad thematic convergence, the essays also share a methodological coherence in the sense that they are predominantly shaped by ethnography — both as a research method and written form — often spiked with oral and archival histories that contextualize my narratives and arguments. The essays that follow are firmly grounded in the historical experiences and ethnographic specifics of Naga society. At the same time, however, I have tried to speak about larger issues and approaches in the study of democracy and elections, kinship and tribes, and the politics of place and identity. As such, I hope this collection is of interest both to those interested in the specifics of contemporary Naga society and to scholars of Highland Asia, India, political anthropology, and conceptual politics and sociology more widely.

A good deal has been written about the Nagas for the past 150 years or so, interrupted, though, by a decades-long hiatus in scholarship after the withdrawal of imperial forces from South Asia and relatedly the eruption of the Indo-Naga conflict that made carrying out research near impossible and in any case secondary to more immediate concerns about life and survival. Among the many writings on Nagas — ranging from colonial monographs to contemporary coffee-table books — the ethnographic genre remains underrepresented, even as a few excellent monographs published in recent years, and several others currently being drafted, are making significant strides in narrowing this gap. The nevertheless still limited availability of contemporary ethnographic accounts of Nagas constitutes a real lack because ethnography and anthropology is based on an intimate knowledge through fieldwork, i.e. it provides a view from below written by people who actually spend their time with the communities they are studying, and is therefore best placed to discuss themes and issues based on the lived experiences, perspectives, and social practices of 'ordinary' Naga men and women. Among Nagas, I found that these local and lived experiences are often very different from what we are told about them by more detached political and historical treatises which predominantly rely on secondary sources (even as these undoubtedly stand by their own merit) and that have long dominated scholarship locally.

The research that informs these essays was carried out between 2011 and 2014. Most of my fieldwork, about fourteen months, ensued in a Chakhesang Naga village I call Phugwumi in my writings, and which translates as 'old village.' Phugwumi is a pseudonym, although readers well acquainted with the Chakhesang Naga will probably not find it very hard to identify the real place and name of this village. Another eight months or so I spent in the Chang Naga village of Noksen in what is now called 'eastern' Nagaland. I place 'eastern' within hyphens here as ideas of place and peoples encompassed by this term have seemingly moved westward in recent decades. Compare, for instance, the territorial stretch of the (now defunct) Eastern Naga Revolutionary Council (ENRC), established in the mid-1960s, with that of the more recently formed Eastern Naga People's Organisation (ENPO). While both organizations claim to represent 'eastern' Nagas, for the ENRC this meant those Naga communities that reside on the Burmese / Myanmar side of the border while the ENPO interprets 'eastern' as encompassing those Naga tribes that remained outside the immediate pale of colonial administration but were administratively amalgamated with 'western' Naga tribes – those who were part of the colonial Naga Hills District – after Nagaland state was created within the Indian Union in the year 1963. As such, the idea of 'eastern Nagas' as residing within Nagaland is of recent invention and best explained as the result of nascent administrative and political developments and aspirations.

The village settings of my fieldwork lent itself to the classic ethnographic model of participant observation in the Malinowskian sense, keeping in mind, however, that 'the locus of study is not the object of study. Anthropologists don't study villages (tribes, towns, neighbourhoods...); they study in villages' (Geertz 1973: 22). I also carried out a large number of formal and informal interviews, both inside the two villages and in urban centres across the state (the last essay in this book offers a few reflections on carrying out fieldwork in Nagaland). But even as 'urban voices' run through several of the essays, the arguments I pursue are probably better attuned to social and political life in rural Nagaland compared to its urban counterparts. In trying to grasp the texture and tide of village life I had many extended conversations with villagers of all ages, genders, and professional backgrounds, including farmers, village leaders, pastors and deacons, government servants, party-workers, and politicians. In both villages I resided with a family, an extended family in Phugwumi and a nuclear family in Noksen. This was not only an unforgettable experience, but, in terms of methodology, helped me to swiftly integrate and better grasp the flow and intricacies of village life, as seen and experienced through the conduit of a family.

Oftentimes I sought out village elders, who have lived through decades of political upheaval and dramatic social change, and spoke with them for hours, often while sitting around the hearth. Their accounts of the past, including memories of colonial officers, intervillage feuds, the onset of the Naga struggle, and the enactment of Nagaland state were rich and revealing, as well as often very different from 'official' versions. The accumulated wisdom, lived experiences, and viewpoints of village elders gave me a broader perspective, while also allowing me to conceptualize how distinctive Naga historical experiences – both embodied and emplaced – continue to have a significant bearing on the shape social and political life takes in the present.

My rationale to study two villages, located at opposite sides of the state, instead of one village (as was long common to traditional fieldwork in anthropology), was guided by the hope, first, to formulate findings and arguments that may be of a more generalized character and, secondly, to be able to draw comparisons and contrasts between places and communities within Nagaland. As such, I have aimed to be both attentive to similarities and differences within the Naga ethnographic field. All the same, it may be immediately and justifiably objected that the essays that comprise this book remain inherently partial (if seen, that is, as a treatise on Naga society as a whole) as they primarily focus on the historical experiences, cultural proclivities, and political socialities of Naga communities within Nagaland and do not say a great deal about Naga communities that reside in Manipur, Arunachal Pradesh, and Assam. They say even less about Nagas living across the border with Myanmar. It is nevertheless my hunch that my arguments and approaches are not altogether off the mark to understand the intricacies, inner-logic, and indeterminacies of social and political life among Nagas residing outside the arbitrary confines of Nagaland state.

When I started my fieldwork, the Indo-Naga ceasefire was in its fourteenth year. Political dialogues between NSCN-IM leaders and interlocutors of the Indian Government were held intermittently in Delhi, but there was still little sign of a political settlement, apart, that is, from never ending rumours. It was also a time in which occasional factional clashes took place, attempts at inter-factional reconciliation were made, and a time that witnessed rising civil discontentment both with factional divides and regimes of taxation put in place by Naga underground groups, as well as with the disposition of sections of Naga underground cadres, or 'national workers' as they are referred to locally.

Significantly also, my fieldwork coincided with the 2013 Nagaland state legislative assembly elections. The ways villagers spoke to one another about politicians and parties, the political practices and principles they adhered to, and the larger vision of 'the political' they articulated are central to several of the essays that follow. On studying elections ethnographically, the famous anthropologist M.N. Srinivas (2002: 11) wrote: 'When it is necessary to get data from opposing groups, as happens during campaigns, the fieldworker may have no choice but to give each side the impression that he is with them. Judging by strict moral standards this is no doubt wrong, but it is difficult to avoid.' I, however, found Srinivas' approach somewhat problematic, and instead I made it clear, when asked by villagers where my political leanings lay, that I had no such leanings, and that neither was there any need for me to favour a candidate or party given that I was not entitled to cast my vote in the first place.

Studying the ways in which elections are performed and talked about at the village level made me realise, for one thing, how global and normative theories of democracy and elections become socially mediated and adapted, as well as interpreted afresh, into pre-existent historical conditions, moral values, and cultural dispositions. Instead of Naga villagers adjusting themselves to the modern democratic ideals and principles, it did not take me long to realise that they were adjusting democracy and elections to their own lifeworlds and uses. It also made me see a discrepancy between liberal democracy's hallmark of party-based elections, individual autonomy and equal voting rights, and Nagas' own normative sense of the good political life that is shaped by values of communal harmony, consensus-building, and complimentary coexistence. This argument is worked out in the next chapter.

All essays published in this volume are reproduced here with permission. Chapter 1, 'Nagas as a "Society against Voting?"': Consensus-Building, Party-Less Politics and a Culturalist Critique of Elections in Northeast India' first appeared in *The Cambridge Journal of Anthropology* 36(2): 113-132. Chapter 2, 'Sovereignty, Integration or Bifurcation? Troubled Histories, Contentious Territories and the Political Horizons of the Long Lingering Naga Movement', was published in *Studies in History* 32(1): 97-116, in a special issue on Northeast India edited by Willem van Schendel and Joy Pachuau. Next, 'Polythetic Democracy: Tribal Elections, Bogus Votes, and

Political Imagination in the Naga Uplands' was published in *HAU: Journal of Ethnographic Theory* 5(2): 121-151. Chapter 4, 'The Making of Tribes: the Chang and Chakhesang Nagas in India's Northeast', was originally published in *Contributions to Indian Sociology* 51(1): 79-104. Chapter 5, 'Performing Democracy in Nagaland: Past Polities and Present Politics' was published in *Economic and Political Weekly* 49(16): 59-67. The chapter that follows, 'Difficult Decolonization: Debates, Divisions, and Deaths Within the Naga Uprising, 1944-1963' was first published in the *Journal of North-East India Studies* 9(1): 1-28, Chapter 7, 'Genealogies of Nagaland's Tribal Democracy' first appeared in *Economic and Political Weekly* 53(24): 41-47. Next, chapter 8, 'Land-Tax, Reservation for Women, and Customary Law in Nagaland' was written as commentary for *Economic and Political Weekly* 52(9): 20-23. Next follows 'Feasts of Merit, Election Feasts, or No Feasts? On the Politics of Wining and Dining in Nagaland' and originally appeared in *The South-Asianist* 3(2): 5-23. Chapter 10 is titled: 'What Makes a Good Politician: Democratic Representation, "Vote-Buying", and the MLA Handbook in Nagaland' and was first published in *South Asia: Journal of South-Asian Studies* 41(4): 806-826. The final essay, 'The Fieldworker Imagined among Nagas' first appeared in a volume edited by Queenbala Marak titled: *Doing Authoethnography* and was published by *Serials publications* in Delhi, pages 303-323.

All the essays in this volume have gained immensely from the comments and criticisms of colleagues and friends. I would especially like to thank T.B. Subba, Arkotong Longkumer, Willem van Schendel, Michael Heneise, Edward Moon-Little, Zhoto Tunyi, Vibha Joshi, Neichute Doulo, Philippe Ramirez, Leishipem Khamrang, Roderick Wijunamai and Kühüpoyo Puro. I also thank my student Karma Pem Dema for helping me compile these essays. My greatest debt, as ever, is to the Phugwumi and Noksen villagers who so graciously and warmly welcomed me into their lives, shared their stories with me, and helped me in all possible ways. To them, I will always remain grateful.

Jelle J.P. Wouters
Thimphu, March 2019

01

NAGAS AS A 'SOCIETY AGAINST VOTING?'

Consensus-Building, Party-less Politics and a Culturalist Critique of Elections in Northeast India

INTRODUCTION

It was potentially scandalous that while voters lined up behind polling booths in the village of Phugwumi, someone wrote the following phrase in the dusty rear window of a nearby parked car: 'Election is an insult to each other by vote'. Phugwumi is a Chakhesang Naga hilltop village located in the tribal highlands of Nagaland in India's 'remote' Northeast. It was polling day for the 2013 Nagaland State Legislative Assembly elections, marking the final episode of weeks and months of frenzied and ferocious electoral politicking in the village. *Athe* (a Chokri term for 'grandfather') expressed his relief that the election season was finally coming to a close. Seated on the portico of his bamboo-walled house, he told me as we sat down for an interview:

> During elections people stop talking to each other, not even saying so much as *'telezüme?'* ['roaming?'[1]] when they pass each other by. Money, greed, whiskies, and no one willing to listen and think what's best for our village. It is shameful. Elections have made our villagers worse!

For Athe, as for most Phugwumi elders, the amoral and self-centred activities of political life, especially in times of elections, were a cause of great concern and frustration. With nostalgic yearning, elders spoke about a time before political parties and elections, when village life was less divided, cooperation more commonplace, and village leaders mature, wise and selfless (*müphrümüvo*).

The pre-electoral era was one that could be remembered vividly because formal democracy arrived comparatively late in the Naga uplands. Seeing the state of India as an invading and colonizing force, the Naga National Council (NNC) resisted and rebelled against incorporation into postcolonial India from the mid 1950s onwards, and successfully boycotted India's first general elections in 1952 and then again in 1957.[2] Earlier, during the colonial era, the (then) Naga Hills District was designated first as a 'backward tract' and then as an 'excluded area'; the 'privileges' of voting for the Imperial Legislative Council and Provincial Council were not extended to either such territories. Consequently, it was only in 1964 — a year after the establishment of the Nagaland state as an envisaged (but failed) political compromise to the NNC demand for independence — that political parties, voting slips and ballot boxes came to impact Naga villages.[3]

But although elections became both regular and participatory in the years following statehood, their societal effects were deemed to be destructive to a pre-existent, culturally inflected 'moral society'. Akio Tanabe (2007: 560) describes such a 'moral society' as a vernacular space 'in which morally desirable human relationships rather than individual rights or political gains are at issue'. What legal and procedural codes of representative democracy and party politics disrupted was the communitarian and political commensality of village life, whose ideals of communal harmony, consensus-building and complimentary coexistence (while not always achieved in practice) were seen as foundational of the good social and political life. Party politics and elections divided and unsettled this traditional *Gemeinschaft* — of the village as a reciprocal community with shared concerns and ends. This experienced societal downfall, at the hands of electoral politics, led a Nagaland minister to propose, on the floor of the State Assembly, that the election system be reformed, since it undermined 'the Naga way of life' (cited in Ao 1993: 211). It also led at least two Nagaland Chief Ministers to espouse that elections would best be done away with altogether, while Naga intellectuals widely agreed that 'party politics has destroyed the harmony of Naga society' (Nuh 1986: 201).

Similar critiques surfaced in the wake of the 2013 state elections, with the locally commanding Nagaland Baptist Church Council (NBCC) singling out elections as 'the biggest force that is eroding the moral foundations as well as the future of the Naga people' (NBCC 2012), and the Chakhesang

Public Organisation (CPO), the tribe's apex body of which Phugwumi is a constituent village, warning:

> It is time to realise that evil practices associated with electoral politics are destroying the good traditional system of our Naga Democracy, the system, which would regard the opponents as worthy and the integrity of everyone would be safeguarded as the rival groups disagree with one another. (*Morung Express* 19-01-2013)

This so-declared 'good traditional system' of 'Naga Democracy' invoked the communitarian ethos and ethics of the pre-state Naga village (Bendangjungshi 2012: 124; Biswas and Suklabaidya 2008: 184; Thong 2014: 158) where 'the collective life took precedence over the individual' (Sema 1986: 10). Any such submission of individual autonomy to village collective life was not generally experienced as forced or repressive, but was part of the ontology of a moral society, and its embedded individual self.

However, this Naga moral society was nonetheless also a 'democratic' one. Naga villages, British civil and military officers observed, 'are thoroughly democratic communities' (Davis [1851] 1969: 324), 'decidedly democratical' (Moffatt-Mills [1854] 1980: xclii), a democracy in its 'extreme' (Hutton 1965: 23), constituting 'a form of the purest democracy' (John Butler, cited in Hutton 1921: 143). Postcolonial scholars similarly characterize the prototypical 'Naga village' as a 'republic' (Vashum 2000: 59), 'ultra-republican' (Kumar 2005: 12), even as the very 'symbol of the republic' (Singh 2004: 12). This home-grown 'Naga democracy', the argument goes, became ruptured and shattered by the arrival of formal, liberal democracy. Udayon Misra (1987: 2193) wrote, 'Nagas always prided themselves as honest and straightforward people', then quoting A. Z. Phizo (who had captained the NNC in its struggle for Naga independence): 'We believe in that form of democratic government which permits the rule not of the majority but of the people as a whole.'[4] Misra continued: 'Anyone even marginally acquainted with the politics of Nagaland would agree that this idyllic picture has undergone a radical transformation'(ibid).

Even allowing for romanticized flagrancies, what remains is that among Nagas, the arrival of political parties, competitive elections and individual and equal voting rights is widely experienced as corrosive and corruptive of an earlier political sociality and moral society that was at once cherished and conceived of as decidedly democratic. Both empirically and theoretically, especially in the light of (normative) democratic theory, this is where the apprehension lies.

4 ■ Nagas as a society against voting

THE MAKING (AND UNMAKING) OF 'MAN THE VOTER'

If the local equation between voting and levying insults is potentially a scandalous one, it is because the act of voting in free and competitive elections is seen as the epitome of political maturity and modernity. Most liberal political theorists contend that casting one's vote is not a mere technicality, which constructs democratic knowledge and authority (cf. Coles 2004), but is rather an emancipatory performance. Voting is seen as 'the most signal emblem of full citizenship in the modern age' (Anderson 1996: 13), and connotative of a universalistic philosophy of individual autonomy and choice, political equality, freedom and rightful self-expression (Comaroff and Comaroff 1997). Competitive elections are further conceived as the only process from which a representative and accountable government can emerge, while they simultaneously serve as a potent reminder that 'power' ultimately resides with 'the people'.

Ideally, in a clean and neatly orchestrated election campaign, contesting parties and candidates clearly articulate their visions, public policies and ideological positions. Electors then individually and autonomously evaluate the merits and demerits of the various positions, propositions and promises made, and on polling day, one may then freely cast a secret ballot. Even as classical anthropological scholarship has long shown how personhood is always and everywhere tied up in social relations (Carrithers et al. 1985; Mauss [1938] 1985), the modern 'man the voter' is superficially stripped from such sociality as he or she is expected to behave as an 'enlightened' and '"enchanted" individual self' (Gilmartin 2012: 411), well adept and ever desirous to deliberate political life in a rational, reflexive and detached manner, as though 'living within society yet standing outside it' (ibid.: 417).

Of course, individual voting based on political parties is just one aspect of a well-oiled democracy, yet competitive elections are 'what most people understand by democracy' (Nash 2004: 194), and in today's global promenade of liberal democracies, free, regular and participatory elections have become the benchmark for most evaluations about how far any democracy flourishes or falters. The contemporary sprawling of liberal democracies notwithstanding, authoritative configurations of 'man the voter' have not been deemed universal for very long. But whereas earlier political theorists and politicians could discuss whether a particular country or place was equipped for democracy and elections, in consideration of varying cultures, historical trajectories and economic conditions, the biggest achievement of the twentieth century, says Amartya Sen, is that a country no longer needs 'to be deemed fit *for* democracy: rather, it has to become fit *through* democracy (1999: 3–4, emphases in original). Consequently, in places whose governments or peoples do not inherently subscribe to norms of elections, or fail to behave as rational and detached voters, such standards presumably ought to be fostered by investing in their *civic culture* (Almond and Verba 1963) and 'political cultural orientation' (Tessler and Gao 2009: 197), based on the liberal maxim that 'politics can change a culture and save it from itself' (Daniel Patrick Moynihan, cited in Huntington 2000: xiv).

Among democratic projects worldwide, India draws special attention, not just because it is the world's largest democracy, but for the democratic and electoral enthusiasm reported all across the nation. Nonetheless, rather than seeing such enthusiasm as the internalization of liberal values, scholars increasingly perceive India's electoral effervescence as evidence of the socially enmeshed, 'territorial' (Witsoe 2009) and 'vernacular' (Michelutti 2007) character of Indian democracy. Across India, democratic practices, Lucia Michelutti (2007: 642) writes, 'have been gradually moulded by folk understandings of "the political" which in turn energize popular politics'. However, India too has its liberalist guards, even as their arguments allow for contextual and cultural frames. Mukulika Banerjee (2014), in *Why India Votes*, explains that Indians vote in large numbers, not because they necessarily expect that an elected government will significantly improve their material welfare, but because elections emerged as 'aesthetic and ritual moments' that promote 'egalitarianism' and 'communitas' as they transcend, even if only momentarily, the deep everyday divisions of caste, class and gender (ibid.: 172). The meaning that ordinary people attach to voting, and the often festive manner in which votes are cast, Banerjee continues, is because voting itself has become understood as a sacrosanct act that encodes 'principles of equality, fairness, efficiency, rights, and duties, all of which are valued ideals' (ibid.: 169).

The remainder of this essay reflects on a very different political context and culture. Most Nagas do not perceive of voting as a celebration of liberalist values, or see it as a sacred duty, but experience it as corrosive of culturalist projections of the good civil and political life. Drawing on ethnography and historical research among Chakhesang Nagas, I postulate that competitive, party-based elections, individual autonomy and equal voting rights are not culturally neutral exercises, but, among Chakhesangs, dissipate and disserve a pre-existent communitarian and democratic heritage. The analysis of this essay does not undermine democracy as an ideal, a spirit or an aspiration, but I do see as provincial – as a reflection (and reflective) of the Enlightenment project (Sahlins 1999) – its current working model: liberal, electoral democracy. Despite its universalistic pretensions, John Dunn (2014: 3) writes, 'liberal democracy does not offer all things to all persons, since all human beings continue to vary widely in their tastes and prejudices and no set of arrangements could satisfy all of them all the time.'

What I offer, in the pages that follow, is neither a grand communitarian theory, as a counter-discourse to liberalism, nor a rustic 'arcadian space' (Shah 2010: 190), but a cosmopolitan culturalist critique against the universalization of a particular and provincial moral and democratic sense. To do so, I situate Phugwumi villagers' political reasoning and attempt to substitute individual voting with collective consensus-making in both the ethnographic *longue durée* and the vernacular, by approaching the form and substance of the enduring political ethos of the prototypical Naga 'village republic' (Wouters 2017a). Next, I focus more broadly on how such past political practices and principles resurfaced as a culturalist critique – and an answer to this critique – of competitive elections. In the process, I reason alongside those Naga elders, intellectuals and even some career politicians 'who have come to realise the evils of the party system and are seriously considering how best to salvage the traditional village unity' (Dev 1988: 27). What they envisage, I will illustrate, is an operational, culturally modulated democracy shaped by consensus-building and selecting leaders. This leads me, in the conclusion, to postulate Nagas as a 'society against voting', an adaptation of Pierre Clastres' (1977) *Society against the State*.

THE QUEST FOR A PRE-POLLING CONSENSUS CANDIDATE

Polling day was still several months away, but Phugwumi was already humming with talk about politics and politicians. State-wise, the Naga People's Front (NPF), which had ruled the state since 2003, sought to complete a hat-trick of electoral victories. The constituency's sitting Member of the Legislative Assembly belonged to the ruling government but with two former ministers and a promising political newcomer also joining the election fray, the constituency's seat was spoken of as especially competitive, and in the wake of polling day, supporters of all four candidates had reasons to believe they were in the driving seat.

While the theme of politics frequently cropped up in the everyday conversations of the villagers, what they discussed and shared did not usually concern party manifestos, public policies or left-centre-right political ideologies. These were not the substance of electoral politics locally. In Phugwumi, akin to places across the subcontinent, 'party ideology was more often than not trumped by social relations' (David Holmberg, cited in Gellner 2009: 127). At stake in Phugwumi, in terms of social binds and divides, was that for the first time two villagers had entered the same election contest. Worse still, the two candidates belonged to precisely the two clans, out of a total six, that had long struggled over standing, dominance and property within the village. While such rivalries and divisions remained mostly dormant in ordinary times, elections, everyone knew, carried the social venom to re-inflate such resentments and grievances with them becoming brooded over aloud. As both candidates were certain to invoke the affective realities of clan and would apply any means (including offerings of monies, feasts and favours) to win over other villagers, the otherwise frisk upland air, so it was feared, would soon thicken. With polling day drawing closer, norms of village cohesion and cooperation — even if occasionally fragile — would then be replaced by competition and the polarization of clan and interpersonal differences, whose after-effects were certain to linger until long after the last ballot was cast.[5]

The same problem had been experienced, years earlier, with the delegation of development projects, policies and budgets from the lower ranks of the bureaucracy down to the village. Phugwumi, akin to all Nagaland villages, was instructed to enact a Village Development Board (VDB) and voting was suggested as the mode to elect those villagers apt to the task. The development monies that poured into the village, however, were substantial, and so became opportunities for profitable (albeit illegal) cuts and commissions. No sooner had this occurred than VDB membership became widely sought after and VDB elections began to appear like state elections, including heated campaigns between villagers, rivalling camps, conflicts and the social production of resentment. Discordance became such that the *Razu Kuhu*, Phugwumi's apex body, intervened and decreed that, henceforward, VDB membership was to be adjudicated through a clan-wise *selection* system in which, every three years, the elders of the six village clans would confer and among themselves — based on intra-clan deliberation and consensus-building — select the most suitable clan member for the post.

It was such lived experiences — the notion that elections and voting create divisions, deepen rivalries and lead to exaggerated individualism — that now informed the villagers' apprehension about having two of their own contesting the election. Well into his eighties, Athe lived through all of Nagaland's elections and he was vocal about the societal and moral destruction they had brought. 'Our memories are long. If a fellow villager contests and we do not wish to support him, he and his relatives, even his entire clan, take it as betrayal and grudges grow.' Another elder agreed:

> In the past we discussed our matters and differences. We had our problems and conflicts, but we also had our own ways of dealing with them. But now villagers say: 'You wait! We'll face each other during the next election' and they then support

rivalling parties and politicians. But every election makes both winners and losers. As a result, differences are no longer settled. They just linger.

In the wake of the 2013 elections, Phugwumi's Razu Kuhu called for a village-wide consultative meeting in which it was resolved that only one candidate should contest and that the villagers would therefore select a 'village consensus-candidate' through public deliberation. The resolution was declared binding, suggesting that if the politician asked to withdraw by village consensus were to refuse to obey — according to India's Constitution and Election Commission he could not be legally barred from contesting — it would be interpreted as disrespecting the will of the village (*müthidzü* or *müthikülü*, which translate as 'the community's voice' or 'the community's thought'), a serious transgression that would impede his, and his relatives', future standing and participation in village life.[6]

While the selection of a consensus-candidate was deemed a necessary procedural adaptation to safeguard the spirit of community, the 'cultural' and 'material' are everywhere closely intertwined. Several theorists have shown how, across India, democratic politics is 'substantially about access to state resources' (Prasad 2010: 142; see also Chandra 2004; Piliavsky 2014ab). Naga politicians, too, have a long track record of privileging their own natal villages, clans and tribes in the dispensing of state resources. On the part of Naga electors, this makes it beneficial for a village to act as a 'voting unit' and particularly to see one among their own capture the constituency. With Phugwumi's constituency counting fewer than twenty-two thousand votes, and with Phugwumi alone possessing close to 25% of these, basic maths suggested that were the village to unite behind a single candidate he would instantly be placed ahead in the polls. However, if both village candidates were to contest, then the village 'vote bank' would certainly end up divided, providing a much-needed village majority to neither. Even if no fellow-villager stood for elections, it had long been common practice for Naga villages to unite behind a particular politician, rather than individual villagers voting for competing candidates. From the beginning of post-statehood democratic politics, village elders often traded the village's collective vote in return, for instance, for the construction of a church, community hall, school building or a bundle of corrugated galvanised iron sheets per house (Aram 1974: 198).

Even though both cultural and material considerations clearly favoured the selection of a consensus-candidate, the resolution failed to materialize. Multiple meetings took place, but it proved impossible to bridge the divisions between the two candidates and their loyalists. With just a few days until election day, the resolution was declared unsuccessful. This failure was to the dismay of many, but especially to Phugwumi elders, who took it as further evidence that the divisive forces of party politics and elections had moved beyond redemption. They were often explicit in criticizing the exaggerated individualism, open contests and competitive self-advancement they witnessed among younger generations during election seasons, and they blamed this on the principle of individual balloting and equal voting rights.

In the past, clan and village elders had been ascribed with special wisdom and acumen – accumulated over a lifetime – and their views, often wrapped in fine speeches and oratorical skills, were respected. While their words never carried the force of law, it was in elders that the maturity and foresight to transcend the mundane and to deliberate village protection and welfare was thought to lie. Elections and equal voting rights had corroded this respect and reverence for the opinions of village elders. Athe reflected thus: 'Whereas in the past our youth would whisper, and were eager to listen and learn from elders, nowadays they shout and will not listen. This is why our village could not agree on a consensus-candidate.' It indicated a social transformation Phugwumi elders felt deeply upset about: 'It is because nowadays the village is ruled by the youth', as was commented frequently when contemporary problems and issues within the village were discussed. Athe again:

> Nobody would dare to voice his aspiration to be recognized as a leader in the past. Such a person would be ridiculed as proud, and not listened to. Young people least of all. But see what is happening today; everyone wants to be a leader, even our youths. They speak loudly, but refuse to think and talk over what is best for the village, instead of what profits them personally. This was not how we used to think earlier.

While Phugwumi failed to pre-select a consensus-candidate, several other Naga villages succeeded as 'a pre-arranged agreement [took] place between village elders and political parties to select the consensus-candidate to be supported by the entire village' (Along Longkumer, cited in Amer 2014: 10). When polling day arrived, with no consensus-candidate agreed upon, Phugwumi fractured as feared into rival groups, to the extent that the Nagaland government declared Phugwumi to be 'hyper-sensitive' and dispatched armed forces to oversee the smooth conduct of polling. Amidst the rising frenzy, some village elders took it upon themselves to mediate differences, by lecturing: 'Soon this election will be over. We will still be neighbours then.'

THE POLITICAL ETHOS AND MORAL SOCIETY OF THE NAGA 'VILLAGE REPUBLIC'

Here I turn to traditional home-grown Naga political theory and praxis, in whose inner-logic, intricacies and ethos I suggest we find answers to Nagas' generally negative evaluation of elections, equal voting rights and party politics. I further suggest that the same body of values and logics helps to explain the attempted procedural adaptation in Phugwumi, which was intended to replace elections with consensus-building and the selection of a leader.

The Naga inhabited hills are usually said to be made up of disparate tribes. Prior to their (partial) incorporation into the British Raj, these were political communities with a fierce history of self-governance. In actual practice, however, both the locus and ethos of political organization was vested not in the tribe but in the prototypical Naga 'village republic' (Wouters 2017a). 'As with all Nagas', wrote the colonial administrator J. P. Mills (1926: 176), 'the political unit of the tribe is the village.' However, this observation must be qualified with a caveat. Namely, that while it was always evident that the centre of political gravity lay (and continues to lie) in the village, Naga 'traditional' politics was diverse, with political systems and sentiments often diverging from one village and tribe to the next. As a general principle, however, 'the commonest system of traditional governance is that there are no real chiefs at all' (Mills 1926: 28). While concurring with this view, political differences, as they existed (and persist), make Naga-wide generalizations a tricky affair, and my characterization of the political sociality inside Phugwumi may therefore be better attuned to certain Naga villages and tribes compared to others.

Much changed after Nagas' enclosure into the colonial and later postcolonial state, but the 'Naga village' found itself remapped at the centre of governance. Through a constitutional amendment, and several others acts, extraordinary judicial and executive powers were delegated to village councils and committees, while, on principle, 'the government tries not to interfere with the village administration' (Horam 1988: 18). One such act is the Nagaland Communitisation of Public Services Act (2001), which entailed the transfer of selected state functions and assets to village-based committees. Its designer, the award-winning bureaucrat Raghaw Sharan Pandey (2010: 22–23), was inspired by the 'rich social capital' inside Naga villages, which, to him, appeared an organic antidote to malgovernance and corruption:

> [The Naga village] is blessed with admirable community bonds reflecting dense and rich social capital, available in amazing

abundance ... The cohesion ... within the villages is of ancient vintage, continuing through generations ... The manner in which a village community conducts its affairs in times of sorrow or mirth, adversity or merriment, is reflective of its genius and to an observer from the outside, is remarkably fascinating. The social capital is clearly seen as performing a governance function.

This sense of community also permeates the early documentary accounts we have of Angami Nagas, of which the Chakhesang Nagas were part until they made a tribe of their own in 1946 (Wouters 2017b). John Henry Hutton (1921: 143) characterized their political form and functioning as a 'debating society'. In addition to political decision-making, 'disputes', Hutton explained, 'when settled at all, were probably settled by a sort of informal council of elders, who would discuss matters at great length, until some sort of agreement was arrived at.' There existed, in days gone by, ritual offices called *Kümvo* (male) and *Imshopüh* (female) in Phugwumi, but their powers were limited and by and large constricted to overseeing village festivals, the observance of *gennas*[7] and agricultural rites. Christoph Von Fürer-Haimendorf (1936: 923) wrote: 'the privileges of a Tevo [*Kümvo* in Phugwumi] are neither numerous nor important. He works in his fields as any ordinary villager does, and in council his voice has no more weight than that of any other man of equal wealth and moral influence.' The *Kümvo* and *Imshopüh* were thus not kings, chiefs, aristocrats or headmen, of which, indeed, Phugwumi had none.

Saying so is not to paint an anarchist history of Phugwumi. Social hierarchies existed, and mattered. For an aspirant villager to climb the social ladder, to expand his personal sway and to increase the sonority of his political voice, the throwing of successive 'feasts of merit' (*zhotho müza*) was a powerful device, a ritualized institution now known in anthropological annals as the Naga Feast of Merit (Fürer-Haimendorf [1939] 1976). Feast-givers were respected as their wealth and generosity revealed their virtue, and their views demanded attention. Bravery and physical strength, in offering protection and through ritually fertilizing the village by bringing in the 'soul matter' (Hutton 1928: 403) of decapitated enemy heads, provided another axis of social differentiation (Tinyi 2017), and in times of battle Phugwumi would usually unite behind one, or multiple, veteran warriors.

Perhaps most importantly, it was the wisdom and acumen associated with ageing that demanded listening ears. 'Age, among the Nagas', Mashangthei Horam (1988: 18) writes, 'has both prestige and power.' In Phugwumi, elders were revered, and their words commanded a respectful audience.[8] Accomplishments in terms of wealth and generosity, physical prowess and especially ageing could therefore result in positions of political prominence. However, Charles Chasie (2005: 102) stresses, 'Certainly no leader was accepted on a permanent basis. The moment the person starts boasting, his downfall would begin.' Village authority, where it existed, remained mostly nominal and resolutions were 'obeyed so far only as they accord with the wishes and conveniences of the community' (Hutton 1921: 143).

With the absence of permanent village chiefs and formal councils, how, then, were decisions ever made? In Phugwumi, it was practices and principles of consensus-building (*küdzükhoküyi*) that governed both political life and moral society. In the village, everyone was allowed to raise their voice in public, at any time, on any topic, proposing any resolution, although it must be emphasized that not everyone's voice was given equal weight. The sonority of one's political voice was set by one's antecedents and achievements, by the merit, virtue and wisdom a person had accumulated over a lifetime. This so-defined 'purest democracy' (Butler, cited in Hutton 1921: 143) of the Naga village was therefore not a 'direct democracy', as a consensus-based, fully and equally participatory and decentralized politics is sometimes imagined (cf. Graeber 2009).

In Phugwumi, the views of the village elderly, as a general political norm, superseded the voices of younger generations whose opportunism and naiveties had to be kept in check. In the cultural etiquette of the past, village youth, while never silenced, were expected to show deference by acknowledging, before speaking in public, the incomplete understanding and limited knowledge that came with being young and unmarried, the absence of fields and cattle in one's possession, and their overall still limited experience of the perils and complications of life. Women, in turn, generally spoke less than men, at least in public, and while Naga women, in general terms, have been thought of as traditionally empowered compared to women in most parts of India (Elwin 1961: 104), their involvement in political decision-making remained, and remains, marginal (Amer 2013).[9] If this 'debating society' or 'purest democracy' now connotes a patriarchal autocracy centred on the old and meritorious, the relations of reliance this produced were not enforced, but entrusted, and ever legitimized by the cultural and communitarian understanding that they had accumulated the merit and maturity to transcend purely personal and clan interests for the protection and welfare of the village at large.

Achieving village-wise consensus, hence, did not rely on the equal participation, or equal weight, of all village voices. It was also often not easy, and could entail lengthy and contentious discussions, but whereas in certain Marxist circles consensus is seen as a euphemism for ideology, or false consciousness, in Phugwumi consensus-building itself constituted the political ideology. Crucially, the essence of consensus-building in Phugwumi was not that all villagers had to endorse the same view, unanimously agree on the settlement of a dispute or wholeheartedly accept the selection of a leader or spokesperson. Often, the decision taken was not the one that could count on the support of the majority, but the one to which the least numbers of villagers strongly disagreed. As such, it was a political system antithetical to the domination of the majority (Wouters 2015: 140–141). It is in this realization that the above-cited statement, 'We believe in that form of democratic government which permits the rule not of the majority but of the people as a whole', reaches full circle.

This principle continues to guide Phugwumi's realm of customary law. To adjudicate decisions, in village council meetings, the principle of voting is never applied.[10] In an interview I had with him, Phugwumi's chairperson explained: 'Voting would only lead to more politics, more competition, and more rivalries. And this would not benefit our village'. Instead, the council prefers to deliberate until they reach an agreement that is acceptable to all its members, even if this means council meetings often become lengthy affairs. In instances where consensus-building proves impossible, the council declares an issue as unresolved or pending, which is preferred over forcing a decision through the divisive practice of voting.

TOWARDS A DEMOCRACY WITHOUT PARTIES AND ELECTIONS

In boycotting newly independent India's first general elections, the Phizo-led NNC not only rejected Nagas' inclusion into the Indian Union but also communicated the cultural incongruity of political parties and elections with Naga life-worlds. 'There is no political party in Nagaland. We don't need it', said Phizo (1951). 'Nagaland need not imitate or adopt foreign institutions [political parties and elections] in matters of political organisation.' In Phizo's view, Nagaland was already democratic by traditional design: '[it] is the very spirit of our country.' The NNC's manifesto thus read: 'In a country like Nagaland, particularly at the present time, [a] party system could never accomplish anything except leading to ruination' (cited in Horam 1988: 321–322).

Phizo instead proposed the continuation of consensus-making as the prime political practice and principle, or what he captured as *mechü medo zotuo* ('the binding will of the community'). As a case in point, Phizo referred to himself as a spokesman, not a leader. 'I can only say what my people want and what they have decided,' he explained. 'The position of a spokesman and a leader is often confused. Like a pilot, a spokesman shall have to follow direction' (cited in Nuh 1986: 95). And when a former Indian Chief Justice once asked him how the NNC elected its leaders, Phizo replied: 'We do not elect leaders, we select them':

> The selection process goes on for several years beginning from the village level where people know each other thoroughly and only people with virtue of integrity and character are accepted to become leaders. Then on the basis of these observations the leaders of the various villages select the most competent person to be the leader. The same is followed through to the national level. Thus a national leader emerges after so many years. (Cited in Mishra 2004: 4)

This traditional and moral vision of selecting leaders was also adopted by the Naga People's Convention (NPC), which brokered Nagaland statehood in 1963. When an interim government had to be constituted, Naga tribes and villages chose their representatives not through elections but 'by their own traditional methods' (Ramunny 1993: 162). When, in 1964, the first post-statehood elections were scheduled, Hokishe Sema (1986: 104), a later Chief Minister, appealed for cultural wisdom: 'I strongly felt that it was too early for the Nagas to fight elections on the basis of political parties ... The system of Tribal Representatives was doing very well and could have continued.' But even as the first elections were fought along party lines, many Naga villages turned inward, applied consensus-building and selected their leaders. In fourteen out of the (then) forty constituencies, candidates were returned unopposed as 'village leaders had met earlier and by consensus had decided who would be their representative' (Ramunny 1993: 161).

Moreover, the six additional seats 'reserved' for Nagaland's Tuensang District were filled without a single vote being cast. Perceived as especially 'backward', Tuensang District was – through a constitutional amendment – given ten years 'respite' from voting. Instead, the Tuensang Regional Council, made up of clan and tribal leaders, *selected* from among its ranks six members for the Legislative Assembly.[11] It was the Naga Nationalist Organisation (NNO) that won the first elections. However, the political discussions that followed saw the resignation of all members of the opposition, by-elections and the manoeuvring of independent candidates, resulting, finally, in all elected representatives joining the NNO government. This made Nagaland's first Legislative Assembly a house without opposition, functioning, indeed, on the basis of internal deliberation and consensus-making.[12]

The following decades witnessed the rise and fall of multiple Nagaland political parties, but their ideological positions were not always clear. This, coupled with frequent party-hopping and the absence of stigma attached to this, led Moamenla Amer (2014: 6) to characterize Nagaland political parties as staunchly 'non-ideological.' This absence of party ideology, in the conventional sense of a left-centre-right political spectrum, showed itself once more in 2015 when all benches of Nagaland's opposition resolved to merge with the ruling Democratic Alliance of Nagaland. 'It will now be a party-less government in Nagaland', the Chief Minister concluded with delight (*Asian Tribune* 2015), adding that with party divisions done away with, the government would work collectively and through consensus-making to bring peace and development.[13]

If the abolishment of party division is constructed, by some, as a first step towards restoring 'Naga community', given that 'contemporary politics and the party-system ... have done great damage to the village unity, dividing many villages along party lines' (Dev 1988: 27), a further culturalist critique propagates the discontinuation of elections altogether. 'Traditionally', writes Charles Chasie (2005: 102), 'we did not elect our leaders ... the notion itself would have been a scandal':

> When you 'go to the people' [as politicians must] you are telling them that you are the best person they could possibly have as their leader! This in a society where even a majority or consensus nomination, to be part of a delegation, is often refused several times by the persons concerned, pleading that they are unworthy. In traditional society, such arrogance and absence of fear of God could result in immediate beatings and social ostracism.

As recently as 2011, the (then) Nagaland Chief Minister declared: 'election is not suited for Nagas.' He then elucidated: 'selection of leader[s] would best suit Nagas' (cited in Solo 2011: 67), thus recognizing that the idea of an '"elected leader" was not in the scheme of life in the Nagas' (Solo 2011: 68). In the 1980s, a former Chief Minister, similarly concerned, had already published a political treatise that advocated the abolishment of political parties and elections, not to undermine Nagaland democracy but to strengthen it. Hokishe Sema (1986: 171-172) envisaged a state-wide selection system, based on multiple levels — village, area and region — of consensus-making. He explained:

> In Nagaland, even the members of the State Assembly, which is the final level, can be selected by the Regional Councils. This system will reduce the increasing expenses of elections

and minimize the corruptions. This is necessary for a good society based on faith in each other and in common values. This does not in any way hamper the power of the State Government, [but] rather helps the progress and thereby good government.

Critics may well argue that much has changed since Naga life-worlds were first and foremost centred in 'village republics', or that ideologies of communal harmony and consensus-making conceal conflicts and power hierarchies within (Nader 1990). Yet many with whom I spoke across Nagaland argued along the lines of Nuh's (1986: 184) evaluation that, 'Unless the present election system is changed, it will not serve the [Naga] people well', and that this change must be in accordance with 'traditional and customary practices.'

NAGAS AS A SOCIETY AGAINST VOTING

Far from a stand-alone case, Nagas' attempt to reintegrate cultural wisdom and moral society into the superficially asocial realm of liberal democracy corresponds to a wider postcolonial critique that perceives liberal democracy and competitive elections as democratically and culturally damaging, rather than liberating. The Comaroffs (1997: 126) elaborate on this as follows: 'democracy through much of the world has increasingly been reduced from the substantive to the procedural, from social movement to electoral process (...); has come to connote little more than the rightful exercise of choice, the satisfying of desire, the physics of pure interests.' For South Africa, Jason Hickel (2015: 2) shows how the values of liberal democracy are experienced as 'morally repulsive and socially destructive.' South Africans draw a connection between democracy and (social) 'death' because the egalitarian projections of liberal democracy corrode age-old kinship hierarchies that are seen as culturally and morally imperative for a desired ritual and lifelong process of what Hickel calls 'fruition.' Their experiences tell them that liberal democracy works to undo 'the ritual work of differentiating persons', dismantle the 'hierarchical structure of kinship' and, in the upshot, returns 'the world to a sterile sameness' (2015: 10).

This narrowing horizon of 'the political' was also part of a deeper culturalist critique that informed the slogan in Phugwumi: 'Election is an insult to each other by vote.' They are an insult because villagers today talk and argue with their voting slips rather than deliberate and build consensus collectively, they now privilege self-advancement over communal welfare, end up selecting self-serving career politicians, and because equal voting rights and participation wrongly equates the experiences, wisdom and foresight of village elders, accumulated over a lifetime, with the immaturities and naiveties of younger generations. It is these social transformations that for many Phugwumi villagers – but especially village elders – reveal the immoralities of party-based elections and individual balloting based on equal voting rights.

This culturalist critique, and the attempted procedural answer to this critique by replacing elections with consensus-building, illustrates a blind spot, not just in political theory but in modern political thinking at large. That is: how do peoples here, there and everywhere themselves imagine the good democratic life? And what if their own cultural and customary theories of arranging their political life diverge from the superficially standard versions of liberal, electoral democracy? And what, moreover, if instead of adjusting themselves to modern democratic ideals and procedures, they wish to apply their agency and cultural creativity to adjust democracy and elections to suit themselves? Can we, in short, imagine culturalist democracies? Most liberal political theorists would not think so. They find the existence of varied cultural interpretations and expressions of the democratic life difficult to accept, even to perceive. They insist that democracy is quintessentially a liberating and transformative force (Bose 2013; Khilnani 2009) that must emancipate individuals from the fetters of traditional cultures and past political authorities.

In a classic treatise, Clastres (1977) established as *Society against the State* those Amazonian tribes, so-called 'primitive', that existed without hierarchical and authoritative leadership, but were nevertheless affluent, cohesive and complex. Because they flourished, they were not *lacking* state structures, Clastres argued, but in their political sociality and cultural proclivities were intrinsically adversarial to the idea of a coercive state. What Clastres critiqued was the universalization of a particular and normative political system, style and sociality, and the subsequent judgement of any society's political position and prestige on precisely those terms.

Nagas' engagement with elections embodies a similar critique; it questions the universalization of a particularistic, political and moral sense of democratic life reliant on competitive elections, individual autonomy and equal voting rights. In voicing their cultural critique and in attempting (and occasionally achieving) procedural adaptations to democratic elections, Nagas communicate an alternative vision and sense of the good democratic life. They are trying, with various degrees of success, to curtail the social havoc they experienced at the liberal hands of democratic elections on their own, home-spun cultural and communitarian theories and praxis of moral society and 'Naga democracy'. If Nagas' traditional political practices, penchants and proclivities make them a 'society against voting', this essay has demonstrated that they are nonetheless a society still premised on democratic principle.

02

SOVEREIGNTY, INTEGRATION OR BIFURCATION?

Troubled Histories, Contentious Territories, and the Political Horizons of the Long Lingering Naga Movement

> *Before you place your order, please decide what you want to eat*
>
> —Sign at a roadside dhaba, Assam

'In this transitional period of history, we the Nagas are in a very delicate position', wrote A.Z. Phizo from Calcutta's Presidency Jail where he had been incarcerated on charges of 'stirring trouble' in the Indo-Burma borderland. The year was 1948. India had just woken up to 'life and freedom', and the Nagas, of whom Phizo introduced himself as a spokesperson, now wanted India to set free the Nagas. His letter continued: 'We occupy a territory at a point of transfusions and we cannot permit Naga territory to be political polemics.' What Phizo invoked was the colonial geo-political objectification (Zou and Kumar 2011), the administrative and cartographic ordering and reordering of a hitherto nonstate upland space, thence transmuting Naga lands from a fringe, rugged and remote, into a crucial and potentially subversive border or buffer zone between India and China, Burma, and at some distance (erstwhile) East Pakistan. '[The Nagas] are not planning Machiavellian politics', Phizo, witty as always, assured, then asserting that it was 'not the nature of the Nagas to be secretive... we never made a secret of our aspiration to be independent again when the British leave India.'

The letter I am quoting from was sent by Phizo to C. Rajagopalachari, the first Governor General of free India,[1] who immediately rejected its contents, as did Nehru, Patel and other Indian leaders (bar, it might be added, Mahatma Gandhi).[2] Phizo, after his release from jail, was to become the fourth President and main ideologue of the Naga National Council (NNC), which came to spearhead the Naga Movement for independence. But while in the 1940s, conflicting interpretations on what was, and what was not, Indian territory, and who was, and who was not, an Indian, were battled with rhetoric, historical narratives, political representations and symbolic acts, when subsequent talks, negotiations, and attempted treaties failed, Nehru ordered in his military and paramilitary forces. 'Troops moved into Tuensang by Oct. 1955', B.N. Mullik, then Director of India's Central Intelligence Bureau recounted, 'and the war with the Nagas started from then' (cited in Vashum 2000: 137).

The subsequent history of the Indo-Naga conflict, which lingers still, is a history of a daring resistance, one defying the odds of a small, initially ill-equipped Naga force holding out despite being outnumbered many times over. But it is also a history of multiple dissensions, coups, rivalries, acts of tribalism, and factional feuds within, over time splitting and complicating the Naga Movement into a myriad of warring underground groups, of which the National Socialist Council of Nagalim (IM-faction) arguably makes the strongest powerhouse today, and since 1997 negotiates with the Centre over a political settlement.[3]

A caveat before proceeding. This essay is one of large summations, small vignettes, and schematic explorations, and those interested in the genesis and evolution of the Naga Movement – its many chapters, complications, and conspiracies – should consult the more detailed, more authoritative works of Horam (1988), L. Ao (2002), Gundevia (1975), Nibedon (1978), Nuh (1986), Iralu (2002), Chasie (2005), among others. Even as this essay aims to contribute to a now budding scholarship on the Naga Movement, it aims to do so only modestly by confining its focus on the divergent political and territorial claims that have, over the decades, been asserted in the name, or against the background, of the 'Naga national question' (U. Misra 1978).

In brief, while the initial claim for a sovereign, independent Nagalim envisaged a political and administrative reordering of a region cut across by the colonial Indo-Burma border,[4] this essay shows how, over time, the Naga Movement increasingly conformed to this international border – at least in praxis – as political attention shifted towards achieving the integration of Naga lands within India but presently divided across multiple states.[5] Recently, another quandary emerged as the Eastern Naga People's

Organisation (ENPO) articulated a demand for the bifurcation of Nagaland through the enactment of a new state to be called 'Frontier Nagaland.' A fourth stance, but one which will not figure prominently here, is one in favour of the status quo of Nagaland state as it was enacted in 1963 as a projected, but unsuccessful, way out of the conflict.

If these divergent political and territorial aspirations – sovereignty, integration, bifurcation (and status quo) – suggest a sinking ever more deeply into a morass of conflicting aspirations, oppositional sentiments, and political disorder, it is amidst such confusion that this essay attempts to historically situate each of these claims, as well as to discuss some of their implications, inner intricacies and indeterminacies, in the upshot serving a heady cocktail of colonial legacies, borders that divide, and post-colonial political imaginations, spiked with shots of old tribal antagonisms and new alignments. The next section will engage, briefly but critically, with reconstructions – politically, scholarly, and lay – of the historical substance of 'Naga-ness', and Naga nationalism.

WHAT IS THE NAGA NATION IF NOT ANCIENT?

In 1929 Naga representatives, under the aegis of the Naga club – the first Naga apex body – petitioned the Simon Commission, which had come to British India to study constitutional reform. Were the British to depart, as rumours had it, they pleaded that 'we [the Nagas] should not be thrust to the mercy of other people... but to leave us alone as in ancient times' (cited in Vashum 2000: 175). Over eight decades on, this petition remains a building block of the 'modern Naga political project' (Kikon 2005: 2833). Not debated or discussed openly, however, was what a return to 'ancient times' would entail, or who the Naga were before colonialism. This altered with the publication in 2000 of what probably counts as the most controversial write-up on the Naga by a Naga: *The Bedrock of Naga Society*. S.C. Jamir, its author, then Nagaland's chief minister, and a known critic, if not of Naga nationalism, certainly of the Naga national movement – and the resistance and violence perpetuated in its name – asked: 'Did we have an independent political existence at all immediately before the British rule or even during the British days? Were we really an independent nation?' Jamir's answer:

> The stark and inescapable truth is that neither did we have a definite and unified political structure nor did we exist as a nation. We were actually a group of heterogeneous, primitive

and diverse tribes living in far-flung villages that had very little in common and negligible contact with each other… In these circumstances, the question of a unified "Naga nation" did not arise (Nagaland Pradesh Congress Committee 2000: 1)

What was controversial about the statement was that it construed the Naga nation as nascent, thus undermining the 'Naga grievance' that the British had wilfully fractured and shattered coterminous and ancient Naga lands, homes, and belongings trough boundaries made in Britain. It postulated that a generic Naga identity had not been the pretext, but the cumulative outcome of a modern Naga political project, concocted and circulated by a small circle of Naga elite. On reading this, Naga undergrounds immediately condemned S.C. Jamir as a reactionary and a traitor, and planned yet another ambush on his life (he had already survived several, as opposed to several of his bodyguards, whom did not), while the Naga Students' Federation (NSF), a commanding pan-Naga body, sought to placate its rage by collecting copies to light a bonfire with them (Daniel 2004: 69). The Naga nation, it was reiterated far and wide, was perennial and historically immutable, as ancient as the proverbial time-immemorial. While cultural and linguistic differences had always been there, as well as occasional feuds within, such had always remained second to an ancient sense of shared 'Naga-ness', or 'Naga-ism' as it was labelled in underground circles (Vashum 2000: 75).

Despite the upheaval and rage the booklet inspired, in the light of existing historical scholarship S.C. Jamir's reading of Naga history almost bordered on plagiarism. In fact, a large amount of ink and debate still goes to historicizing and explaining the rise of Naga political consciousness, and in tracking the historical antecedents and catalysts of the movement for Naga independence, creating an expansionist body of scholarship that is at once so contested and so unimaginative, and predictable. Invariably, such reconstructions commence with the colonial archive and retell and reiterate, for instance, Woodthorpe's (1888: 47) observation that the term Naga 'is quite foreign to and unrecognised by the Naga themselves', Robinson's (1841) remark that 'they know themselves by the designations of their respective tribes only, and not by any name common to all races', or Hutton's (1926: xv) statement that it is 'exceedingly difficult to propound any test by which a Naga tribe can be distinguished from other Assam and Burma tribes which are not Nagas.'

It is despite such vintage observations that in recent years it remains remarkably possible to present as novel and revelatory claims that 'the Naga nation is not "given" in nature; instead it is continually being constructed' (Nag 2013: 5). What is tirelessly showcased is how a generic Naga identity and nationalism is historically forged, as a response and reaction to colonialism, prompted by the Naga participation in both World Wars,[6] articulated against the perceived 'Indian occupation', the cumulative effect of mass conversions to Christianity, or enacted through the witticism and charisma of Phizo as a 'swayer of men' (Horam 1998: 27), and in the upshot thus invented, constructed, and imagined (e.g. Nag 2013; Joshi 2013; Wettstein 2012; Franke 2009; Baruah 2003), making one wonder what kind of modern nation is not historically contingent and imagined, or where we may be able to find such an historically immutable nation.

Rather than concluding with, new analytic avenues emerge by premising that the Naga, akin to all but decaying identities, is a nation-continually-in-the-making, a modern political project on the move, then progressing, then faltering, and always an 'evolving concept that is difficult to pin down' (Longkumer 2010: 206). Such a premise, rather than novel or even noteworthy, only follows local demotic discourses that differentiate strongly between tribes, clan, and villages, and takes seriously the pervasiveness of stereotypes, prejudices, and occasional antipathies that reproduce such differences. It also merely recognises the differential mythic narratives of origin and migration, the different languages and cultural expressions every few miles, the blood-soaked histories or raids and retaliations within, and the continuing acts and sentiments of tribalism that inform the intra-Naga politics of belonging and difference. Thence, if Baruah (2003) propagates the 'confronting of Naga constructionism' as the only way out of the ethnic politics and violence that permeate the Indo-Naga conflict, this well ignores that articulations of difference and disjunction are, and have always been, intrinsic to stories Nagas tell about themselves. Crucially, however, as Baumann (1996) explained us, demotic articulations may persist quite independently from a dominant discourse or ideology – in this instance the deliberate and discursive production of a unified, ancient Naga identity – which may, nay must, persist for official, instrumental, and political purposes.[7]

Why S.C. Jamir's statement drew such disapproval, then, is not necessarily because his historical reconstruction was inaccurate, but because as a prominent public leader he spilled into the public sphere what many thought belonged to what we might call the private realm of 'historical intimacy' – a somewhat skewed adaption of Herzfeld's (1997) 'cultural intimacy' – or aspects that are locally known but considered a source of political discomfiture and therefore best left out of the public arena in favour of a more instrumental, more promising political sociality. The problem therefore appears less of praxis and more of theory, and while theories of nationalism have long freed itself from the dangerous depths of primordialism and complicated Ernest Gellner's argument pertaining 'the nationalist imperative of the congruence of political unit and of culture' (1983: 121), political and layman understandings of nationalism remain crucially hinged on the notion that to qualify as a nation today, and to have one's political aspirations counted as legitimate, one must be able to account for a perennial, historically immutable, culturally homogenous, and territorially delimited identity.

Relevant research on Naga nationalist politics, then, lies not merely in recurrent efforts to deconstruct the dominant narrative of ancient Naga unity (although, this too merits the scholarship it abundantly receives), but in better understanding the political potential and purposes of divergent Naga nationalist narratives (of which the 'ancient Naga-ness thesis' is, as we will see, but one variant) to either subdue or support present political borders and arrangements, necessitating us to appreciate, once more, that instead of the past shaping the present, contemporary politics often mould understandings and articulations of the past. The pages that follow partially seek to apply such an approach by situating divergent Naga political and territorial claims in an 'unfolding history of the present' (Comaroff and Comaroff 2012: 118).

NAGA SOVEREIGNTY: WHAT DOES IT MEAN?

Following ten years of heavy militarization, guerrilla warfare, and widespread misery, 1964 witnessed the first Indo-Naga ceasefire. Subsequent peace talks however soon became deadlocked. Gundevia, India's interlocutor, recalled thus: 'All sorts of words like "independence" and "self-determination" and "sovereignty" were bandied around but I often wondered whether the connotation of several of these difficult words was the same in Angami, Ao and Sema or Lotha' (1975: 133). To enable legible conversation, 'Kevilaye' [sic] a brother of A.Z. Phizo, 'acted as the interpreter from Angami [not a few NNC leaders belonged to the Angami Naga] into English and from English into Angami, sentence by sentence from our side of the table to the other and back' (ibid.). While Gundevia evidently spoke with some disdain when he lamented the 'impossibility of translating high-sounding English words into the relatively less developed languages in the hills' (ibid.: 138),[8] his remarks draw attention to the problematic cultural and historical transitivity of 'sovereignty' and 'self-determination' (and 'independence') as the modular forms of post-colonial political space and political subjectivity.

Our ethnographic and historical record confirms the need to historicize and 'provincialize' (Chakrabarty 2000) the modern dogma that territorial sovereignty should be 'fully, flatly and evenly operative' (Anderson 1991: 19). In earlier political space – in South Asia and beyond

– sovereignty was more often 'galactic' (Tambiah 1977), 'theatrical' (Geertz 1980), 'monastic' (Chatterjee 2014), wholly absent (Scott 2009), or partial and overlapping, while borders were usually faded, fluctuating, and porous, until the gradual usurpation of such vernacular possibilities through the imposition and local infatuation – or the sustenance of a 'derivative discourse' as Chatterjee (1983) frames it – of imperial notions of stern sovereignty and territorial exclusivity, reinforced by the 'European myth' of Cartesian and cartographic political borders (Leach 1960). Indeed, when the British Raj expanded its sway into the swamps and highlands of India's Northeast, they 'had to first contend with the conditions of overlapping territoriality and sovereignty, which characterized the indigenous polity of the region' (S. Misra 2005: 222), and if British-Naga relations quickly ran amok this was not in the least because of a British policy of 'pushing the hill tribes up into the hills' (Karlsson 2011: 70) by declaring as wastelands and tea-gardens swathes of lowlands over which upland Nagas had long exerted notional control, had negotiated rights on, or extracted tributes from (Wouters 2011). On the other hand, as Leach wrote: 'In this region [upland Burma but also the hills of Northeast India] the indigenous political systems which existed prior to the colonial expansion were not separated from one another by frontiers in the modern sense and they were not sovereign Nation-States' (1960: 50).

That 'sovereignty' – both in theory and practice – is particularistic and thence polymorphous can be read into Phizo's 1951 Plebiscite speech.[9] While calling India a 'sovereign country', Phizo (1951) showcased his own understanding of sovereignty by quickly adding that many Indian citizens were not living sovereign lives:

> What is the lot of Indian cultivators? They are mere tenants in their own soil and not the sovereign owners of their own land as in our country. Most of the Indians live in rented houses in all the towns and cities though they may appear to be onlookers as 'big gentlemen' behaving and speaking very good English like the British.

This Phizo (1951) saw as different among the Naga: 'land belongs to the people as private property, and every family possesses land. We uphold every person as sovereign: man and women alike. Every family is a landlord; but, there is no landlordism in Nagaland... land being so owned by the people who are in their person sovereign.' Phizo's theorising of sovereignty corresponds with what elders in the Chakhesang Naga village I shall call Phugwumi remembered about Phizo's visit to their village in the early 1950s. One elder recalled thus:

> He spoke about socialism, the Naga Nation and that we had been an independent people since time-immemorial. I did not understand all of what he said that time, but we of course supported that all our land, cattle and possessions should remain ours, and ours alone. Phizo explained that the Indians, if we would not resist them, would count our land and cattle and make us pay taxes over them, and that we would so lose our freedom

But if Phizo's deeper understanding of sovereignty was less about state, courts, and police, and more in terms of ownership over land, cattle and communitarian ethics, such vernacular conceptualisations only ill-fitted the post-colonial political episteme of spatialized nation-states (Biolsi 2005: 240).[10] It is here that Samaddar's (2008) conjunctions of the emergence of the 'political subject' – as a reaction to new political theories and praxis brought by colonial rulers – appears illustrative, and indicative of the specific political rhetoric and demands forwarded by Phizo, and his NNC. It was during colonial rule, Samaddar writes, that legal reasoning became crucial not just to political argumentation and resistance, but also came to inhibit a 'cognitive dimension', and this new political thinking spilled over in the spheres of community and customs (2008: 14). Phizo was aware of this, and after qualifying that 'Nagas are not legal minded' (cited in Nuh 1986: 89), he lamented: 'almost every Indian leader is a lawyer, and these learned people, who search for a flaw in legal system or try to produce one when there is none... This is the danger. We already see their tactics.'

Thence, even if notions of sovereignty carry a problematic historical and cultural transitivity, in protecting the Naga and envisaging their political future Phizo had little choice but to fare political modernity by making his own the near obligatory and modular categories of 'nation' and 'territorial sovereignty'. Implicitly, this was also advised by the Peace Mission, which in its attempt to facilitate the 1964 peace negotiations urged the NNC to formulate 'a clear conception and precise picture of what is meant by independence and sovereignty' (Srikanth and Thomas 2005: 66). Any Naga, or indigenous, constellations of belonging and self-determination would, as Phizo probably realised, run the risk of legal subversion by the 'Indian lawyers' he so feared. As a result, Phizo did not so much advocate a return to 'ancient times' – as Naga representatives had pleaded to the Simon Commission – but socially produced a new Naga political space and imagination, and on purpose.

With territory as a kernel of this new political space, Phizo readily portrayed the history of the Nagas as evolving 'in a compact geographic unit with clearly demarcated boundaries before the advent of the British' (cited in Nuh 1986: 101). A 'compactness' which the British dissevered:

> The Naga were divided by the British administration into three major units. About one-fifth of the Naga population with that much in proportion of our land were administrated from British India. About the same proportion was administrated by British Burma. And approximately sixty percent of the population occupying a territory of about seventy percent of Nagaland were left untouched and undisturbed, who were absolutely independent (ibid.).

Given that 'in the national order of things' (Malki 1997) a nation without a fixed and clearly delineated territory is not considered a nation at all, the nascent NSCN, in framing the Naga territorial encompassment, edited out the qualifications of 'arbitrary' and 'roughly' (see Baruah 2003: 322) from the following depiction of Naga and their land by J.H. Hutton, and promoted it as the historical boundaries of the Naga:

> The expression Naga is useful as an arbitrary term to denote the tribes living in Certain parts of the Assam hills, which may be roughly defined as bounded by the Hukong valley in the north-east, the plains of the Brahmaputra valley to the north-west, of Cachar to the south-west and of the Chindwin to the west. In the south, the Manipur valley roughly marks the point of contact between 'the Naga' tribes and the very much more closely interrelated groups of Kuki tribes – Thado, Lushei, Chins, etc. (Hutton 1926: xv).

While political projections of the Naga nation were thus also shaped by the authoritative grammar and vocabulary of political modernity – its benchmarks and modular forms of homogenous nations, fixed territorialities and absolute sovereignties – paradoxically, perhaps, it now appears that a political settlement may be located by taking seriously the historicity of sovereignty and exploring a return to vernacular, or indigenous, understandings and arrangements of political space, in the process envisioning a new type of political society that is at once traditional and modern.

Towards this end, the NSCN-IM leadership, in its political dialogue with the Centre, proposed 'shared sovereignty' based on a 'federation of India and Nagaland', thus recognising both the 'uniqueness' of Naga history (in relation to 'Indian history') and unavoidable modern relations of interdependence. Such a 'special federal relationship', even if connoting the 'political exotic', only conforms, as Samaddar notes, 'to a historical pattern along which the Indian state had developed in the past, except for the 200 years when the colonial centralised model of military despotism based on continuous physical conquests and annexations developed and subsequently became the sole possessor of the political imagination of the ones colonised' (2008: 164). Such a rethinking of sovereignty is not just intellectually expedient, but has proven politically possible elsewhere in the form of indigenous spaces imagined, struggled over, and achieved by American Indians, and which includes instances of tribal sovereignty within an ancestral homeland, co-management of overlapping territories, supra-tribal rights, and hybrid indigenous spaces, making Biolsi (2005: 240) conclude that in the United States, 'the nation-state, it turns out, is only one among several (perhaps many) political geographies imagined, lived, and even institutionalized under modernity by American Indians.'

THE DEMAND FOR INTEGRATION

If a burgeoning literature now shows how international boundaries carry colonial and contentious imprints, often perforating pre-existent social practices, ethnic affinities, and historical continuities (Van Schendel 2005; Gellner 2013), what often escapes scholarly treatment is that borders *within* may equally inhibit imperial legacies and might equally work to divide what is expressed and imagined as similar. Moreover, if India's Northeast is readily construed as an ultimate borderland surrounded, as it is, by five nation-states, the region's special post-colonial political dispensation of 'cosmetic federalism' (Baruah 2003), one of relatively small states and still smaller autonomous 'ethnic homelands', also renders it an ultimate *internal* borderland, with its many borders constituting prime sites of contestations, conflicts, 'cartographic anxiety' (Krishna 1994) and 'apprehensive territoriality' (Van Schendel 2013: 268).

While the NSCN-IM, in its dialogues with the Centre, professed readiness to absolve its demand for absolute territorial sovereignty, it remains firm on the unification of Naga territories within India.

> We will never compromise on our demand for the reunification of the Naga homeland. We were divided first by the British and then India perpetuated the divisions. The NSCN wants a unified Naga homeland and we will either have it or we will fight for it (Muivah cited in Samaddar 2009: 182).[11]

Amidst boundaries that divide, the Nagaland-Manipur border remains especially emotive and contested given the multiple communities

— Tangkhul, Rongmei, Poumai, among others — that identify themselves as Naga within Manipur, as well as the sizeable territories they claim as ancestrally theirs.[12] The remainder of this section first offers an insight into the historical delineation of this boundary, then briefly discusses the demand for its redrawing, and ends with certain dissenting voices, doubts, and protests in favour of the territorial status-quo.

In 1887, George Watt had recently returned to London from a boundary expedition in Manipur, and the Royal Anthropological Institute invited him to address its members. Watt started his lecture with praise for a set of earlier lectures and articles by Colonel Woodthorpe, by then an acclaimed veteran on the Naga Hills. Woodthorpe's descriptions of the Angami Naga and adjoining tribes in the Naga Hills District, Watt explained his audience were of 'the Northern neighbours of the hill tribes of Manipur.' He then continued: [they are] so intimately related to one or two of the Manipur tribes that they can with difficulty be separated from them.' It is therefore not just a little surprising then, one might contend, that Watt's duty, and those of associated officers, was precisely that: separating the 'northern' from the 'southern' Nagas through a fast and firm boundary.

In pinpointing this boundary, Watt let himself be led by geographical features:

> To the north and northwest of Manipur, one of the most important ranges (the Barail), culminates in Japvo, a peak over 10.000 feet in altitude. From this elevated mass transverse spurs connect the neighbouring parallel ranges. These links not only determine the watershed of the rivers which are to traverse the valleys of Manipur from those one might be almost pardoned for viewing as the northern extensions of the same valleys into the Naga country, but along these very transverse spurs may be traced the line which demarcate the Nagas of the north from the Nagas of Manipur (cited in Elwin 1969: 449).

But even as Watt spoke of 'geography', his and his fellow colonial officers' interpretation of the rugged hills and stretching valleys was invariably shaped by political contemplations, and if historians now deem the colonial caste-wise enumeration of India's populace as a technology of power and political subjugation (Cohn 1986), much the same can be said of the crafting of territorial divisions. In this instance the political imperative was to 'separate the Angami Nagas [who staunchly resisted British enclosure] and all the inferior tribes subject to their influence... from the Nagas of Munnipore [sic]' (cited in Mishra 1998: 3273). As early as 1824, Manipur had ceded into a British protectorate. The Manipur king, belonging to the Vaishnavite Meitei community of the Imphal Valley, claimed notional control over – and in some instances mythic narratives, shared festivals, ritual alignments and marriage alliances with (see Saha 2005) – adjacent upland tribes, and which the British deemed it politically pious to recognise (and objectify). However, demarcating the hilly expanse of the Manipur valley kingdom was always going to be a fraught exercise given that 'the territories of Muneepor [sic] have fluctuated at various times with the fortunes of its princes' (Pemberton 1835: 20). This begs a set of important questions: whose territorial claims should count, and whose should not? What historical moment should be taken as the benchmark for such claims (to compare, any claim that the political ordering of Europe should be based on the status quo of, say, 1943 at the height of Nazi expansionism would instantly be rejected as ludicrous)? And what should be considered as justifying claims of political supremacy (e.g. territorial rights, military victories, taxes, tribute)? Such reflections in boundary-making, if at all pondered over, certainly came second to realist considerations of '[colonial] administrative convenience, diplomatic, and security reasons' (Shonreiphy 2014: 42).

Despite abounding uncertainties, in 1843 Bigge and Gordon proposed a boundary whose delineations, after subsequent correspondence and the snubbing of complaints, was more or less finalised in 1872 (Venuh 2005: 38).[13] This boundary, once implemented, drew quick resentment as Johnstone, then British Political Agent to Manipur, duly put to paper:

> There was a long boundary dispute between Manipur and the Naga Hills. The boundary has been most arbitrarily settled by us when the survey was carried out, so far as a certain point, beyond that it was vague. Manipur claimed territory which we certainly did not possess, and which she had visited from time to time, but did not actually hold in subjugation (Johnstone 1971: 93).

After the British departed, the boundary remained and became a bone of post-colonial contestations. As opposed to the demand of sovereignty, which remains the domain of Naga undergrounds, this desire to unify Naga lands within India finds articulation across the Naga political spectrum. For instance, a resolution unanimously adopted by the Nagaland Assembly in 1994 goes:

> Whereas, by quirk of history, the Naga-inhabited areas have been disintegrated and scattered under different administrative units without the knowledge and consent of

the Nagas... Whereas, the Nagas irrespective of territorial barriers have strong desire to come together under one administrative roof... the Assembly, therefore, resolves to urge upon the Government of India and all concerned to help the Nagas achieve this desired goal... (cited in Chasie 2005: 61).

Naga civil societies too demand this, and in 2010 the Naga Hoho – a pan-Naga apex body – went so far as to state that 'henceforth, we derecognize any artificial boundary lines drawn across out ancestral lands in the so-called Manipur state' (cited in Shonreiphy 2014: 44), while within Manipur, Naga civil bodies submitted multiple memoranda to the centre to express 'the desire and aspiration of the Nagas to live together as a people under one political roof', and that this is justified by 'historical facts.'[14]

However, there are also dissenting voices and doubts. Among them, Scato Swu, who headed the Revolutionary Government of Nagaland, which separated from the NNC in the 1960s, and whose experiences in the Naga national movement convinced him that 'Nagas would not be able to live together. We will fight among ourselves as there is a lot of tribal politics' (cited in Horam 1988: 53). Such instances of tribal discrepancies occasionally manifest themselves on 'state-lines', suggesting the emergence of new alignments, and 'on many occasions the NSCN(K) served "quit notice" to Tangkhuls to leave Nagaland. The Nagas of Manipur were considered "impure Nagas" as they were not part of the crucial phase of the movement' (Sharma 2011: 195). But even if not present, or under-represented, in the initial years of the struggle, when Tangkhul Nagas joined in large numbers, Horam (1988: 27), a Tangkhul himself, narrates how 'they were not welcomed by the few Naga tribes for fear that they would monopolise Naga leadership and the best jobs.' The extent of 'anti-Tangkhul propaganda by fellow Nagas', he continued, 'was difficult to understand by all non-Nagas' (ibid.).

The prospect of Naga integration also remains staunchly opposed by the states potentially affected by the redrawing of state boundaries, and whose governments invariably insist on the integrity of their territories, thus indicating that boundaries – even if historically contentious – have also solidified, producing new entitlements and territorial alignments. In coursing between the 'territorial imperative' (Harvey 2009: 171) and the 'dangers of [territorial] belonging' (Van Schendel 2011), local pundits have begun to explore possibilities of 'de-territorialized integration' for instance through cultural and emotional means, or supra-tribal institutions. Recently, and amidst ensuing political negotiation, the Naga People's Front (NPF) took a leap by expanding its party scope beyond the territorial confines of Nagaland (after changing its name from Nagaland People's Front), thus trying to unite Nagas across states behind their party. During Manipur's elections of 2012, the NPF filed twelve candidates in Naga dominated constituencies, of which four turned victorious. And while this result was hailed by the NPF who called it an electoral success and 'a forward journey of Naga integration', it was downplayed by Manipur's Congress Party, which interpreted its victory in eight of the constituencies as evidence that the majority of Naga votes aligned to the political status-quo. While the conversation on Naga integration is set to continue, recently another territorial quandary emerged: a claim for the bifurcation of Nagaland state.

THE WISH FOR BIFURCATION

While demands for sovereignty and integration resent and reject existing borders, lamenting their delineation 'from the drawing boards in distant places' (Chasie 2005: 35), in recent years an ostensibly contradictory demand emerged, one not for less, but for *more* boundaries and *more* divisions among the Naga. In 2010, the Eastern Nagaland People's Organisation (ENPO), representing the interests and aspirations of six tribes (Konyak, Chang, Phom, Sangtam, Khiamniungan, and Yimchunger) articulated a demand for the bifurcation of Nagaland through the enactment of a new state to be called 'Frontier Nagaland.' In support of this demand, mass rallies ensued in places across Eastern Nagaland, while towns and roadsides were decked with banners reading: 'We demand Frontier Nagaland', or 'Justice delayed is justice denied. We want Frontier Nagaland.' This act was widely seen as undermining the larger 'Naga cause': 'they [the ENPO] cannot be said to be in support of the integration issue while they are demanding a separate state of their own' (Shonreiphy 2014: 44). Or in the words of a Nagaland Minister: 'the Naga people – be it the NSCN(IM) or the NSCN(K) and NNC – they all had been fighting for the sovereignty of the Nagas, whereas some group [now] tries to divide the Nagas' (cited in *Kangla* 04-03-2011).

The ENPO, however, did not necessarily see it that way, and its office holders variously emphasized that they did not intend to obstruct on-going political dialogues. Their demand was to be understood and engaged with at a different level, as a response to a continuing development deficit they experienced across Eastern Nagaland. This dearth of development, they insisted, was not accidental but the cumulative result of skewed government priorities and projects. The statehood demand revolves, Khiamniungan (2014: 77) writes, around 'claims that [in] almost all the decision making or policy matters... [advanced Naga tribes] played the determining role.'[15]

But besides narratives of neglect, there was also a historical backdrop as the projected boundary between 'Nagaland' and 'Frontier Nagaland' largely coincided with the erstwhile colonial division between 'administrated' and 'un-administrated' Nagas. In a remarkable twist of reasoning, spokespersons of 'Frontier Nagaland' did not condemn colonial rule, but lamented its historical absence among them, as this had, they explained, thwarted their educational attainments and wider upliftment. Chingwang Konyak, a prominent politician from the area narrated thus: 'It is a process of civilization that administration extends from administered to 'un-administered areas', but whereas the Naga Hills District gradually came under British administration from 1866 onward 'there was a big tract of land between the Naga Hills and Burma which was not administered' (2012: 1)

Of the Chang Naga, part of this 'un-administrated' area, J.H. Hutton wrote in 1929:

> The Chang is one of those Naga tribes which occupy the hinterland, as it were, of the Naga Hills district, stretching back to the high range, which divides Assam from Burma. Only two small Chang villages of mixed population fall far enough west to come within the boundary of the administered district, the bulk of the tribe being situated in the area of loose political control which forms a buffer between the district and the still unknown tribes which occupy the slopes of the high range on both the Assam and Burma sides (1987[1929]: iii).

When Eastern Naga villages figured in colonial documents, often so in relation to raids and plunders into British administrated areas, the villages' names were usually preceded by such adjectives as 'trans-frontier', 'trans-Dhikhu' (the Dikhu being the river that broadly demarcated the end of British controlled areas), or 'free Nagas.' Eastern Nagaland's prolonged non-state existence also has ramifications in terms of Naga nationalist narratives, and which made a key informant I address as *Abou* (a Chang classificatory term for father) posit, in the context of decades of bloodshed and misery, that the Eastern Nagas should not have joined the Naga Movement given that they were already *de facto* independent:

> We were called 'free-land' and 'free-Nagas' and we belonged to no-tax land. When the British left they advised the Indians; you should cater to them for a few years and after that they can be on their own. But then A.Z. Phizo came to our Chang area and propagated an independent Nagaland consisting of both administrated and non-administrated Nagas. Because our

forefathers were mostly illiterate, they did not understand the implications of Phizo's plan and followed him, thus we ended up fighting for an independence and freedom we already had.

Even if Abou's reasoning appears somewhat fanciful (and does not necessarily represent an uniform view held across Eastern Nagaland) as there was no sign that newly Independent India was *not* to expand its administration, his evaluation nevertheless corresponds with Elwin's (1957: 3) observation that 'the leaders of the Naga National council, and those who follow them by conviction, are not the Nagas who have had least to do with the outside world, but those who have seen most of it.' That the present-day Eastern Naga tribes should fall outside British administration Elwin had deemed bad policy in the first place:

> Even after the Naga Hills District had been brought under ordered Government, the wild and rugged tract to the north-east remained. It was populated by martial tribes; there were no communications and no money to build or maintain them; and despite constant urging that it was inconsistent to develop one part of the hills and neglect another (1961: 27)

While hardly any administrative attention or resources was directed to trans-Dikhu Naga villages, in legal terms the area was brought under British nominal control in 1902, and in the Government of India Act of 1935 'Tuensang was defined by as a '"tribal area" within India' (Elwin 1961: 27). Crucially, however, the Tuensang Area (which broadly overlaps with the whole of Eastern Nagaland today) was not classed as an extension of the then Naga Hills but brought under the North-Eastern Frontier Agency (NEFA), which extended northwards into what is today known as Arunachal Pradesh. It was only in 1963 that the Tuensang Frontier Division was separated from NEFA and aligned with the Naga Hills District to form the new state of Nagaland. This unison, even if advocated and brokered by the Naga People's Convention (NPC) (see Sema 1986), in which Eastern Naga leaders were represented, however was not on equal footings, or so asserts Chingwang Konyak:

> [When Nagaland State was created in 1963] there were hardly any graduate from Tuensang [Eastern Nagaland]. Even Matriculates were very few, so people of the present ENPO areas could not get in the Government Services. But from the present advanced tribes, many were recruited into the Nagaland Civil Service, Nagaland Police Service, and other services (2012: 6).

With affective bonds of village, clan, and tribe readily superseding normative projections of impersonal statehood and detached governance, the ENPO today laments that state employment and benefits quickly became usurped by the kin and wider tribesmen of the already 'advanced tribes' who came to adjudicate the state machinery, thus perpetuating their comparative class distinction. It is perhaps here, in the sphere of state allocations and entitlements, where instances of the tribalism that long thorn the Naga Movement assumes full force, in the process creating new resentments and divisions, but also fresh aspirations and alignments. While many 'Western' Nagas appear ready to admit that the Eastern tribes comparatively lag behind, their take on the situation remains different. When the (then) Chief-Secretary of the Nagaland Government visited the Chang village where I was carrying out fieldwork on the occasion of the 22 Chang Gazetted Officers meet, he asked those present to rethink their claim for 'Frontier Nagaland.'

> I am going to speak from my heart, and there might be certain things which you [The Chang Gazetted Officers] might not like to hear, but in that case please bear with me… The ENPO is in confusion, because when they submitted their representation I observed that 99.99% of their grievances have to do with development. These are development issues which can be solved with proper planning, good leadership and special packages. We Nagas can't live divided. If we are not united we will fall.

In other words, if the colonial division and disseverance of Naga territories lies at the crux of demands for sovereignty and integration, the demand of 'Frontier Nagaland' roots in a history of colonial absence and of experiences of post-Nagaland statehood marginalisation. ENPO's demand for *more* boundaries and *more* of the Indian state suggests that the state and boundaries are no longer just sites of resentment among the Naga, but now also manifest themselves as lucrative entries to state resources well worth struggling over.

CONCLUDING REMARKS

At the historical face of it, current Naga territorial predicaments, the disputes, the violence, suggest the British 'messing up', and of independent India instead of rectifying wrongs, perpetuating them. But things are hardly that simple, and the armadas of Naga nationalism and the arbitrariness of colonial borders and policies connect and disconnect in complex ways, as the aspirations for sovereignty, integration, and bifurcation illustrate.

What remains undisputed is that Nagas, akin to the colonial subalterns subjugated and marginalised elsewhere, had little or no say in the drawing of borders, whose delimitations were instead concocted and chiselled at the convenience of the colonial administration and later confirmed and congealed (but also added to) in the post-colony. Even as boundaries in South and Southeast Asia did not dwell on the catastrophic notion, once popular in colonial Africa, that straight lines make uncomplicated borders, they hinged on arbitrary considerations, political motives, and bird-eye perspectives all the same. Consequently they not just truncated what was, or came to be, Naga political consciousness across two countries and four states, but also cut across single tribes, split villages, and, in at least one instance, runs through a house, as is the case for the dwelling of the chief of the Konyak Naga village of Longwa (Shonreiphy 2014: 42).

But the story of the Naga is not just a story of a colonially subjugated people seeking a return of their freedom, their territory, and to fulfil their perennial destiny as a nation. There are other stories to be told. Among them, the notion that history, collective memories, and nationalist narratives need not coincide (and not only among the Naga), but that 'to release a different imaginary concerning the past is to release a different imaginary as to future possibilities' (Harvey 2009: 181). Naga nationalism, as a motion, praxis, and political project, after all, hinges on 'future time', not 'time past', and its political projections, first voiced by A.Z. Phizo and his NNC, were products of their time, which is reliant on, and responsive to, the rise to hegemony of the modular form of the territorial nation-state (Biolsi 2005), in the process producing a new Naga political space, sociality and subjectivity. But the Naga story is also a story of old tribal loyalties and differences, new alignments, fresh entitlements, and a gradual (if still contested) embeddedness into colonial and post-colonial state structures, arbitrary but now long-standing territorial divisions, and development programmes and aspirations, all adding to a current multiverse of claims and counter-claims. Thence, if the Indo-Naga conflict is especially protracted and vexed, as is so often asserted, this is not only an aftermath of fraught colonial policies, the sole result of failed treaties and backfiring policies, or because decades of military confrontations did not identify a clear victor, but also because over the years different Naga groups came to propound differential, and at times ostensibly conflicting, political and territorial claims. The Centre, on its part, looks on and insists, as does the owner of the Assam road-side *dhaba* quoted in the epigraph, that before the Naga place their order they first decide what they want to eat.[16]

03

POLYTHETIC DEMOCRACY

Tribal Elections, Bogus Votes, and Political Imagination
in the Naga uplands

POLLING DAY IN PHUGWUMI

07:00 AM. Polling Day. Phugwumi, Nagaland.
Villagers thronged near the gate that led toward the Government High School in whose classrooms electronic voting machines had been installed the previous day. The gate was guarded by rifle-clad soldiers who hailed from places across India and had been dispatched to the faraway – for them – and remote Naga uplands to ensure the smooth conduct of polling. On receiving a nod from their commandant, two jawans unlocked the gate. Polling began.

07:10 AM. Polling halted.
'Why are you carrying so many voting slips?' the commandant snapped at a village elder wrapped in a colorfully embroidered shawl to keep out the February cold. 'One man, one vote. That's the rule!' The commandant scaled up his voice, seeing that nearly all voters had multiple slips in hand. His interference was met with loud disapproval. 'This is our village,' one villager known for his fortitude, stepped out of the queue and protested. 'Don't tell us how to play democracy!'

Little could the army commandant know that Phugwumi's Village Council had endorsed 'household voting,' a decree that empowered the head of each household to cast the votes of his dependents. 'Household voting' was thought to have several advantages. First, it would render it unnecessary for villagers who resided elsewhere, particularly students, to travel home to vote as someone could vote for them. Second, it facilitated the polling of the roughly two thousand bogus or proxy votes the village was proud to possess and in the run up to Polling Day had struggled hard to protect from proposed deletions (more below). It was also seen as more effective as it shortened queues. In any event, it had long been seen as a man's duty to represent his family in the political sphere, and it was only in rare instances that members of the same household voted differently as this was understood as showing discord within the family.[1]

07:30 AM. Voting still on hold. Tension mounting.
Everyone agreed that this election was of a different kind as it was for the first time in Phugwumi that two of its villagers had joined the same fray, a political circumstance nearly all villagers lamented. In an attempt to prevent intravillage divisions and differences from flaring up, the villagers had tried to select a village 'consensus candidate' to whom the village votes and proxies were then to be allotted. Multiple rounds of meetings, however, had not led to a consensus and both politicians had entered the fray, competing for the constituency's seat with each other and two more candidates from close-by villages.

07:45 AM. Both village politicians arrived at the school compound.
After a ferocious campaign, which had divided the village into political camps, the two village candidates now acted in unison. The commandant's decree of 'one man, one vote' risked the polling of the village's bogus votes, which the Village Council, in the absence of a single consensus candidate, had resolved to divide equally over both candidates. As Nagaland constituencies and margins are comparatively small, such additional votes could well mean the difference between winning and losing. The two politicians confronted the commandant, telling him, in clear terms, that his jurisdiction was confined to the maintenance of law and order, that he had no business in lecturing the villagers on how democracy works. For a while the commandant stood his ground, drumming up electoral principles to his defense, but with two irate politicians challenging his authority, and the atmosphere around him turning exceeding volatile, he eventually gave in.

Household voting was allowed to resume and bogus votes polled.

INTRODUCTION

This ethnographic snapshot depicts Polling Day in a Chakhesang Naga village I call Phugwumi, where I was carrying out research when the 2013 Nagaland State Legislative Assembly elections ensued. Reports and tales from villages across Nagaland, a small, hilly, and tribal state tucked deep into India's Northeastern region, indicate that Phugwumi's way of 'playing democracy' might hardly constitute a case of local deviance. But if inflated electoral lists, 'household voting,' and the effort (albeit in this case a failed one)[2] to agree on a consensus candidate appear ready fodder for judging Nagaland's democracy as dissolute and perverse, and for regulating it to the dubious chambers of democratic deficits and electoral ills, as is indeed commonly done (Misra 1987; Singh 2004; Dev 2006; Amer 2014), this essay seeks to flick the paradigm. It explores what happens to our understanding of what procedural democracy means and is about when we interpret Phugwumi's engagement with elections not necessarily as deviant and deluded but simply as empirical data based on particularistic historical and cultural inferences and logic in need of explanation, even theorizing. Proposing thus, this essay asks, what do ordinary Naga men and women actually make of the procedural democracy they are made to engage with (cf. Comaroff and Comaroff 1997; Paley 2008)?

While much has been said about the need to decenter the ideas and idioms of, among others, liberal democracy, the subject, and popular sovereignty that largely emerged out of European thought and history, from where they then swelled into universalistic and normative projections (Chatterjee 1986; Chakrabarty 2000), the core tenets of liberal democracy — which besides regular trips to the polling booths, free press, universal adult franchise, secret balloting, and an open multiparty system hinges crucially on voters behaving as 'enchanted individuals,' at once part of society and capable to deliberate and act autonomously from it (Gilmartin 2012) — remain the benchmarks (and conjure the temporal and transspatial definition of democracy) against which existing democracies are evaluated.[3] Put differently, while global democratic theories provide everyone the right to vote, they do not allow voters everywhere, Ashis Nandy (2002: 4) writes, 'the right to bring their odd cultural ideas and morality into the public sphere,' in the upshot precluding and impeding local understandings of the substance and guiding principles of politics and 'the political.'

Stressing the veracity of Nandy's 'odd cultural ideas and morality,' not as deviances but as carriers of political modernity, this essay distances itself from the preconceived notions that make 'normative democracy' (see Nugent 2008) in favor of the 'analytic openness' Julia Paley (2008: 3–4) rightly deems crucial 'to explore how anthropological perspectives might take understandings of democracy in new and unanticipated directions.' To do so, the pages that follow invite attention away from the constrictive canons and creeds central to most political and democratic theories and argues toward recognizing the polythetic nature (invoking Needham [1975]) of democracy by providing central stage to democracy's contingent character and its open-ended, ever-evolving construction (Paley 2002), its multivalence (Gutmann 2002: xviii), its particularistic moral idioms (Piliavsky 2014a), and the longer histories that usually lie behind contemporary political and electoral practices as they manifest themselves locally (Witsoe 2013), but so without fully discounting the authoritative presence of circulating, global discourses and dominant assumptions steadfastly and staunchly propagated by international organizations and national Election Commissions.

Modern democracy, I will argue, is to join the ranks of core anthropology topics such as kinship and ritual to be accepted and approached as amorphous and polythetic (Needham 1975), as not constituting a defined and discriminable class of political phenomena, molded by a distinct and universalistic assemblage of liberal democratic theories, that can be measured, evaluated, and objectively ranked (as is attempted, for instance, by the organization Global Democracy Ranking) but as a broad, open-ended, and multivalent political construction that locally manifests itself as indissoluble to – in its ideas, idioms, and praxis – the particularistic socio-historical substances, social bonds, and struggles over standing and sway that shaped 'the political' long before the authoritative entrance of liberal and procedural democratic institution. Democracy, then, too, is an 'odd job word' (Wittgenstein cited in Needham 1971: 7); handy to describe and classify societies and a term easy to invoke at will, but so at the analytical risk, to transmute Leach's classic phrase, of merely creating a class labeled (liberal) democratic societies that may be as irrelevant for our understanding of actual democratic practices, principles, and imaginations as 'the creation of a class of *blue butterflies* is irrelevant for the understanding of the anatomical structure of lepidoptera' (Leach 1961: 4; emphasis in original).

Among modern democratic projects worldwide, postcolonial India draws special attention, not just for its status as the world's largest democracy but for the democratic and electoral effervescence reported all across, the unprecedented political participation and opportunities for upward mobility democratic institutions and elections provided for the poor, lower castes and other oppressed rungs of the society, the resultant 'million mutinies' for change (Kohli 2001: 14), its spotless democratic record (bar a brief interlude of emergency 1975–77), and its unfailingly high voter turnouts.[4] To account for India's democratic enthusiasm anthropologists have now foregrounded popular perceptions of democracy and elections (Banerjee 2008) and invoked the term 'vernacular democracy' to grasp the ways in which democratic practices 'have been gradually moulded by folk understandings of 'the political' which in turn energize popular politics' (Michelutti 2007: 642; cf. Tanabe 2007; Neyazi, Tanabe, and Ishizaka 2014). Crucial to democracy's vernacularization, or indigenization, is its inevitable 'territoriality' as Jeffrey Witsoe (2009: 64) proposes to capture how democratic politics become absorbed into often purely local and always animated contestations over dominance and subordination, which in his ethnographic setting of Bihar involved numerically preponderating lower castes taking on the traditional hegemony of upper castes (cf. Jaffrelot 2002). Thence if such plotting of the 'vernacular map' of India's democratic experiences is the devise, what we might need a pinch less of are discussions of institutional factors and functioning, formal analyses, Gini-coefficients and positive correlations, party manifestos, official rhetoric, and left-center-right political spectra, but instead locate new departures in the crucial insight that 'party ideology is more often than not trumped by social relations' (Holmberg cited in Gellner 2009: 127; cf. Chakrabarty 2008).[5]

Clifford Geertz (1973: 311) anticipated this turn when he argued already long ago how 'a country's politics reflects the design of its culture.' He continued, 'one the one hand, everything looks like a clutter of schemes and surprises; on the other, like a vast geometry of settled judgments,' only to conclude, a little dismayed: 'what joins such a chaos of incident to such a cosmos of sentiment is often extremely obscure, and how to formulate it is even more so' (Geertz 1973: 311).[6] Such 'extreme obscurity' between culture, broadly conceived, and modern politics may however be much diminished by rigorously studying democracy bottom-up and through approaching politics – both its acts and articulations – in the vernacular and in the ethnographic *longue durée*,[7] thus clearing the stage for the study of 'actually existing politics' (Spencer 2007: 178) without reducing them to assessments in terms of, what Alain Badiou (2010: 7) calls sarcastically, 'the good little democrat's handbook.' By attempting thus, this essay also answers to Witsoe's (2011: 621) plea that the multifarious experiences of Indian democracy requires 'positive theorization' with 'positive in the sense of not being reduced to the frameworks of analysis that have emerged from, and formed part of, liberal democratic models of governance or even that derive from critiques of liberal democracy.' Thence, a Phugwumi villager exclaiming 'don't tell us how to play democracy' is not to be seen as evidence of immature or misled political imagination but an invitation to explore a vernacular political modernity, one that offers a critique to conventional democratic theory and practices but that is crucially informed, as I seek to show ethnographically, by particularistic historical and cultural practices and principles that have remapped themselves as 'changing continuities' (Schulte-Nordholt 2005) unto the new democratic arena.[8]

In what follows I will argue toward more profound anthropological engagements with democratic politics and elections by situating them in both the vernacular and ethnographic *longue durée*. The locus and ethos of the pre-state (Chakhesang) Naga polity, which revolved around village and clan loyalties and rivalries, and whose internal deliberations were crucially guided by the normative principle of consensus-making, are to my way of reasoning crucial ingredients to capture contemporary and local conceptions of 'doing politics' and of arranging 'the political.' With Polling Day drawing near, we will discuss two episodes that stood out in Phugwumi. First, the villagers' desperate (and successful) attempt to protect the village electoral list from the state-initiated deletion of 'bogus votes,' and, second, the villagers' (unsuccessful) attempt to agree on a 'village consensus candidate.' This is followed by the conclusion, which draws out the larger theoretical issues invoked in the anthropological study of democracy. But first a few words about the ethnographic setting.

THE SETTING

As the vernacular experience of India's democracy is now slowly being plotted (Michelutti 2007, 2008; Berenschot 2011; Witsoe 2013; Piliavsky 2014ab, 2013; Ruud 2003), this so far remains to the exclusion of India's Northeast. And if this is only characteristic of the region's wider scholarly identity as a 'geography of ignorance' (Van Schendel 2002), in the contemporary world of Indian democracy this marginal engagement also persists because theories and concepts in vogue to capture South Asian democratic life-worlds find little or no historical and social roots among Nagaland's tribal and predominantly Christian populace.[9] Absent, in Nagaland, are politics of caste relations and equations deemed so central elsewhere (Srinivas 1955; Gupta 2005), age-old and '*Jajmani* infused' patron-client relations scripted afresh unto the democratic playing field (Piliavsky 2014b), or politicians (even entire castes) associating themselves with, or seen as avatars of, particular gods and deities (Michelutti 2004; 2008). Absent, too, are Dalit parties trying to unsettle upper caste dominance as is reported for South India (Gorringe 2011), or the unfolding of a 'silent revolution' with lower castes successfully seizing political power across North-India (Jaffrelot 2002). The study of Nagaland's democratic experience, its local character, inner-logic, and substance, then, offers another entrance into the multiverse of Indian democracy.

Before proceeding, it must be qualified that Nagaland might not be a straightforward place to study Indian democracy as the legitimacy of the Indian state is locally challenged and undermined by a long lingering claim for Naga independence. It was in its quest for independence that the Naga National Council (NNC), then led by A. Z. Phizo, boycotted the country's general elections of 1952 and 1957 (see L. Ao 2002: 49). It was only after the creation of Nagaland state — as an autonomous state with the Indian Union — that elections became regular and gradually also participatory (Amer 2014), even though the NNC and nascent nationalist Naga groups continue to condemn such elections as 'Indian elections imposed on Naga soil.'[10] Over time, the NNC's standing and sway faltered, but not necessarily the Naga Movement, which is today forwarded by (rivaling factions of) the National Socialist Council of Nagalim (NSCN), whose strongest powerhouse, the NSCN-IM, currently finds itself in a long-drawn ceasefire with Delhi (although at the time of writing, many rounds of negotiations had not yet culminated into a definite political settlement). While any account of Nagaland's democracy may not be considered conclusive without a discussion on what is locally called the 'underground factor,' this will not figure centrally in this essay, which instead focuses on the substance and idiom of elections as it unfolded itself at the village level.[11]

This village level is provided by the Chakhesang Naga village of Phugwumi, which akin to many Naga villages sits perched high on a hilltop from where it stands guard over its neatly excavated paddy fields below.[12] The village's social texture is shaped by clans, of which there are six: Tunyi, Puro, Kezo, Vero, Yhobu, and Thira. Clan feelings tend to be strong in the sense that the six clans are thought of as natural units with their members having specific physical, behavioral, and mental predispositions, as well as sometimes specific historical narratives of migration and settlement, while certain patches of forest and fields around the village are clan-owned and the influential positions of Village Chairperson and Village Development Board secretary rotate clan-wise. In the prestate and colonial past Phugwumi was known and feared as a 'warrior village' and exerted widespread influence and tribute — 'they were dreaded by all around as a blood-thirsty people, who think nothing of murder for the sake of plunder,' as the colonial officer John Butler (1855: 208) wrote about the Phugwumi villagers — a historical disposition of standing and supremacy, which, I will show, most villagers saw as 'natural' and inevitable to see itself reflected and remapped onto the new democratic arena.

In terms of demography, Phugwumi is a large village, the largest of the constituency, which counted eight more villages and a modest administrative hub. In 2013, the constituency's electoral list tallied below 22,000 votes. As such, Phugwumi's constituency was small, which is akin to other Nagaland constituencies but very different from those in most parts of India.[13] Of the 22,000 total votes, Phugwumi alone possessed nearly 5,500. This numerical preponderance made Phugwumi center stage during elections as its internal electoral dynamics could well be, and often had been, decisive in the overall election outcome. In this the 2013 state elections was to be no different.

STUDYING ELECTIONS IN THE ETHNOGRAPHIC *LONGUE DURÉE*

While voting has been construed as a technique through which democratic knowledge and authority is constructed (Cole 2004), and voter turnouts as a sign of people's faith in the political system of democracy (Lukes 1975), in Phugwumi balloting must also be understood as an act 'after the fact' (Geertz 1998), comparable to the last Arabian Night preceded by a thousand equally enticing others. It is the substance of these proverbial thousand nights, and many more, that makes the social archaeology of voting decisions in Phugwumi today. Perhaps it is this misconception – that an election constitutes a short, spasmodic event, and is thus unsuitable for the prolonged inquiry characteristic of anthropology – that for long prevented anthropologists from fully endorsing democracy and its elections as a prime field of ethnographic inquiry.

Those few anthropologists who did venture beyond the numerical assessments of democracy often ended up interpreting them using the advanced anthropological idiom of ritual (Abeles 1988; McLeod 1999). Thus an election is seen as a 'ritual drama' (Nimmo 1985), as an elaborate rite in the Victor Turner (1969) sense complete with a liminal in-between phase (Herzog 1987) and the fostering of communitas (Banerjee 2011) caused by a temporary flattening of hierarchies as otherwise socially elevated and aloof politicians turn 'beggars' for votes. Like a proper 'ritual of rebellion' (Gluckman 1954), the election ends with a reaffirmation of the institutional status quo of procedural democracy. For India, too, it is held that through the act of balloting 'Indians reaffirm the unity of the nation and the investment of power in the rulers by the ruled' (Hauser and Singer 1986: 942). In the latest edition of this 'election-as-ritual' approach, Banerjee (2007, 2011) emphasizes the festive, almost sacred ethos elections have taken on in West-Bengal, and more widely across the Subcontinent. People flock to voting booths, Banerjee says, not because they are sufficiently naïve to expect that their welfare will change from one election to the next, as their previous experiences tell them it will likely not, but because they perceive the act of voting as a sacred expression of citizenship; as a signature of 'patriotic faith in the idea of India' (2007: 1560). Banerjee's interpretation certainly lands in troubled waters in Nagaland where voter turnouts readily pitch over 80 percent (Amer 2014), and is so both significantly higher than West-Bengal and the national average (which usually counts around 60 percent), but whose inhabitants often distance themselves (and are distanced from) ideas of India and 'Indianness' (Wouters and Subba 2013), and where a resistance movement against the Indian state continues to hold sway, eliciting considerable local support. If not out of patriotic faith, what then explains, in addition to proxy voting, the electoral effervescence in Phugwumi and across Nagaland?[14] The following ethnographic and historical discussions offer a few initial insights.

While democratic politics was initially not a core part of my research, after elections were scheduled it soon etched itself at the very center of it. This was not only because it attracted my interest (which I must confess it did) but also because politics soon submerged Phugwumi's entire social landscape. Suddenly, the theme of politics seemed to crop up in almost all everyday conversations, whether they were held in the paddy fields, around kitchen fires at nights, or on the whitewashed steps leading to the village church. Such discussions, however, generally did not involve the party manifestos, political ideologies, or government policies most political theorists would want voters here, there, and everywhere to discuss. Instead they revolved around bonds of kinship, historical narratives, village and clan loyalties, and for some, it should not be denied, about the monetary offers candidates were likely to make in return for their votes.[15] Such 'political talks' often zoomed in on disagreements or grievances gone unaddressed, ranging from land disputes, intervillage differences, incidences of thieving, adultery, and unfulfilled promises, to intravillage clan (and personal) rivalries over local standing and dominance, and while such past episodes remained mostly dormant in 'ordinary times' as Polling Day drew closer they became recalled and brooded over aloud.

A former Phugwumi politician, for instance, narrated how his candidacy had been hindered by the perceived conduct of some of his relatives during his father's and grandfathers' times:

> They were well-built, strong, and excelled in village wrestling. Those days, 'might' often meant 'right' and they became somewhat domineering in their behavior and got themselves landed into disputes. Much has changed since, but the

villagers remembered this. Many therefore felt reluctant to cast their vote for me. I was held accountable for deeds done long before I was even born.[16]

He had also expected, but only marginally received, electoral support from one particular clan:

> In the past, we [the former politician's clan] acted as their elder brothers. They were small in numbers but we saw to it that they were treated at par with other village clans. We protected them. When I contested, I reminded them about this part of our village history but in the end many of them voted for another candidate.

'Politics runs very deep in our village,' or so I was told repeatedly.[17]

A political agent of one of the candidates explained further: 'Our villagers don't vote based just on the present. They also see the past behavior of the ancestors, relatives, and clan-members of the candidates. If there is some problem or controversy there, the candidate will find it difficult to win.' Given this deep social archaeology that influenced local voting decisions, for me as an 'outsider' to grasp the villagers' political reasoning there was no shortcut to first grappling with Phugwumi's social history in its entirety, including how its six clans were said to have come to their present location, when they arrived, and their reputation and standing within the village. How during the precolonial era the village had grown into a monopolistic protection racket, one that raided nearby villages and levied widespread tribute, and how such tributary relations extended into the colonial and, in some cases, the postcolonial era. But also the intricacies, conspiracies, and rivalries internal to Phugwumi, which involved clan struggles, contests over status and standing, and disputes over land and property. It was such narratives, not parties, manifestos, and ideologies that turned into the stuff and substance of local electoral politics.[18]

To better understand such a remapping of 'old politics' onto new political arenas, we might do well to first take a step back. In 1933, Christoph von Fürer-Haimendorf, the first trained anthropologist to carry out prolonged fieldwork among the Naga, accompanied J. P. Mills, the then Deputy Commissioner, on a tour deep into Angami Naga territory, visiting a number of villages, some in the vicinity of Phugwumi. In each village Fürer-Haimendorf watched how 'hordes of clansman' (1939: 12) approached J. P. Mills to bring before him their disputes and disagreements. Quarrels mostly concerned 'land and the succession to property or the claims of a betrayed husband, suing the seducer of his wife, or the damage that one man's cattle had done to another man's crops.' All along, J. P. Mills 'very patiently worked through the tangle of accusations and defense, and finally passed judgments' (1939: 12). It befuddled Fürer-Haimendorf: 'Why is it that the Angamis of those remote villages, whose economy had then not been disrupted by an outside force, were unable to settle disputes among themselves and brought the most trivial quarrels before the Deputy Commissioner?' The answer was perhaps not the breakdown of tribal jurisdiction Fürer-Haimendorf suggested, but may be sought in the villagers' agency to appropriate and rework the colonial machinery to their own benefits. Put differently, colonial offices and officers came to provide ordinary Naga villagers with new avenues to work through preexisting divisions and differences, and new ways to settle long-standing struggles over clan and village status, standing, and sway (cf. Spencer 2007: 84–87).

It is a similar inner-logic, I pose, that came to characterize Nagas' engagement with poststatehood institutions and ideas of procedural democracy. While reasoning in a very different context, Jonathan Spencer subscribes to the possibility of such a reading when he concludes for rural Sri-Lanka:

> If party politics had not come to the village, the villagers would have had to invent them. Politics had simply provided a new idiom in which villagers could express the kinds of division that had long existed. As such, electoral politics was simply the latest in a line of institutions which villagers had appropriated for their own uses. (2007: 84–85)

What new democratic institutions and practices locally provided for the villagers, Spencer had already proposed a decade earlier, was 'an apparently bounded and structured social arena in which to work through all manners of purely local tensions and differences, while nevertheless seeking more of the good things and social standing that follow from access to the state' (1997: 9). Challenged here, as does the ethnography of Phugwumi, is the conventional view that elections and voter turnouts express 'the symbolic affirmation of the voters' acceptance of the political system and their role within in' (Lukes 1975: 304). Confronted, too, is the fancy that citizens in India cast their ballots as a ritual act of patriotic fervor to the idea of India. What emerges as crucial, to the contrary, is to look at how democratic ideas and practices become vernacularized and territorialized. How preexisting divisions and struggles over local standing and dominance, pace Spencer (2007, 1997), etch themselves at the very center of democratic imagination, stirring the electoral effervescence in ways it does in Phugwumi.

THE HISTORICAL SUBSTANCE OF THE NAGA 'POLITICAL'

In a necessarily abridged form, this section sketches the historical and cultural setting in which democratic practices and principles locally unfolded and became enmeshed (cf. Michelutti 2007). It does so in an attempt to locate, what John and Jean Comaroff (1997: 127) call, a 'native political anthropology,' one that engages with particularistic histories and vernacular cultures of participatory politics. It is through the ethnographic unpacking of such vernacular political narratives and practices, Comaroff and Comaroff well illustrate, that we may arrive at a critical appreciation of local democratic forms and functioning.

The prestate history of the Naga has been painted as a history of 'village republics,' of independent and semi-independent units. 'As with all Nagas,' wrote the colonial officer J. P. Mills (1926: 176), 'the real political unit of the tribe is the village.' Over time, most authorities on Naga history tell us, 'each village emerged [as] independent and had its own history' (Venuh 2005: 15); they were at once 'sovereign and self-sufficient' (Nuh 2002: 15) and functioned as a 'compact and well-knit society' (Shimray 2007: 40). In broad strokes, this was how British officers first encountered the Naga:

> At the time of the first British acquaintance with them many villages were still isolated from their neighbours by thickly forested hills and by rivers unfordable for several months in the year, and they tended to be on terms of head-hunting warfare with their nearest neighbours, or at best of an armed and ever suspect truce, almost every village being an independent political entity. (Hutton 1965: 19)

Casual parallels have been drawn with ancient Greek city states: 'if the Greek had city-states, in Nagaland every village is a small republic' (Namo cited in Singh 2004: 14) or 'the ancient Naga possessed [a] political spirit like the people of Ancient Greece' (Singh 2004: 13), even though, unlike Greek city-states that engaged in extensive trade, the Naga village was a 'distinct economic unit' (Horam 1992: 60), one that 'grew in isolation' (Bareh 2001: 115).

Although such reconstructions of Naga pasts are not misinformed, they are overdrawn. For one, the focus on isolation fails to account for historical relations – whether raids, trade, or tribute – certain Naga villages had with peoples of the adjacent Assam plains (Wouters 2011; Devi 1968). It also underestimates the frequent intervillage struggles over local dominance, the tributary relations that thence emerged, and the rise to local hegemony of especially powerful villages (Hutton 1921a: 11). Phugwumi was one such village and by the time British forces started surveying the hills, it had established itself as a local hegemon – a British officer estimated the village to be inhabited by as many as 2,000 fierce and feared warriors (Butler 1855: 195). But while British pacification – Phugwumi's local supremacy took a blow when it was attacked and subdued by a British-led force in 1851 – put a halt to most (though not all) intervillage raids, this did not cease intervillage rivalries, even though it stopped its most violent expressions in terms of hitherto reported headhunting. Today narratives of such battles, heroic deeds, brave warriors, and the subduing of others villages, remain an essential and proud part of Phugwumi's repertoire of oral history, even though church pastors and deacons now preach that this pre-Christian, 'heathen' past is best forgotten.

A mere focus on the locus of the traditional Naga polity, as vested in the village, would also overlook the variety in its political ethos, any characterization of which must start with acknowledging its heterogeneity. Digging through the Naga archives we find accounts about chiefs and democrats (Jacobs et al. 1990), nobles and commoners (Fürer-Haimendorf 1973), village councilors (Mills 1926), clan elders (Mills 1922), powerful chiefs (Fürer Haimendorf 1939; Hutton 1921b), and the conspicuous absence of chiefs (Hutton 1921a). Phugwumi was a village without kings or chiefs, and was loosely ruled, village elders recall, through debate and consensus-making usually led by clan elders or other villagers who had gained social prominence,[19] and when such deliberations broke down, as they did occasionally, through the muscular principle of 'might is right' – 'the Naga Hills was peaceful,' the Assam Administrative report of 1890 states, 'except for one serious riot at the Angami village of [Phugwumi], in which one man was killed and several wounded.'[20]

Finally and crucially, sole focus on the 'village republic' conceals the pivotal axes of clan and *khel* (ward) within; for the Angami Naga J. H. Hutton (1921a: 109) qualified, 'although the village may be regarded as the unit of the political and religious sides of Angami life, the real unit of the social side is the clan. ... The rivalry or antagonism of clan with clan within the village has coloured the whole of Angami life' (1921a: 109), and such 'enduring patterns' (Fortes 1949) of clan continue, as we will see, to shape understandings of 'the political' inside the Naga village.[21]

If such historical insights complicate the thesis of the Naga village republic, it does not fully negate it, and 'some [probably all] Naga communities are organised very strongly around the principle of the village as a unit' (Jacobs et al. 1990: 71). From this follows that 'the village rather than a group of villages or a tribe is the natural unit of organisation and hence the correct basis of investigation' (Horam 1992: 60). This remains so in the poststatehood era as the 'village republic' became etched at the center of local governance. Through the Nagaland Village Council Act of 1978 and later Nagaland's unique Communitisation of Public Institutions and Services Act of 2001 (Pandey 2010), extraordinary judicial and administrative powers were delegated to the village levels, while as a general principle, 'the government tries not to interfere with the village administration' (Horam 1988: 18). In terms of identity articulations, too, the Naga village remains a prime marker, even though Nagas have long ceased to live solely in their villages. This corresponds to a wider trend in India's Northeast where 'Every village … has its own identity, and although many people have left their villages and settled in urban areas for better educational and medical facilities they continue to identify themselves with their respective villages' (Subba and Wouters 2013: 194). It was this historical texture, one embroidered with rivaling 'village republics' and also of clan struggles within, into which modern democratic institutions and practices became locally woven and tailored.

PROTECTING THE VILLAGE ELECTORAL LIST

Polling Day was still several months away when news seeped into Phugwumi that the government had scrutinized the village's electoral list and had identified as many as two thousand or so bogus votes; double entries, names of villagers long deceased, and of persons who no longer resided in the village or had never lived there. The government, it was said, was now preparing to delete these votes and that would instantly cut Phugwumi's voting strength by roughly a third. Inside the constituency, Phugwumi had not been the only village convicted guilty of maintaining an inflated electoral list, but nowhere was the proposed deletion proportionally as high. Phugwumi villagers received the news with anger, even outrage, and it was soon interpreted as a deliberate attempt on the village's historical standing and poststatehood political preponderance.

It did not take long for suspicion to befall a senior local politician known for his political acumen, who hailed from a village located on an opposite hill range. While a minister in the past, he had been defeated in the previous election, in no small parts because of low votes from Phugwumi.[22] Even fewer in Phugwumi were likely to endorse his candidacy this time, and the politician had therefore resorted to shrewdness, acting in connivance with those bureaucrats allied with him from the days he held office, to enhance his electoral prospects by reducing Phugwumi's voting power, or so it became suspected in the village. There were other signs pointing toward his involvement. The politician's proven vote-bank, a cluster of three villages including his natal one, had hardly been affected by proposed deletions, which rather than a reflection of the accuracy of their electoral lists was quickly interpreted as part of a large and crafty political scheme being put in place. Moreover, in recent press statements he had come out strongly in support of the elevated democratic principle of 'one man, one vote,' a sudden political ideal the villagers now understood as him having skillfully prepared the political grounds to unfold his electoral strategy of weakening Phugwumi.

More discomforting still was the realization that no nonvillager could possibly possess sufficient intimate knowledge of the village to differentiate genuine from bogus votes. An 'inside hand' was suspected, a fellow villager gone against his own people. 'Lured with money?' 'The promise of a government job?' 'A lucrative state contract perhaps?' Guesses were many and hidden accusations soon thickened the air. 'Nobody can defy our village,' A*the* remarked in dismay. 'This goes far beyond the election. This is affecting our village as a whole.' The Village Council, in an emergency meeting, decreed that should the 'inside hand' be identified he would face instant excommunication for seven years, a punishment that equaled Phugwumi's customary sentence for homicide.

To be sure, few in the village insisted that the proposed deletions were entirely unfair, as most knew that the Election Commission deemed bogus votes as perverse political practice. What was objected however was that the proposed curbing of the electoral list, rather than an outcome of official, detached, and impartial procedures, appeared a political attempt to downsize the village's standing and sway. For most, the village's inflated electoral list was understood as a reflection and remapping of the village's prestate hegemonic past. Given that in the modern political arena power and influence were no longer obtained by the might and bravery of village warriors but by numbers of votes, many in Phugwumi thought it was not just justifiable but historically inevitable that they would dominate numerically on the constituency's electoral list, and for which, in addition to its already large number of inhabitants, the addition of 'extra votes' had long been the prime method.

If an inflated electoral list and proxy voting — or the voting of 'dead souls' as Staveley (1972) called it for ancient Greece and Rome, which along with inventing procedural democracy also first invented its circumvention — is condemned as distorted electoral practice characteristic of a weak state and perverse political parties (Birch 2011: 37), in Phugwumi the casting of such proxies drew on an inner-logic of historical relations of intervillage dominance and subordination, a set of relations subsequently recast as the effect of democracy's vernacular territoriality.[23] Similar sentiments reasserting the 'village republic' revealed itself in a colloquial distinction between 'home' and 'escape' votes. Homegrown democratic theory taught that without solid 'home support,' or the votes from a contestant's natal village, it was nearly impossible for any politician to conquer his constituency. 'Escape votes,' in turn, referred to those votes villagers polled for candidates of other villages when a fellow villager was also contesting the fray. While 'escape votes' were not unusual, they carried a dubious moral quality as it was understood that those promising their votes to a nonvillage candidate must be doing so out of certain material interests, or perhaps had been monetarily induced, thereby privileging their purely personal considerations over those of kin and village loyalties.[24]

Besides promising to punish the 'inside hand,' Phugwumi's Village Council also dispatched a summon letter to the politician, offering him an opportunity to defend himself against the accusations. The summon, however, went unheeded, and when he also ignored a second and a third call letter, the Council took it as further evidence of his complicity and proscribed him and his party members from campaigning within the village's territorial jurisdiction. As no redress could be expected from the politician, council members called on the offices of the Additional District Commissioner in the nearby administrative town and subsequently on the District Commissioner posted in the district headquarters, located on an arduous five-hour drive away. The District commissioner, however, in his official capacity, had merely lectured Phugwumi's delegation on the principles and practices of 'good democracy' as outlined by India's Election Commission, and which well justified the deletion of the village's bogus votes. Phugwumi's efforts were further hindered by a rising prominence of a 'one man, one vote' slogan popularized by the locally influential Nagaland Baptist Church Council (NBCC).[25] And when during a courtesy visit to the village a few weeks later, the District Commissioner publicly defended the 'one man, one vote' principle, chances of retaining the bogus votes seemed all the more slim.

Seemingly against all odds, the Village Council persisted in pursuing the matter with the district administration, and in a last ditch effort another delegation took off for the district headquarters. It was during this visit that matters — as they were recounted to me by one of the delegates that evening — took a dramatic turn. As they pleaded their case once more, a state functionary remarked that more bogus names had been identified on Phugwumi's electoral list and were also being prepared for deletion. On hearing this, some of the delegates burst into anger, a rage fueled by frustrations cropped up for months. 'If you [the government] continue to harass and insult our village,' one of them had uttered forcefully, 'how do you expect us to be able to control our village youth?' Given that during times of conflict, or intervillage tension, village youth, in both past and present, quickly converted into village defense forces, the question posed was a rhetorical one, hinting at the possibility of unrest, of violence even. The deeper meaning of the statement was too obvious for the officer, a Naga himself, not to recognize. While still on their return to the village the Council's chairperson's mobile phone rang. The call came from the offices of the District Commissioner. In the brief conversation that followed the chairperson was assured that the administration was in no way prejudiced or ill-disposed against Phugwumi and that their grievances would be looked into.

Although it was impossible for the administration to rescind all deletions without gambling its authority to govern, the vast majority of them were revoked, making for a small political loss the villagers were now ready to settle for.

THE FAILED CONSENSUS CANDIDATE

If the previous section illustrated the remapping of the 'village republic' onto the new democratic arena, this section will focus on the micropolitics within Phugwumi, which mostly centered on sentiments and idioms of clan. In our wider body of political ethnography clan-politics is often associated with places in Central Asia, where despite massive state-led campaigns to foster national, civic identities, 'in all regions of each country, most people strongly identified with their local clan networks, not with ethnic groups, and certainly not with either the democratic opposition or the state' (Collins 2009: 1). As a social institution, clan is not usually seen as salient to the Subcontinent where identities and loyalties of caste continue to reign: 'politicians are obsessed with "caste,"' writes Lucia Michelutti (2007: 645).[26] With castes altogether absent among the tribal and Christian Naga but with clans assuming political significance, Phugwumi, and the Naga more widely, thus provides a contrary case.[27]

It was the first time for Phugwumi to have two of their own contesting the same fray. What especially worried the villagers was that the two candidates belonged precisely to those two clans that had long disagreed and struggled over standing, dominance, and property within the village.[28] It did not take long before Phugwumi's predicament was talked about as an interclan contest, both by voices inside and outside the village.[29] Here the problem was not simply that all fellow clan-members were obliged to vote for the candidate of their clan – after all, bonds of kinship can at times be as divisive as they are uniting – but that there was always a tension between one's expected loyalty and conformity to one's clan and more civic or private considerations.[30]

When it first became evident that two villagers aspired to contest the election, most in Phugwumi immediately objected. For one, they feared that it would lead to the breakdown of the village community into different groups, causing rivalries and resentments whose effects would be felt until long after the last ballot would be cast.[31] Second, it would divide the village vote-bank (including its proxies), and while it had always been an illusion for the entire village to unite behind a single candidate, in a village with as many votes as Phugwumi had, gaining a solid majority of 'home votes' would nevertheless put a candidate instantly ahead in the polls. Such village majority support would also provide the candidate with sufficient leverage to lay claim on the total of village proxies, thus further strengthening his position. 'One minus one is zero,' as one village leader captured Phugwumi's predicament, implying that were both to contest they would cancel out each other's prospects. This would not just be unfortunate in the context of Nagaland's (somewhat arbitrarily dubbed) politics of patronage and clientelism in which Members of the Legislative Assembly (MLAs) are invariably expected to privilege their natal villages, and their loyalists especially, in terms of state benefits, and which makes it lucrative for a village to have one of their own elected into the assembly, but also because a village producing an MLA would instantly witness a rise in its local standing and repute.[32] 'We have to keep our village together,' Athe opined. 'We should not allow two villagers to contest.' Others added that producing two candidates would cast shame on the village: 'It will show to the outside world that we are not united within.'

Following on popular opinion, the *Razu Kuhu* (the village's self-created apex body), in consultation with the Village Council, called for a consultative meeting to deliberate the matter. In the mass gathering that followed (although among them only few women were present) and that lasted throughout the day, multifarious opinions and views passed the venue, perspectives often preceded by long and detailed narrations of village and clan histories. 'Our village was not established just yesterday,' as it was explained to me during the meeting. 'We can't discuss today's politics without first discussing the past.' As the meeting prolonged, consensus emerged that only one villager should be allowed to contest. It was therefore resolved that the village community was to select a 'consensus-candidate' to which all villagers were socially and morally expected to submit their votes (although they could still vote for one of the two nonvillage candidates if they so desired), as well as given all the village's bogus votes.

If this resolution to 'select' rather than to 'elect' a candidate goes against the grain of universalistic and normative projections of autonomous voting, in Phugwumi (and among the Naga more widely) the act of balloting was subject to a sustained culturalist critique as it was seen as unduly dividing the village into 'our side' and 'their side,' thus challenging the widely noted communitarian ethos of the Naga village (Bendangjungshi 2012: 124; Biswas and Suklabaidya 2008: 184; Thong 2014: 158).[33] A. Z. Phizo, erstwhile President of the Naga National Council (NNC), captured this communitarian and consensual spirit as *Mechü medo zotuo*, which roughly translates as 'the binding will of the community.' Or in the words of another early Naga intellectual, 'We believe in that form of government that permits the rule, not of the majority, but of the people as a whole' (Sahkrie cited in Nuh 2002: 16).[34] Poststatehood Nagaland politicians have voiced similar culturalist critiques. On the floor of the Nagaland assembly, a minister proposed that Nagaland's election system be reformed, for the present election system went against 'the Naga way of life' (cited in L. Ao 1993: 224). A former Nagaland chief minister publicly advocated the replacement of the election system by one of selection, which he deemed 'necessary for a good [Naga] society based on faith in each other and in common values.' He insisted that this would 'not in any way hamper the power of the state government, rather helps the progress and thereby good government' (Sema 1986: 171–72). Most recently, it was another Nagaland Chief-Minister who remarked that 'election is not suited for Nagas,' then elucidating that 'selection of leader[s] would best suit Nagas' (cited in Solo 2011: 67), thus recognizing that 'the idea of 'an elected leader' was not in the scheme of life in the Nagas' (Solo 2011: 68).

Principles of 'selection' and 'consensus-making' (*Küdzükhoküyi*), even if endorsed culturally, could nevertheless be a highly contentious process.[35] Crucially, however, the essence of achieving consensus was not that everyone must hold the same opinion; the meeting's outcome, the resolution adopted, or the leader chosen was usually not the one to which the largest numbers of villagers agreed but the one to which the least numbers vehemently disagreed. As such, it was the tyranny of the majority in its reverse. This principle continues to reign in the state-protected realm of Phugwumi's customary governance. 'We never vote,' as Phugwumi's chairperson told me. 'We discuss until we reach an agreement among all [nineteen] council members.' As a result, council meetings were often lengthy, occasionally stretching for days on end. If no agreement could be reached a case or issue was declared unresolved or kept pending, which was preferred over forcing an outcome through the divisive practice of voting or raising hands. On the whole, consensus-making, even if a long-drawn exercise, was regarded as more cohesive as it reified a sense of community, skirted open competition, avoided disputes, and thence minimalized the risk of instigating disharmony within the village community. In the colonial era, this stress on deliberation and consensus-making made J. H. Hutton characterize the Angami Naga as a 'debating society.' He wrote, 'disputes, when settled at all, were probably settled by a sort of informal council of elders, who would discuss the matter under dispute with one another, the parties, and the general public at great length, until some sort of agreement was arrived at' (Hutton 1921a: 142–143).[36]

To select a consensus candidate, the Razu Kuhu called for a second meeting. However, for reasons I won't detail here, clan-members and supporters of both politicians remained firm behind their candidates, citing reason after reason to justify why their candidate, and not the other, should be named Phugwumi's consensus candidate. The meeting failed to resolve the situation, as did subsequent rounds of talks and attempted negotiations. Worth noting is that in one such meeting it was proposed that elders from a certain clan – let's call them clan C – should act as a mediator between the clans of the rivaling candidates as this would be in accordance with clan C's historical role as a barrier, bridge, and occasional arbitrator between both the clans. While this proposal did not achieve endorsement, that it was suggested perhaps further illustrates the centrality of clan reasoning in the micropolitics of the village.

While this failed attempt to agree on a consensus candidate frustrated most in Phugwumi, it pleased a small section of villagers. They were the party workers of the sitting MLA (during the previous election there had been no candidate from Phugwumi) who belonged to another village. They had withstood the primordial pulls from clan and village and continued to support their candidate who, during his past tenure, had reciprocated their electoral support by brokering them privileged access to the lucrative echelons of state. The sitting MLA now found his actions paying off in their continued loyalty, even though he had to assure and reassure to continue to provide them with such material benefits was he to retain the constituency's seat. Well aware that should Phugwumi unite behind a single candidate, the sitting MLA would stand little chances of winning, his party-workers had attempted, and with notable success, to sidetrack the village quest for a consensus-candidate by willfully appropriating elevated principles of democracy to their own uses: 'Is not the selection of a consensus candidate undemocratic? Can not any person contest if he wants to?' 'Should not all villagers decide by themselves whom to cast their vote for?' 'Are we not living in a free country?'[37]

CONCLUSION

Put together the various ethnographic incursions and historical subtexts and what we witness emerging is a Naga vernacular political modernity, or a homegrown democratic theory revealing itself. Such cultural readjustment is no doubt fraught with occasional contestations and incongruities — and will continue to evolve — but crucially relies on historical charters and a cultural inner-logic of its own, centering, in Phugwumi, around preexistent notions of the 'village republic,' clan sentiments and struggles, and the normative rule of consensus-making. Even if Phugwumi elders now lament how increased individualism, as well as monetary incentives offered by politicians, have started to corrode the communitarian ethos of the village polity (of which the villagers' failure to settle on a consensus candidate was seen as symptomatic), the ways elections are understood, talked about, and 'played' remain best understood as 'changing continuities' (Schulte-Nordholt 2005) of preexistent ideas and idioms of politics and 'the political.'

If this essay has been a persistent plea for more profound anthropological engagements with modern democracy and its elections by joining Paley (2008: 4) in arguing toward 'an awareness of democracy's open-ended construction,' it also calls for extending all of anthropology's complexities into its comparative analysis. Rodney Needham (1975) argued that topics central to the study of anthropology like systems of descent, marriage patterns, and residence should be understood as categories whose members bear overlapping (what Wittgenstein famously called) 'family resemblances' to each other, as well as to members of other categories, but do not exhibit a single and exclusive defining feature that until then, mostly monolithic definitions of, for example, matrilineal descent or patrilocal residence, supposed. Needham soon gathered a wide following and scholars now recognize the amorphous and polythetic nature of nearly all social phenomena they study, ranging from religion (Southwold 1978), ritual (Liénard and Boyer 2006), medicine (Ross 2012), to art (Morphy and Perkins 2006: 12) and even genital cutting (Lyons 2007).[38]

Such polythetic reasoning however has largely eluded the study of democracy and perhaps the field of political anthropology more widely. Even if we may readily agree that democracy does not possess a single and exclusive defining criterion, its evaluation is nevertheless grounded in an a priori and normative checklist of institutions, procedures, practices, and values that most liberal political theorists insist can, even should, be tutored into existence here, there, and everywhere (e.g., regular elections but voters *selecting* a consensus-candidate, or free media but villagers 'de-enfranchising' individuals by introducing household-voting conventionally fail the cut of good democracy). It is with some resourcefulness that the spirit of Needham's polythetic reasoning – thus recognizing democracy as an amorphous and polythetic concept – might result in approaches to modern democratic life-worlds less constricted by the indexes and instructions of the 'good little democrat's handbook' (Badiou 2010: 7), in the upshot helping us to broaden and resignify our political imagination.

In short, if a 'positive theorization' (Witsoe 2011) of India's multifarious democratic experience (and not only India's) is the device, this programmatic turn must rely on the recognition that modern democracy too is best understood as a polythetic phenomenon, as not exhibiting a set of exclusive characteristics and defining standards by which any democracy's well-being can thence be judged, but that modern democracy – its institutions, ideas, and practices – are characterized by an amorphous range of variations, differential understandings, marked multivalences, and distinctive constructions, to be understood in historically particularistic and relativistic frames. While this should not be a license to bring all performances of politics within the fold of democracy, recognizing the polythetic and contingent nature of democracy would importantly bestow levels of historical agency and cultural imagination on the recipients of modern democracy to adapt, reappropriate, and rework democracy and its elections according to their distinctive life-worlds. Thus enabling them to become the repositories and enactors of their own versions of democracy based on their, returning to Nandy (2002: 4), 'odd cultural ideas and morality.' If anything, the case of Phugwumi illustrates how the villagers, rather than adjusting themselves to the elevated principles of modern democracy, have long applied their agency and rich political imagination to adjust democracy and elections to themselves.

In conclusion, let us return to this essay's main question: 'what does democracy mean and what is it about among the upland Nagas?' Politics, Michel Foucault once said, 'is the continuation of war by other means' (cited in Witsoe 2011: 620). Without overstretching the analogy an illustrative linkage may be drawn among the Naga between contemporary democratic politics and prestate episodes of intervillage warfare and intravillage clan rivalries. For the Angami Naga (then still including the present-day Chakhesang Naga), Hutton (1921a: 109) observed how in times of intervillage war deep-seated clan antagonisms would temporarily be suspended and the villagers come together in unison. Such unity, however, was often fragile and in periods of relative peace 'the village would from time to time break out into riot, while it is incessantly troubled by internal bickering. In almost every dispute between two men of different clans the clansmen on each side appear as partisans and foment the discord' (Hutton 1921a: 109). As an intellectual exercise, replace 'war' with 'elections' and

Hutton's argument appears to stand today with Phugwumi acting in unison to defend itself from the proposed curbing of their electoral list, which they saw as a deliberate attempt on the village's political standing, but with the subsequent breakdown of the village community as the result of (although not necessarily fully determined by) clan competition within.

As for the election outcome, the mathematical equation of 'one minus one is zero' proved to be correct. On Polling Day the village vote bank, including its bogus votes, became divided between both candidates, while about fifteen percent of the votes 'escaped' the village. As a result, the sitting MLA retained his seat while the two Phugwumi candidates ended in the third and fourth positions respectively.

04

THE MAKING OF TRIBES: THE CHANG AND CHAKHESANG NAGAS

Known for its social, linguistic and cultural heterogeneity, India's Northeast is often presented as an 'ethnic mosaic' (Bhaumik 2009), a 'rainbow of people' (Rajkumar 2010), an 'ethnic explosion' (Nibedon 1981) or an 'anthropologist's dream' (Narahari 2002: 5). However, far from a neatly separated assortment of communities, the region's social diversity is layered and especially complex. 'India's Northeast', Ramirez writes, 'is emblematic of the regions where it is not only the extent of diversity that seems immeasurable, but also its irregularity' (2014: xvii). Usually such so-called 'social irregularities' — here understood as the reckoning of kinship and belonging, cross-cutting the superficially standard tribal and ethnic groups and boundaries — are discarded as misfits, idiosyncrasies and anomalies, or as the proverbial exceptions that demonstrate the rule of tribe and ethnic group as core social signifiers. This essay negotiates a different road; it moves beyond tribal essentialism by proposing central stage to such presumably 'social irregularities' as encountered ethnographically. In doing so, it formulates both a historical critique against dominant categorisations of the region's social landscape and suggests alternative ways of analysing local patterns and reckonings of relatedness, identity and belonging.

Drawing on ethno-historical perspectives and ethnography gathered from the small and hilly state of Nagaland, and specifically from those who today identify themselves as Chang and Chakhesang Nagas, the pages that follow illustrate how local social practices, expressions of kinship, and other forms of reckoning identity readily defy our everyday anthropological and administrative vocabulary. Across India's Northeast, this lexicon adopted by scholars – but equally by politicians, bureaucrats, litterateurs and local elites – to reconstruct, reckon and represent identities is vested in the authoritative discourse of 'ethnic group' and, in our context, 'tribes'. Despite local infatuation with the term 'tribe' now, it is not a vernacular category and its cultural transitivity, as I seek to show, was problematic. When put to practice, the denominator of tribe worked to conceal, even restrain, social spaces and historical possibilities that existed – and occasionally persist – before, beneath, betwixt and between categories of 'tribe', social possibilities I will tentatively capture as 'pre' or 'a-tribal' histories, 'trans-tribal' belongings and 'new' tribal formations.

In the upshot, then, this essay questions the mechanical use of the old and frequently betrayed category of 'tribe', including its folk sociologies and suppositions of perennial, immutable, relatively homogenous and discrete entities.[1] The uncritical usage of this category, I postulate, worked to absorb and usurp past (and present) 'social irregularities' instead of analysing them, and transmitting them further as vernacular social patterns and real historical possibilities of the reckoning of identities and belonging. Even if the following exercise to think outside the conceptual realm of tribe remains preliminary, it is our enduring incapability to venture beyond the contemporary tribal (and ethnic) paradigm that seems to constitute the greatest malady of the contemporary anthropology of India's Northeast.

THE IDEA AND IDIOM OF TRIBE AND THE NAGAS

Today peopled by 16 state-recognised Scheduled Tribes (STs), Nagaland is referred to as a 'tribal state'. Locally, ideas, idioms and sentiments of tribe inundate social life. Identities are recognised tribe-wise. The 'tribe' has become a prime category of governance including tribe-specific reservations and development allocations. Constituencies are more or less delimited on the basis of tribal territories, while acts of tribalism and inter-tribal antagonisms regularly make headlines.[2] And yet, as an idea, idiom and praxis 'tribe' is exogenous to Nagas (and India more widely) and was for long not a prominent mode of reckoning and expressing identities.[3] Scholars variously emphasise how 'originally the term [tribe] was used in African contexts and was transferred to British India' (Berger and Heidemann 2013: 6),[4] and that 'prior to the colonial era the use of a generic term to describe tribal peoples was, on the whole, absent' (Xaxa 2005: 1363). In fact, when the concept of tribe was first propagated to chart and categorise Nagas, British officers soon realised its problematic local translation. Captain Butler remarked that

> These various tribes all dovetail into each other in a most remarkable manner, and it is impossible to assign to them any hard-and-fast limits, or to say that beyond certain limits a tribe does not extend; for not only do we often find men from two or even three tribes living in the same village but in many cases villages belonging to the same tribe are separated from each other by those of several other tribes.[5]

No matter how hard they tried, Captain Butler and other colonial officers found it difficult, often impossible, to clearly define and delineate Naga tribes. But then, who expected them to arrange their lives in the form of fairly homogenous, linguistically undivided, culturally coherent and territorially defined tribes in the first place? The answer, in hindsight, was given by J.H. Hutton, formerly the British District Commissioner of the (then) Naga Hills when, roughly 30 years after his retirement, he reflected: 'The present [post-colonial] administration of the area, for one thing, have gone still further than we did in my time in *particularizing tribes*' (1965: 16, author emphasis).

Little analytical heed is paid to this process of 'particularising tribes'. This situation contrasts with the long flourishing body of historical research that shows how the colonial regime increasingly felt the need to classify, chart and categorise Indians into distinct and hierarchically linked social groups and, while not inventing, certainly promoted a caste paradigm of social life (Dirks 2001; Inden 1990). Similar analyses do not figure prominently in the social histories of tribes.[6] While adequately reviewing the history of how tribes have been conceptualised surpasses the scope of this essay, historical (and still popular) portrayals of what a tribe is relied on notions of a cultural aggregate, a historically constant entity, residence in a discrete territory and the sharing of a unique language. To illustrate, 'The Imperial Gazetteers of India in 1891 first defined a tribe as a "collection of families bearing a common name, speaking a common dialect, occupying or professing to occupy a common territory"' (cited in Mukherjee 2013: 810). In 1967, a Joint Parliamentary Committee reproduced such views when it asserted 'geographic isolation' and a 'distinctive culture' as core characteristics of tribes (cited in Atal 2009: 23–24). But also an anthropologist as acclaimed as Fürer-Haimendorf could talk about the 'cultural background of the individual tribes' (1982: 3), thus apparently suggesting that each tribe had a unique and unified culture. Of late, this discursive conflation between identity, culture, language and territory has found new and fertile soil in the transnational indigenous movement, of which the Nagas have become an enthusiastic part (Karlsson 2003), and whose discourses, publications and sessions tend to promote essentialist and historically stable reconstructions of so-defined indigenous communities (Kuper 2003).[7]

Such discursive essentialism of 'tribe', however, is easily defied by lived realities, certainly so in India's Northeast. For the Assam-Meghalaya borderland, Ramirez (2007: 91) documented fundamental local disassociations between ethnic labels, languages, social patterns and cultural features. Ramirez highlights an entirely different social world and reflects that

> In the field, the objects of my observations have been all sorts of limits and anomalies, especially those pertaining to the assumed correspondence between societies, cultures and ethnicities. This involved, for instance, people claiming to belong to group A but speaking a language commonly associated with group B, or following social rules assumed to be typical of group C (2014: xix).

This essay adds to such complexities as well as extrapolates Ramirez's (2007, 2011, 2014) attempt to move past the ethnic (and tribal) paradigm as being applicable to the Nagas and amongst whom it finds fertile ground.

A 'PRE-TRIBAL' VILLAGE?

We start our exploration of atypical social phenomena in Nagaland's Tuensang district and in a hilltop village called Noksen, counting roughly 220 houses today. Noksen is a Chang Naga village. Or so it appears in government statistics, in documentations and reports, on the villagers' personal documents, while it is also the box villagers invariably tick when called upon by census officials. In official discourse, in short, there exists no confusion that Noksen is a Chang Naga village. Yet, lingering beneath this identification as Chang, a section of villagers simultaneously articulate an alternative identity, insisting that, deep down, they are not really Chang – or were not always Chang – but belong to a community called Ya. Who, then, were, or are, the Ya? And how they came to be known as Chang? The following is an exercise in conjectural history or a story 'as told by village elders.'

Noksen is divided into four exogamous clans: Oungh, Kangshou, Lomou and Houngang.[8] Clan feeling is strong in the village in the sense that the four clans are thought of as natural units, each possessing its own peculiarities and distinct qualities. Beneath this division into clans, however, there exists another axis of identity which cross-cuts clan divisions as villagers also refer to themselves as either 'Chang' or 'Ya'. When asked about one's *pang* (clan), villagers rarely mention, say, Oungh or Lomou but qualify that they are either 'Ya Oungh' or 'Chang Oungh', 'Ya Lomou' or 'Chang Lomou'. This division is also mapped unto other domains of the village's social life-world. For instance, while Chang serves as the lingua franca, those who identify themselves as Ya also speak a language called Noksei. While all Ya in Noksen portray fluency in Chang, only few belonging to the village's Chang segment speak more than a few incidental phrases of Noksei.[9]

One reason why Noksei is known but to a few Chang is that the Ya-Chang linguistic divide largely corresponds to a territorial division within the village as most of the Ya households reside clustered in one of the four village *khels* (wards) called Longpha. If an overlap of 'blood' and territory, or clan and khel, is observed in numerous villages across the Naga Hills, the core variable that structures the village's settlement pattern in Noksen is not clan but language group. Divergent cultural practices denote another dimension that separate the Ya and the Chang, even though nascent Christian influences and the advance of formal education led both groups to adopt 'Biblically approved customs'. In the process, certain traditions that were seen as 'heathen' and 'demonic' were discarded and which, in part, resulted in a streamlining of their cultural practices. Nevertheless, of the few old village women who flaunt face tattoos, it can safely be assumed that they are from village Chang as Ya women traditionally avoided facial tattoos. And while those who decease in the village are invariably buried in a tidy cemetery today, in the pre-Christian past it was only the village Chang that opted for burials. The Ya exposed their dead on bamboo frames in a designated place outside the village before ultimately, after a ritually sanctioned process, disposing the skull and bones across a cliff considered sacred.

Another distinction lies in their different mythical places of origin. Akin to the adjacent Ao Naga, the Ya point to a place called Longtrok where they are said to have emerged from six stones. The village Chang, however, derives its origins from a now deserted place on the Changsang hill range. Despite their shared mythical place of origin with the neighbouring Ao Naga, Ya elders however refute any reconstruction that the Ya were Ao Naga before they became Chang, thus defying Mills' conjecture that going by linguistic affinities, the Ya might have been Ao before they became Chang:

> Then there are villages such as Longla and Noksan[10] which have long been under Chang chiefs and have adopted Chang dress and custom, though an Ao dialect [as Mills classed the Noksei language] is current in them together with Chang (1922: 2).[11]

What, then, is the story of the Ya and their apparent enclosure into the Chang fold? While exact dates and narratives vary, in broad strokes oral history tells of a time when the Ya were numerous and mighty and Noksei (which, akin to the name of the language was also the name of the village, although 'Ya' was also used) was viewed as a warrior village that was feared widely as the perpetrator of numerous raids on nearby villages.[12] For reasons that remain contested, Noksei – then solely inhabited by the Ya – got into a conflict with Tuensang village, a village Hutton (1929: 48) was to term as the Chang's 'chief village' and he recounted that it was 'one of the biggest Naga villages I have been in, and must have about 700 houses' (ibid.). If earlier the Ya of Noksei were thought to have numbered an equally large, if not larger, number of households, a devastating epidemic – narrated locally as involving acute dysentery – led to a reduction and weakening of the village population. Tuensang village, on the contrary, was at its height as well as expansionist in its ambitions when Tuensang warriors ultimately attacked Noksei. They routed its population and many Ya died and those who survived sought refuge in the jungle and neighbouring villages. For several years, Noksei remained deserted, until a few Ya survivors resolved to try and re-establish the village. With Ya-Chang enmity still raging, they approached certain Chang warriors both for protection and the proposal to jointly re-establish the village.[13] This desire of the Ya to return, against many odds, follows a wider local sequence highlighted by Mills: 'Even if the greater part of the invaded village does retreat out of range, as sometimes happens, some are almost sure either to remain or to creep back to an existence inglorious but secure' (1922: 9).

Though it is hard to determine the exact year of Noksei's re-establishment, conjectural calculations through the tracing of genealogies seem to point to the second half of the 19th century. What can be said with more certainty is that the re-establishment of Noksei (which eventually came to be spelled as Noksen) involved a change of social arrangements versus the previous Ya polity. For one, the Ya adopted Chang clan titles (as well as gradually the Chang language) and in doing so, pledged their political allegiance to them.[14] The Chang also acquired the right to first select the lands they wished to cultivate and so came to possess the most fertile fields down the village. But in spite of overall Chang suzerainty, the Ya were able to reconstitute their age group system, of which the Chang segment became part and which, while practiced extensively among the neighbouring Ao Naga, is otherwise not generally thought of as a Chang custom. In the process, the Ya also laid claim on the position of Head of Generation (as part of the age group system), a customary arrangement still in place, and still a position exclusively meant for the village Ya. But if the Ya resumed charge over the traditional politico-ritual domain, the village Chang eventually took to electoral politics, and of the four MLAs Noksen produced after the inception of Nagaland statehood in 1963, none belongs to the Ya.

The social history of Noksen indicates that historical trajectories, language, cultural practices and tribal affiliations do not necessarily match, despite dominant discourses of tribe and contemporary folk sociologies trying to fuse such elements. More crucially, the Ya's historical trajectory permits the question whether the Ya were initially not a tribe but a 'pre' or 'a-tribal village'? The historical possibility of such a 'pre-tribal' village can also be read in the historical case of Yacham village, of which Mills recounted:

> Yacham and their small neighbour Yong, for instance, speak a dialect resembling Chongli [an Ao language] but follow Phom or Konyak customs to a great extent. Yacham recently told me that they really did not know what they were – Aos would not recognize them as Aos and their trans-Dikhu neighbour would not accept them as kinsmen (1922: 2).[15]

Here, the question to ask is precisely when and why did it became problematic for the inhabitants of Yacham to not belong to a tribe? The answer would likely tell us a thing or two about the emergence, institutionalisation and local infatuation of the idea and praxis of tribe among Nagas.

Returning to the Ya, their possible 'pre' or 'a-tribal' existence, with them affiliating themselves with no identity larger than their own village, appears a real historical possibility.[16] If indeed so, they, in some sense, *became* tribal only after being defeated at the hands of Tuensang village and made part of a then expanding Chang identity. If such a reading of Ya history already defies dominant tribal essentialism, it would also suggest that the Chang tribe, as it exists today, was not a 'historically given', the result of collective migratory waves or an entity validated by tradition, but to some extent the cumulative outcome of a process of crude expansionism. It is a historical sequence Hutton already hinted at: 'In all directions the [Chang] parent village of Tuensang has thrown out offshoots which have conquered and practically absorbed the neighbouring tribes, and which have spread the influence and the mixed culture of the conquerors'(1987: iii-iv).

TRANS-TRIBAL CLAN IDENTITIES

In this section, we remain in Noksen and elaborate on the four village clans but only to find that they are hardly the constituent components or sub-units of tribes, the way most classic anthropological approaches construe (cf. Ramirez 2011: 92).

'I do not understand. You belong to the Oungh clan of the Chang tribe. How then would you marry a girl from the Pongener clan of the Ao tribe, the Angh clan of the Konyak tribe, or the Thonger clan of the Sangtam tribe amount to incest?' My informant shook his head: 'You do not understand. The Oungh, Angh, Pongener and Thonger clans are the same.' 'But how can it be?', I countered. 'The Chang, Konyak, Ao and Sangtam are different tribes. They speak different languages, follow different cultural practices, customs and traditions, and reside in different territories. How can then any issue of incest ever arise between them?' But while my informant was ready to agree to that from all aspects, the Ao, Konyak and Sangtam tribes were different from the Chang, he insisted that the Oungh, Angh, Pongener and Thonger clans were nevertheless the same and that with clan-exogamy the rule, marriage between them was prohibited. After this conversation, it did not take me long to find out that all four village clans articulated similar affinities with clans from other tribes.

That these inter-tribal clan belongings initially stunned me was clearly my problem, not those of my informants and other villagers to whom I subsequently expressed my confusion. To them, there was nothing unusual about performing kinship and observing incest prohibitions across tribal boundaries. Why, then, did it so confuse me? The answer, in hindsight, appears fairly simple. Classic accounts of tribal societies had taught me to view a tribe as a composite of clans and lineages, well-illustrated by the putative model of unilineal descent groups and segmentary lineage systems documented for pre-state Africa in which a tribe was thought of as segmented into clans, clans into lineages and lineages into households or homesteads.[17] Of course, I was never taught that tribal identities emerged in isolation; ever since Barth's authoritative theorising of ethnic identity as the result of social interaction and not, as was previously asserted, based on an inventory of cultural traits, it was recognised that cultural boundaries are not the same as ethnic ones. For instance, in the Swat Valley of Pakistan, group boundaries were fuzzy and movements across always a real possibility. Thence, a Pathan could become a Baluch for economic and political reasons. Barth, however, reasserted ethnic identity as 'superordinate' (1969: 17) and ethnic boundaries as 'canaliz[ing] social life' (ibid.), thus precluding possibilities of trans-tribal social domains with, for instance, a particular

Pathan clan or lineage expressing kinship or belonging with a certain clan among the Baluch. If these 'African' and 'Swat' models may be adequate in their respective ethnographic settings, they cannot enable us to comprehend the historical configuration of clans among Nagas as a single clan may be represented in more than one tribe, even if under a different denominator.[18]

Long ago, Hutton (1921b: 135) already observed how 'a [Naga] clan often identifies itself with a clan belonging to a neighbouring tribe', while J.P. Mills wrote:

> There is a system of intertribal corresponding clans existing in all the Naga tribes.... A Lhota will say, for instance, that his clan is 'the same' as some particular Ao clan. That Ao clan in turn will say that they are 'one clan' with some particular Konyak clan, which in turn has a corresponding Phom clan, and so on.... A Sema who comes and settles in the [Lotha area] becomes a Lhota and incorporates himself into the clan corresponding to his old clan. If he or his children go back they slip into their old clan again (1922: 82).[19]

Colonial administrators dismissed such trans-tribal kinship ties as artificial and fanciful: 'such identifications, while sometimes apparently not unreasonable, would frequently seem to be entirely supposititious, and will not bear investigation' (Hutton 1921b: 135). According to Hutton:

> The truth is that it is exceedingly useful to persons of different tribes to establish definitely an identity of clan. If a man's hosts in an alien village regard him as of their clan, he is at any rate safe from being cut up by them, even though others of their village may feel no compunction in taking his head, and this aspect of clan feeling has undoubtedly caused men to go out of their way to claim reciprocally an identity of clan on the slenderest pretexts. Once established, such a theory rapidly gains ground, as traders of both the tribes affected by it are only too glad to take advantage of it.[20]

While social binds are everywhere as malleable as social divides, such an entirely constructivist reading of corresponding clans would discount folktales and conjectural history that point to shared agnatic descent traced by clans today present across different tribes, the invocation of common apical ancestors, a recalling of similar places of mythical origin or totemic roots (assuming the form of phratries), as well as similar ritual qualities associated with clans across tribes.[21] Among the Chang and various other

Naga tribes, clans were traditionally associated with ritual dispositions and qualities, and while the coming of Christianity mostly erased such ritual associations from the popular mind, they are remembered by village elders. Among the Chang, the Oungh made up the priestly clan and was bestowed with performing most village rituals. It was from their ranks that the 'Ounghbo', which roughly translates as 'announcer' but who usually functioned as the village's nominal head, was traditionally selected. Next, the Houngang clan was associated with village defence and its members assumed leadership in constructing and maintaining defence walls. The Kangshou clan traditionally adjudicated over the start of the annual agricultural cycle, a responsibility symbolised by the ritual sowing of the first seeds and which only a Kangshou clan member was entitled to do. Finally, the Lomou clan was ascribed with special powers to keep epidemics away from the village and birds, insects and rats from houses and crops – a ritual duty equally crucial given that a failed harvest would usually induce instant starvation. The four clans were also associated with specific rituals, feasts and festivals in the village. This division was strict in the sense that it was ritually sanctioned and if, for instance, a non-Kangshou would adjudicate over the start of the agricultural cycle or a non-Houngang assume leadership in village defence, divinely induced misfortune was thought to be certain.

Noksen elders tell that neighbouring Naga tribes are arranged, if not always exactly the same, along similar traditional politico-ritual lines. This division offers an entrance into notions of trans-tribal clan belonging. Even if none of the villagers could tell me their 'corresponding clan' from the more distant Yimchunger or Khiamniungan tribes, they insisted that they would be able to identify it by interacting with villagers there about their traditional politico-ritual division, with those clans occupying similar roles 'naturally' constituting the same clan. While more comparative research is needed, this correspondence in ritually sanctioned duties and privileges is well documented for the Oungh clan in relation to the Angh clan, which among the Konyak is considered ritually superior and the repository of hereditary chiefs (Fürer-Haimendorf 1939), as much as, among the Chang, the ritual office of Ounghbo was associated with the Oungh clan. A similar ritual linkage can be drawn with the Pongener clan among the Ao, of which Mills wrote:'[The Pongener is] considered, probably correct, to correspond to the Angh clan among the Konyak, and has many privileges in the way of shares of meat and the right to wear certain ornaments' (1922: 13).[22] This traditional prominence was associated with an Ao origin myth in which three males and three females emerged out of six stones with the Pongener apical ancestor emerging first (Ao 2004: 161).

While such trans-tribal belongings can be read and interpreted differently, taken together they seem to suggest that among Nagas, clan identities both preceded and long prevailed over tribal identities. Such clan (or perhaps phratry) belongings did not fully dissolve with the emergence of the 'idea' and 'praxis' of tribe, thus explaining how the same clan could come to 'belong' to multiple tribes simultaneously without ever completely discarding their shared belonging. Moreover, that trans-tribal clan belongings continue to be socially reproduced in the 'demotic discourse' (Baumann 1996) of villagers, as they also do in the Assam-Meghalaya borderland (Ramirez 2014) and among the Kachin in neighbouring Myanmar (Robinne 2007), must make us critically interrogate and reconsider the historical relationship between clans and tribes.

THE MAKING OF A NEW TRIBE: THE CASE OF THE CHAKHE-SANG

Can tribes be made? Invented almost at will? Or constructed anew in the same way as, say, one can dismantle a vehicle and assemble it into something else? Perhaps they can. In the 1950s, Verrier Elwin observed how 'tribal groups in Nagaland are forming new affiliations and using names hitherto unknown to Anthropology' (1961: 5). The Chakhesang Naga is one such new affiliation. As a tribe, it entered administrative and ethnological annals in 1946, in August of that year to be precise (Vitso 2003: 1), which is when the tribe was assembled through a merger of different language groups hitherto part of other tribes.

Who, then, are the Chakhesang Naga? Parts of the answer lie in its nomenclature. 'Cha' stands for a language group known in full as Chakru (or Chokri), while 'Khe' represents an adjacent language group known as 'Khezha'. In the colonial ordering of peoples, both the Chakru / Chokri and Khezha were classed as Eastern Angamis. Even so, Hutton emphasised that to his mind, it were the Western Angamis who were 'Angamis *par excellence*' (1921a: 15, emphasis in original), 'real Angamis', and 'Angamis proper' (ibid.: 23). In Hutton's acquaintance with them, he found Western Angamis generally taller compared to Eastern Angamis and while Western Angamis wore leg ornaments more often, Eastern Angamis were keener on brass armlets. Again Western Angamis used longer *daos*, (broadswords) while Eastern Angamis decorated their houses with more ingenuity. Western Angamis chewed tobacco whereas Eastern Angamis preferring to smoke it. While most mithuns belonging to Western Angamis were wholly black in colour, the Eastern Angamis were black and yellow pied (Hutton 1921a). None of these differences, trivial as they may seem, however, lay at the basis of the Eastern Angamis' decision to break away from the Angami fold to form a tribe of their own.

The 'Sang' part of the new tribe's nomenclature was derived from the Eastern Sangtam tribe whose inhabitants resolved to leave the wider Sangtam tribe to join the new tribe in the making. It is reported that the name Chakhesang was 'unanimously selected...in a joint public meeting in order of the alphabetical serial of arrangement giving full recognition and equal respect to each individual sub-tribe's entity...[and that] the name Chakhesang was approved on the day it was formed by the British Government' (Vitso 2003: 21). On closer inspection, however, the nomenclature, while representing the largest sub-units, did not represent all those who joined in as two Rengma villages also pledged their allegiance to the Chakhesang (Elwin 1961: 5), while a cluster of Poumai villages also came to identify themselves as Chakhesang[23], as did a few Sumi Naga villages or Sumi-speaking segments of Chokri- and Khezha-speaking villages. If this appears as a complex mixture, what then catalysed their merger?[24]

To start with, the term Angami itself was exogenous, while the added qualification of 'Eastern Angamis' was arbitrary (Hutton 1921a: 15–16). Some argue that this initial misclassification and a subsequent dissonance between ascribed and self-identity lies at the roots of the Chokri and Khezha separation from the Angami fold as 'the unique feature of the Chakhesang tribe was not given much interest by the [colonial] administrators or the scholars' (Chakhesang Student Union 1997: viii). This, however, may only be one part of the story as it does not explain why (then) Eastern Angamis, in separating from Western Angamis, with whom they shared obvious cultural and linguistic affinities, aligned with the Eastern Sangtams with whom such similarities were less pronounced. Conversations with elders in Phugwumi, the Chakhesang Naga village where I conducted field work, lead me to highlight another sentiment, the probability of another force that was at work in the making of the Chakhesang. I postulate that the creation of the Chakhesang may also be read as both a reaction and aspiration, one defined in response to a growing sense of deprivation both Eastern Angamis and Eastern Sangtams perceived vis-à-vis certain other parts of the Naga Hills, particularly the Western Angami territories which came to house the seat of colonial administration. The amalgamation of disparate groups into the Chakhesang tribe was therefore the result of 'negative solidarity', as Subba (1988) explains the frequent fission and fusion among communities in places across India's Northeast. Such impromptu and flexible 'tribal solidarities', he writes, are 'adopted', not 'inherent', 'temporary' rather than 'permanent', but always, and crucially, directed at pursuing shared interests or mitigating common grievances (ibid.: 375).

It was in the territorial jurisdiction of Western Angamis, especially in and around Kohima (Nagaland's state capital today) that the British established their headquarters. Over time, this culminated into proportionally higher levels of government employment among Western Angamis, inspiring levels of material progress that was further augmented by the establishment of missionary schools (to compare: the first school among the Eastern Angamis was established 37 years after education was introduced among Western Angamis (Chakhesang Student Union 1997: vii)), health clinics and opportunities for commerce and trade. It was amidst such rising inequalities that Phugwumi elders recall the inequitable treatments they started to experience at the hands of the Western Angamis who were gradually becoming more 'advanced' during their intermittent visits to Kohima to procure salt, deposit taxes, trade or to visit colonial offices. Going there, they also witnessed how Western Angamis absorbed most of the government benefits and saw among them evidence of profits and progress they could not find in their own areas. Against this background, the creation of the Chakhesang tribe may, to an extent, be understood as a protest against skewed government priorities and growing disparities, as signifying an expression of shared neglect among members of the Chokri, Khezha, and adjoining Eastern Sangtams – releasing sentiments of 'negative solidarity' that surpassed, if only temporarily so, the cultural and language differences amongst themselves. Their amalgamation, then, relied in part on the conviction that forming a sizeable, separate tribe would place them in a stronger position vis-à-vis Western Angamis and the state, and help them, as Bareh too argues, 'receive maximum development benefits (2001: 228).'[25] If indeed so, this would provide a historical counter-point to the thesis of unstructured, amorphous 'jellyfish tribes' (Yapp 1983) in which the fragmentation and disintegration of tribes is construed as a strategical move to keep the state away (Scott 2009) because, to the contrary, the Chakhesang invented and defined itself in relation to the state and the material incentives it had to offer.

That 'negative solidarity', however, is as much about fission as fusion can be discerned from the eventual partial break-up of the Chakhesang tribe in 1990. The Eastern Sangtam component opted out with its leaders citing discontentment with the meagre development benefits that their villages received compared to the ranges inhabited by the Chokri and Khezha. Their separation, however, did not involve their return to the Sangtam tribe but manifested itself in the construction of yet another tribe – the Pochury. In establishing this tribe, Bareh writes: 'the Pochury elites have made great efforts, requesting the government to give Pochury official recognition (2001: 94).' As a result, a Pochury of sufficiently advanced age today has, during the course of his life, shifted his tribal belonging thrice, from Sangtam to Chakhesang to Pochury. For those imagining and representing tribes as ancient and historically immutable, now there is something to account for.

This departure of the 'Sang' component also led to the opening of a discussion on the tribe's nomenclature. The Poumai component, for one, had long expressed the desire to see an acronym of theirs integrated in the tribe's name and with the 'Sang' opted out, a renaming of the tribe as 'Chakhepo' (with 'po' standing for 'Poumai') was proposed by some of its leaders. But while this matter was extensively deliberated by the Chakhesang Public Organisation, the tribe's apex body, the change of nomenclature failed to garner sufficient support with those arguing against it citing the hassles a change of name would entail in today's world of ever more complex bureaucratic paperwork. The arduous process it takes to acquire state recognition was a deterrent and so what was stressed was that the name 'Chakhesang', despite it having grown into a misnomer, must be considered as inclusive of all those wishing to identify themselves as such.

DEMARCATING THE CHANG NAGA

If, as a tribe, the Chakhesang is a novel formation, so, Hutton wrote, was the Chang Naga:

> The Chang are a new tribe. Their chief village – Tuensang – has only existed for eleven generations, and a number of their clans now regarded as pure Chang in blood, and speaking no other language, are known to have had an origin from Konyaks from Angfang, or Yimtsungr from somewhere else (1929: 46).

Such historical contingency goes against the grain of those Chang folk sociologies and representations which invoke the locally popular term 'since time immemorial' and which usually entail a step-wise collective migratory wave from present-day Mongolia or China to Tuensang with lengthy stops in what is today Myanmar. Arguing not against but alongside Chang folk sociologies – which exist in their own right – this section outlines the possibility of an alternative, more contingent historical narrative that substitutes images of a historically immutable identity to one of modern 'tribe-making'.[26] The narrative of the Ya *becoming* Chang provides one such case. But there are many more to be told. The Oungh clan of Tuensang village, Hutton observed, was formerly 'part of a Konyak village which was split after being defeated by Tobu [village], the other half going to Angfang' (1929: 47).[27] Within Tuensang village, the Oungh clan mostly clustered in the Bilaeshi khel where they maintained their own identity and cultural expressions. While, for instance, the other village clans buried their dead, the Oungh, like the Ya, placed their corpses on *machans* [bamboo platforms], in the same manner as Hutton observed in 'some Konyak villages' (ibid.). And if nearly all Tuensang village women wore face tattoos, they differed in 'the chin patterns between the Ung clan and the others' (ibid.: 50). The Oungh clan also had not forgotten its defeat at the hands of Tobu and expressed continued enmity towards this village (ibid.: 47). In Tuensang, the Oungh clan assumed a priestly status, but this did not safeguard them from occasional scorn: 'As the Ung-clan is usually spoken of with contempt it doubtless represents a conquered population acquainted with the god of the soil' (Hutton cited in Mills 1922: xxxii). Such sentiments notwithstanding, Hutton also emphasised how 'although the two cultures [Oungh and Chang] are yet incompletely fused, the people themselves have blended completely, and the physical type which has resulted from the hybridization of the two tribes is not only very pronounced, but excessively vigorous' (1987: iii).

While this process of the Oungh clan being gradually absorbed into the Chang fold defeats views of a historically stable Chang social demography, it would add to the rationale behind the formation of the Chang Committee in 1945. At the time of its establishment, so I was told by its president, the Chang Committee propounded two central objectives, in addition to the wider rationale of advancing Chang welfare. First, to permanently pacify the area by resolving feuds that lingered both between and within villages. Second, and crucially here, to ascertain which villages could reasonably said to be culturally and customarily Chang. To the Committee, back then, this second objective must have appeared as daunting as the desire to foster peace. This was because cultural forms, historical trajectories, language and political affinities were often found disjoined locally, of which the case of Tuensang village's Oungh clan appears exemplary.

Many such cases existed. For 'Waoshu village', Hutton observed how its inhabitants were 'mixed Chang and Konyak' (1929: 56), while about Hakchang village he wrote how its inhabitants 'still speak the Chang language and wear the Chang tattoo, but in appearance and custom they are entirely Konyak' (ibid.: 51). Hutton's emphasising 'still' seems to indicate that he saw them as Konyak on-the-make, a prediction proven wrong as Hakchang is a Chang village today. Hutton encountered similar 'mixtures' across the area. About the Sangtam villages 'Chatóngrê' and 'Chimongre', he wrote how its inhabitants 'had a good deal of Chang blood, and are very much under Chang influence and will sooner or later turn into Chang, I fancy' (ibid.: 45). Hutton's prediction never materialised as both villages identify as Sangtam today. Hutton was also wrong about the Chang future he predicted for Chongtore, which 'although Sangtam, had a very strong admixture of Chang blood, and builds its houses in the Chang manner' (ibid.: 46).

The Chang Committee also had to consider historical instances of a village, or a segment of it, changing its political affiliation from one tribe to another. The historical trajectory of Litim village, neighbouring Noksen, indicates such a sequence. While located on a hilltop today, oral history tells that earlier it was located further down the slope. It was there that an internal feud broke out between clans leading the village to split. One section moved upward and settled at its present location, placing themselves under the notional protection of Noksen, while the other section moved further afield and came to inhabit a village known today as Alisopur, located a few hours walk away. While sharing a common descent and for long a joint residence, Litim today identifies as Chang and Alisopur as Sangtam.

But even as the Chang Committee gradually succeeded in defining and demarcating the Chang tribe, the levels of manufacturing and moulding it required made it a protracted and initially often inept process. A Chang pastor who had researched the growth of Christianity among the Chang narrated, when I visited him, that in his study of Church registers, he had found that in the 1950s, the Chang suddenly 'lost' roughly 900 Christians. The reason, he eventually discovered, was not the revival of past animism he had first suspected but the direct result of a cluster of Chang villages having 'converted' to the neighbouring Phom tribe.[28]

CONCLUDING REMARKS

Amongst the greatest social ruptures that has taken place among Nagas during the 19th and 20th centuries were the emergence, institutionalisation and local infatuation with the idiom and praxis of tribe. While the exact outlines that led to the spread of tribal essentialism, manifested in today's 'time-immemorialism', demand further ethno-historical research, this process was undoubtedly subject to the colonial production of knowledge (cf. Cohn 1996) and wider processes of state-making. Colonial writings and policies sought to regulate and regiment what was perceived as the locally encountered 'ethnographic chaos' (Jacobs et al. 1990: 19). This desire was grounded in the state's imperative towards the standardisation of any 'social hieroglyph into a legible and administratively more convenient format' (Scott 1998: 3) and the idea and idiom of tribe was intended towards this end.

British civil and military officers pursued the concept of tribe despite being aware of its problematic cultural transitivity as the central organisational principle locally. Besides Butler's (1876) remark on the absence of 'hard and fast limits' of Naga communities, Mills (1926: 176) admitted that among

Nagas, the 'real political unit' was not 'tribe' but 'the village', while Hutton (1921a: 109), for the Angami, observed how the 'real unit of the social side is the clan'. And yet, when the colonial government ordered monographs to be written on the peoples they governed, they were invariably composed tribe-wise, for example *The Lhota Nagas* (Mills 1922), *The Ao Nagas* (Mills 1926), *The Rengma Nagas* (Mills 1937), *The Angami Nagas* (Hutton 1921a) and *The Sema Nagas* (ibid. 1921b), in the process working to authorise 'tribe' as the prime category of both administration and identification. Such social imaginaries stayed when the British left, to the extent that the contemporary anthropology of India's Northeast 'relies strongly on the categories provided by colonial depictions' (Ramirez 2014: 5).

It would, of course, be rather fanciful to bestow the British colonial regime with sufficient power to forever fix local identities. In fact, across India's Northeast,

> ...many of the colonial labels are not only lying in disuse, but are being contested by those who were labelled so and some of them have successfully replaced the colonial labels such as Abor with Adi, Dafla with Nyishi, Mikir with Karbi, Lalung with Tiwa, Lushai with Mizo and so on (Subba and Wouters 2013: 204).

Discussions on nomenclatures and the desire to change these are also present among Nagas, for instance, a call to replace 'Lotha' with 'Kyong'. What the British administrative and ethnological ordering of the social landscape did seem to institutionalise, however, was the discursive, semantic and technical means for representing identities in an idiom and discourse of tribe.

But if the category of tribe is undoubtedly the way most Nagas nowadays perceive, experience and articulate their social environment, this essay has shown that the idiom, idea and praxis of tribe did not always exist in the same form and force as it appears today. It seems the tragedy of 'tribe' that it has led to a nearly irreversible usurpation of alternative social spaces and identifications that existed before, beneath, betwixt and between Naga tribes – all possibilities that shake the foundations of dominant tribal essentialism. This realisation invites us to a dilemma which, I pose, ought to be at the heart of the anthropology of Nagas, and of India's Northeast more widely, namely, how to account for the observation that social organisation – both past and present – is based on interpersonal, village, and clan networks which cut across tribal and ethnic groups with clearly permeable boundaries and yet most people maintain a view of the whole society as made up of homogenously partitioned and neatly bounded entities purportedly in existence since 'time-immemorial'?

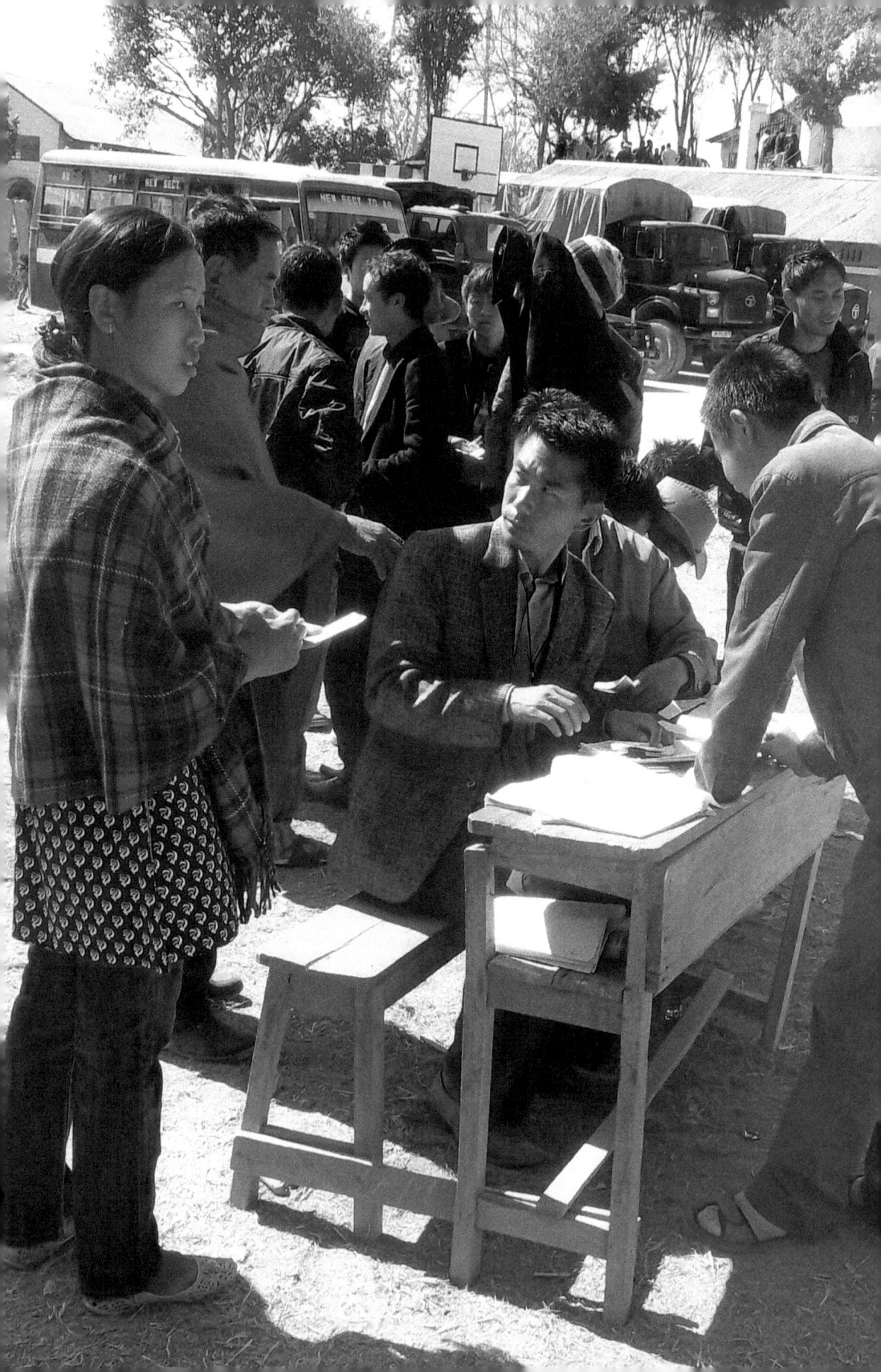

05

PERFORMING DEMOCRACY IN NAGALAND: 'PAST POLITIES' AND 'PRESENT POLITICS'

Electoral politics, tradition, and culture interrelate in complex ways, and this relationship is not always easy to discern; it is often elusive but always present. Geertz recognised this long ago; 'One of the things that everybody knows but no one can quite think how to demonstrate', he postulated, 'is that a country's politics reflects the design of its culture' (1973: 311). Geertz continued, in his distinctive prose, 'on the one hand, everything looks like a clutter of schemes and surprises; on the other, like a vast geometry of settled judgments.' He then concluded, a little dismayed, 'What joins such a chaos of incident to such a cosmos of sentiment is often extremely obscure, and how to formulate it is even more so' (ibid.). In this essay, I will attempt, rather optimistically, to elucidate some of this 'extreme obscurity', even though I am not talking, unlike Geertz, about a country as a whole, but about a state within a country. This state is Nagaland and the setting is the 2013 state legislative assembly elections, which took place while I was conducting ethnographic research in the area.

In 1985, on the floor of the state assembly, a prominent Naga minister proposed, in vain, that Nagaland's election system be reformed for the present election system went against 'the Naga way of life' (cited in Ao 1993: 224). This statement, while controversial then, had long been preceded by A Z Phizo, the erstwhile president of the Naga National Council (NNC), which struggled for Naga independence, and who argued that 'There is no political party in Nagaland. We do not need it.' All things considered, he continued,

'Nagaland need not intimate or adopt foreign institutions [modern democracy] in matter of political organisation.' In Phizo's view, Nagaland was already fully democratic by traditional design, '[it's the] very spirit of our country' as he put it, hence, they would not require political parties and elections to 'become' democratic.[1] Most recently, it was Nagaland's chief minister who reportedly remarked that 'Election is not suited for Nagas', then elucidating that 'Selection of leader[s] would best suit Nagas' (cited in Solo 2011: 67).

This statement by the chief minister is not to be interpreted as an attack on the idea of democracy, but rather as a perceptive reading of traditional Naga polities, which, although highly diverse, share a common rejection of the principle of voting, or for that matter to raising one's hand in support or opposition, which is seen as dividing the community into 'our side' and 'their side.'[2] It is perhaps for this reason that, in the village where I was conducting field research, somebody wrote in the dust that had gathered on the rear-window of his car: 'Election is an insult to each other by vote.' Put differently, 'The idea of an elected leader was not in the scheme of life in [sic] the Nagas' (Solo 2011: 68). This does, of course, not imply that public deliberations, political divisions and conflicts were unknown within different Naga polities, far from that, but that voting or 'raising hands' was not the preferred strategy of decision-making. Yet, despite Phizo's evocative rejection of electoral politics, and later statements in his support, parties and elections not only seeped into Nagaland, but etched themselves at the very centre of Naga society.[3]

However, rather than approaching the introduction of modern democracy as a radical disruption of past political practices, this is a study of continuities and connections, of linkages between past polities and present politics. Rather than accepting new democratic principles at face value, I will show that Naga tribes possess the agency to appropriate, reinterpret and rework the idea of modern democracy along the lines of their own traditional polities, ideologies, and pre-statehood political cultures. That Naga tribes are both the repositories and enactors of their own particular versions of democracy, appropriations which may run counter to some of modern democracy's elevated principles, but which are, on the whole, a great deal closer to their traditional lifeworlds.

ACCEPTED WISDOM

Conventional assessments of Nagaland elections, both scholarly and commentarial, often invoke its alleged criminalisation, the interplay of money and muscles used to ensnare voters (Dev 2006; Misra 1987; Singh 1986), or on 'Operation Election' (Sen 1974), pointing to the large presence of armed forces in the area. While it is hard to deny that Nagaland's electoral politics routinely deviate from textbook versions of free and fair elections, as it does in many places across the globe, there is much more to Nagaland's democracy than mere manipulation, disorder, corruption and occasional violence. After all, the richest or most generous candidates do not automatically win, nor do threats and intimidations inevitably prevail. This essay, while not downplaying 'electoral ills', departs from the popular condemnation of Nagaland's elections as a mockery, if not a slur on democracy. Instead, it argues towards a more contextualized, a more culturally embedded understanding of Nagaland's electoral processes, one which renders bare the incongruence between modern democracy and different traditional Naga polities, but also one which bestows Naga communities with the agency to remould, tailor, and adapt modern democracy to their own uses and advantages.

Prevailing descriptions about traditional Naga polities have been about chiefs and democrats (Jacobs et al. 1990), nobles and commoners (Fürer-Haimendorf 1973), bodies of elders (Mills 1926), powerful chiefs (Fürer-Haimendorf 1939) and the absence of chiefs (Hutton 1921a), sovereign village states and village republics (Mills 1926; Venuh 2005; Singh 2008), extreme egalitarianism (Woodthorpe 1881), clan rivalries (Hutton 1921a), and, on the whole, represented as a continuum with hereditary autocracy, if not near dictatorship, and radical democracy at its opposite ends, with (a section of) the Konyak Naga usually associated with the former and the Angami Naga as the most obvious example of the latter. While such terms are obviously simplifications of complex, multilayered Naga political systems, I propose, and at the risk of being accused of overestimating the relationship between culture, traditional polities and contemporary electoral politics, four models — The *angh* (king or chieftainship) model, the village consensus candidate model, the clan candidate model, and the household model — which I think help to understand how different Naga electorates elect their representatives. These four models, I argue, are best understood as extensions, or a remapping, of different traditional Naga polities, thus, building upon pre-existing political practices.

As such, I submit that Nagaland politics is not a politics of manifestos, party ideologies, competing long-term visions, public platforms, and debates. Although these do play a role, they are of little help in understanding how Naga electorates vote as they do.[4] Nagaland electoral politics is a politics of many things, most of them outside the scope of this essay, but what I want to emphasise here is that it is a politics of 'primordial' affiliations of clan, village and tribe, and of a remapping of traditional polities unto the democratic playing field. While democratic elections are essentially a modern exercise, highly bureaucratised, rationalised and reliant on technology – this essay shows that, in Nagaland, who gets 'voted in' largely hinges on traditional modes of decision-making and age-old loyalties.

My data are primarily 'declarations of support', as they appeared in plenty in Nagaland dailies in the months and weeks preceding the 2013 election.[5] By relying primarily on newspaper declarations, my evidence is, admittedly, perhaps more anecdotal than it is methodical, although I concur with Gupta's (1995: 385) reasoning that newspaper reports must be understood as 'cultural texts' and 'socio-historical documents', and can be a great asset for 'thick description', and that it is unfortunate that they are often treated with 'benign neglect by students of contemporary life.'[6] The household model is also based on ethnography, as it was among the Chakhesang Naga, whom I include under this model, that I was conducting fieldwork during the 2013 Nagaland state assembly elections.

It must be emphasized that the four models of electoral politics proposed here are 'ideal types'. Most certainly, they are not deterministic, and, in reality, they are perhaps as often defied as adhered to. Then again, within the same Naga tribe and constituency multiple models might compete and intermingle. And while for the purpose of clarity I associate each model with one or more particular Naga tribes, this does not suggest that the model applies either exclusively to them, or that all units falling under its tribal designation practise it in exactly the same way. While my current data does not suffice to fit all Naga tribes into one of the four models, I suspect that further research would render this feasible, at least so conceptually. The above safeguards notwithstanding, I do maintain that the four models outlined below are useful to 'think along with' as they provide certain insights into Nagaland's ostensibly so intricate electoral politics.

ANGH OR CHIEFTAINSHIP MODEL

The first model, in prominence among the Konyak Naga, and in a somewhat less pronounced manner practiced by the Sema (now Sumi) Naga, is the *angh* (king) or chieftainship model. The basic premise of this model is that the traditional leverages of Konyak and Sema aristocrats have, to an extent, been remapped unto the democratic playing field with traditional rulers now influencing the voting patterns of their 'commoners.' While this does not imply that the political opinion of traditional aristocrats is necessarily definite, it suggests that their political stance tends to preponderate over the majority of 'ordinary villagers.' After the introduction of democracy a few

Konyak anghs joined the election fray themselves, so blurring the division between traditional leverages and post-statehood constellations of power, but most kept to their traditional area of jurisdiction, turning themselves from 'kings' into 'king-makers.'

In the past, before their enclosure into the state, Konyak anghs reigned over a village or a cluster of villages, and their powers were hereditary, autocratic and sacrosanct.[7] In the words of the colonial administrator J H Hutton (1965: 23): 'The Ang [sic] is a repository of fortune, virtue, or life-principle of his village'. Hutton continued: 'In some villages he is, or was, so heavily tabooed that he must not touch the ground' (ibid.). About the angh of Mon, the present-day district headquarters of the Konyak area, Fürer-Haimendorf wrote: 'like other chiefs the Ang [sic] of Mon was an autocratic ruler who had power over life and death of his subjects' (1974: 9). On the whole, anghs expected 'deference from the villagers as well as parts of their crops and labour: they could exercise sexual rights over the women of the commoner (*Ben*) clans' (Jacobs et al 1990: 71).

The village's *morung*, or bachelor's dormitory, in the past was similar across a number of Naga tribes and the place where unmarried males lived together, and where deliberations were held. It was usually an appendage of the angh's private residence (Hutton 1965: 23). About the Sema Naga, Hutton wrote elsewhere that their traditional chieftainship was not sacred, but secular, but that like the Konyak anghs their powers were hereditary. The chieftain families, he observed, 'form an aristocracy in the literal sense of the word' (1921b: 150). A Sema village was usually called after its founding chief, who was the 'lord of the manor' (ibid). As a general principle, the chief's house served as a meeting place, as well as a dormitory for the village unmarried males. Their customary obedience to their chief, Hutton concluded, 'makes the average Sema more ready to accept discipline and orders generally than Nagas usually are' (1921b: 27).

While the introduction of the state bureaucracy diminished the absolute authority anghs and chiefs once enjoyed, they continue to have a large say in village affairs, and, by extension, in who will be elected as the member of the legislative assembly in their constituencies. In the wake of the 2013 state assembly elections the following 'declaration of support' from a Konyak Naga village appeared in the Nagaland dailies: 'The Zangkham Village citizens ... unanimously resolved to support and vote for the young and capable NPF [Naga People's Front] aspirant candidate ...' This declaration, promising collective vote from the entire village, was signed by the chief angh, and countersigned by the local party president. Another Konyak Naga village declared in the newspapers that 'Anghs, GBS [*Gaonburas*][8], Councils and Youth of Chi, Leangha and Goching villages firmly resolved and select ... as an intending NPF candidate', a statement which was endorsed by the chief angh-cum-chairperson of Chi village, the angh-cum-chairperson of Leangha village, and the chairperson of Goching village, the last one presumably not holding the title of angh. Similarly, the angh of Tizit village published a declaration, countersigned by the village council chairperson, announcing that his village had 'unanimously resolved to support ..., the intending candidate.' In yet another Konyak constituency, the angh of Nokzang village declared his support for one candidate in the newspaper, and promised that all the 1,329 voters of the two villages over which he presided would be cast in favour of the NPF. If the angh is not the principal actor, he may assume the role of mediator or facilitator, as seemed to have happened in the village of Tangnyu, from where the following 'declaration of support' was dispatched: 'The Council of Tangnyu village had called a meeting at Chief Angh's Palace ... and decided to support and strengthen the Independent Candidate.'

In case of the Sema Naga, aristocratic families now tend to hold the state introduced offices of gaonbura and village council chairperson, although representatives from non-aristocratic lineages also hold these offices. It was under the auspices of the head gaonbura, that Sunito village conducted a general meeting in which it was 'resolved that we will support solid franchise to the NPF candidate.' In a similar vein, it was a gaonbura, chairperson, and the secretary of Unity village who stated in the newspaper that, 'We, the Sumi Community Council reaffirms the decision ... to fully and sincerely support the intending NPF candidate.' On the whole, however, it appears that Konyak anghs have a comparatively larger say in contemporary electoral politics compared to the traditional aristocrats among the Sema, although, obviously, context matters.

While the views of traditional aristocrats no longer carry the force they once did, the 'declarations of support' cited above suggest that anghs and chiefs have, in parts, been able to remap their traditional leverages, now playing a prominent role in local electoral processes. Hence, for an aspiring politician in the constituencies where this model is in vogue the essence of the matter is to win over the traditional anghs and chiefs, trying to persuade them to use their influence to his support. To be sure, this model is not deterministic. Long ago Hutton already wrote that 'a strong Ang [sic] had very considerable power, but a weak one tended to act as his fellow-clansmen advised him' (Hutton 1965: 23). The Sema Naga, in turn, have a long history of dissent and the break-up of villages over contests over leadership. The same dynamics apply to electoral politics today, and with their traditional powers now diminished by the state bureaucracy, anghs and chiefs perhaps more than ever depend on their own character and charisma to assert their authority.

THE VILLAGE CONSENSUS CANDIDATE MODEL

The village consensus candidate model, which holds that a village tends to vote en bloc for a particular candidate, figures most prominently among the Ao Naga people, although it is also practised in various villages belonging to other tribes. In this model, the unit of voting is not the individual, but the village. The village's collective vote is deliberated at the level of the village council (*putu menden*) and the village's apex body called the *senso mungdang*, which freely translates as the gathering of all male citizens, although female citizens are now increasingly part of these gatherings. A senso mungdang is only held sporadically, and if such a meeting is deemed desirable, as it often is in the wake of an election, the newspaper is used to summon all citizens residing outside the village to return home, thus, for instance,

> Süngratsü Senso Mungdang and Village Council jointly informs to all the citizens of Süngratsü village that all male and female citizens should reach the village on or before the 18th February 2013 positively for the ensuing State Assembly Election ... Any member not complying with this order will invite strict disciplinary action from the Senso Mungdang and the Village Council.

The political resolution adopted during the senso mungdang proceedings is final, and those who try to go against it risk to be condemned as 'traitors' and to be sentenced under customary law. Put differently, the political opinion of the village majority supersedes those of individual voters, who, even if they ideologically or otherwise disagree with the selected village candidate, are expected to cast their votes for him.

As in the case of the traditional aristocrats, there are traditional precedents to this voting strategy adopted among the Ao Naga. In the past, the Ao Naga polity has been depicted by colonial officers as the most intricate, multilayered and complex political system among all Naga polities. It consisted, as it still does, of a number of councils, ranked hierarchically and based on age-groups, with one such age group taking the lead for a set period of time. Unlike the Konyak and the Sema Naga, 'there are not in the Ao tribe any hereditary chiefs' (Hutton 1965: 21). Rather, 'the control of affairs lies with a council' (Mills 1926: 177). Mills continued: 'To debate matters of importance all the councillors (*Tatar*) will meet' (ibid.: 182). The locus of authority was thus vested in the village council, which was 'composed of elders representing various clans and kindred for fixed, if fluctuating periods' (Hutton 1965: 23). They were to rule over the village, upholding the common good, with non-councillors expected to submit to their authority. This body of village councillors was assisted by a range of subsidiary bodies made up of junior age groups, who would, in time, rise up to become councillors themselves.

This age-wise ranking started with the induction of young boys into the village morung, which took place only once every three years 'with each batch taking on entrance certain menial duties to be performed till the entry of a fresh draft three years later, when the former took over a superior status' (ibid: 24). Although life in the morung was abandoned on a person's marriage, he would belong, for the rest of his life, to the same grade as the cohorts of his entry in the morung, and eventually rise up to become part of the leading age-group in the village (Mills 1926: 177). Among the Ao Naga, membership of the village council was the 'zenith of any ambitious village career' (Hutton 1965: 24). During this period, a man represented his kindred on the council and was entitled 'to share all meat killed in public feasts, as fines from village offenders, as presents to the village, or killed for entertainment of distinguished strangers' (ibid). Unlike the position of angh or chief, whose authority could last for many years, often till their death, the position of a councillor was not permanent but temporary, and after a designated period of time, 'the whole body of councillors goes out of office at once, and no one can be re-elected however influential he may be or however short a term of office he has enjoyed' (Mills 1926: 183–84). This vacating of office often went contested; at times it was even violent, with the office holders reluctant to relinquish their privileges, and the new generation all too eager to assume village leadership (ibid: 181).

Today, Ao Naga villages continue to be organised into councils, although the introduction of the state has introduced new arenas and institutions through which non-councillors can now assert power of their village, at times competing with the traditional authorities. Despite this occasional tussle between 'modern' and 'traditional' constellations of authority, the dispositions of the traditional Ao Naga polity appears to have reconstituted itself in the sphere of electoral politics, with councillors assuming a leading role in adjudicating the collective vote of the village. Among the Ao Naga, this often results in the selection of a village consensus candidate; a village resolution which is subsequently declared in the local dailies, and signed by the president and secretary of the senso mungdang. To illustrate, the Nokpu village declared, 'As resolved in its General Meeting held the Nokpu *Senso Mongdang* [sic] hereby declares to support the candidature of ... in the forthcoming State General Assembly Election

... Any person found to be defying the decisions made by the Nokpu *Senso Mongdang* [sic] shall be dealt with accordingly'. Merangkong, another Ao Naga village, declared, 'Merangkong *Senso Mungdang* in a general meeting ... unanimously resolved to extend full support to the Independent Candidate for the forthcoming legislative assembly election.' It was further resolved that 'Heavy penalty and strict action will be imposed against any citizen of Merangkong who acts against the aforesaid resolution.' This village consensus candidate model can also work the opposite way around, with a village resolving not to give any vote to a particular candidate, as the following statement suggests, 'The Yaongyimsen Kosasanger Tatar passed the decision that not a single vote will be voted in favour to the Congress Candidate.'

This model does not apply to the Ao Naga alone. A Chang Naga village also publicly endorsed a particular candidate and subsequently promised that 'the Village Council is fully responsible for bringing the absolute majority.' Going against such a village resolution can have dramatic consequences, as evidently happened in Yangzitong village. Here the village's apex body announced the expulsion of five of its villagers for a duration of six years for publishing a newspaper 'rejoinder' against the selected village consensus candidate. The village apex body justified its decision to expel them by stating, 'Any [electoral] resolutions are issued in the interest of citizens and not to some persons or a handful of people. As such a press statement issued by few individuals has directly insulted the 'Suro Pumji', which is an apex body of the citizens.'

In constituencies where the village consensus model is in vogue, democratic politics is less about election than it is about selection, and voting is not so much an individual exercise as it denotes collective action with each village, in a way, turning into a 'single vote', which a candidate can either win or lose in its entirety. Hence, to get elected a successful candidate must seek the support of a number of village councils (*putu menden*), with the backing of the village apex body, the senso mungdang. In this model, large villages assume larger powers as their collective vote can instantly put a candidate ahead in the polls. This has led at least two Ao Naga villages to join hands by combining their collective vote; the Mopungchuket and Süngratsü villages announced that they, in a joint session, had 'resolved to jointly declare their support to the Congress candidate for the forthcoming State Assembly Election.' This declaration further read: 'it is informed to all the citizens of both the villages to abide by this joint declaration'. As most villages declare their village consensus candidates months or weeks before the actual elections, the outcome of the state legislative elections among the Ao Naga is often already known before the first ballot is cast.

THE CLAN-MODEL

The third model proposed here is the Clan-Model of electoral politics and is perhaps most prominent among the Lotha Naga, although the rhetoric of clan unity and clan-wise electoral support is also prominent amongst various other Naga tribes. In this model the locus of electoral politics does not reside in the traditional aristocrats or in village councillors, but in the clan leaders. As each Lotha clan, generally, has members across Lotha villages, preponderating numerically in some and constituting a minority in others, Lotha electoral politics is more of an inter-village affair compared to the first two models. The clan-model suggests that electoral politics is predominantly a tussle between competing clans with each clan uniting behind a particular candidate, subsequently trying to convince other clans to align with them. In a recent study, Ovung, himself a Lotha, argues that, 'every serious treatment of Lotha politics finds clan as the most important determinant in patterns of political life' (2012: 122). 'Clan-thinking', Ovung continues, 'dominates and the question of clan numerical strength always arises' (ibid).

In principle, the clan model implies that each Lotha clan selects a political candidate amongst its members, or alternatively declares its collective vote to a particular candidate belonging to another clan. On the face of it, this model suggests that, compared to numerically small clans, larger clans have more opportunities to push one of its members into the assembly. While this holds true as a general principle, no single clan carries enough votes to do so alone, and clan-members often live in different constituencies thus weakening their collective voting power. As a result, every clan and candidate must seek alliances with other clans in order to win the election. In this model, the most effective tactic of a political party to thwart another party's candidate is to try and set up a rival candidate in his clan, so potentially splitting the candidate's vote bank.

Why clans should be so central to Lotha electoral politics is perhaps a little more difficult to discern compared to the first two models. However, its relative importance might well relate to the Lotha's traditional landholding system, about which the colonial administrator Mills (1922: 97–98) remarked, 'Compared to other Naga tribes a very large proportion of the land in the Lhota [sic] country is clan land, which is held in common by all members of that particular clan in the village'. Mills then continued: 'Every year the members of a clan in a Lhota [sic] village meet and apportion out the land which each is to cut that year ... Strangely enough this delicate operation never seems to result in a quarrel' (ibid). Seen from this angle, the primacy of clan among the Lotha is directly related to the primacy of agriculture and its clan-based landownership pattern, a traditional disposition towards a clan-based social organisation, which now appears to have been reasserted into the democratic arena.

About a month before the February 2013 elections, the Ngullie Lotha clan came out with a public declaration, informing that, 'a general meeting of the Ngullietsu Ekhung [all Ngullie union] was held in Yanthamo village and attended by more than 2000 Ngullies' clansmen representing all the villages'. During this meeting they resolved to select a certain veteran Ngullie politician as the 'official Candidate from the Ngullies clansmen'. The public declaration further qualified that although the Ngullietsu Ekhung did not want to 'infringe on the exercise of democratic rights by any individual', they had 'blessed and endorsed' the candidature of the veteran politician, then adding that 'no individual member is above the Ngulliestu Ekhung' and that any violation of its resolutions may compel the Ekhung 'to take measures as per customary norms and practices'.

Even if a public declaration is not done under the banner of a single clan, the clan remains the unit of measurement, as the following declaration shows,

> the ... RJD [Rashtriya Janata Dal] campaign committee would like to express their gratitude and appreciation to the undermentioned supporters ... for extending wholehearted support to the RJD candidate ... 23 households of Patton's clan from Pangti village, 50 households of Kikon's clan from Yanshum Khel [ward] of Pangti village and Sungro, 21 households of Ngullie's clan from Yanshum khel of Pangti village and Sungro, 48 households of Ngullie's clan from Yondon khel of Pangti Village and Sungro.

Two other newspaper declarations coming from the Lotha area read: 'The Enny Clan of Old Changsu village with 25 households declare unconditional support to the NPF candidate', and '34 households under Tsopoe's clan of Pangti village ... have unanimously decided to support ... in the ensuing General Assembly Election'. In certain cases, the clan-model among the Lotha gives way to the village consensus candidate model as evidently happened in Tsungiki village, where the village council came out with a statement endorsing a particular candidate as the 'official candidate of our village', further adding 'Given the fact that, it is the first time we humbly appeal to all the neighbouring villages to support our village candidate.'

While clan unity during electoral politics is actively pursued, it is often more an ideal rather than an actual reality. In the period preceding the election numerous clan declarations, rejoinders and re-rejoinders emerged in the newspapers with clan representatives disputing the resolutions adopted by their clan leaders, or with a clan in a certain village promising its 'collective clan vote' to a different candidate than their clansmen from a neighbouring village. To illustrate, in one village eight members of the Ezung clan questioned, using the medium of the newspaper, the 'declaration of support' published by their village council chairperson who was a member of the Ezung clan, accusing him of spreading 'cheap propaganda.' This disjuncture between clan political rhetoric and actual practices is also shown by Ovung (2012). While emphasising that clans are the units of electoral politics, and indeed that, no serious view of Lotha politics can exclude the importance of clan, Ovung's survey about clan's internal harmony and integration shows that, compared to ceremonies (including marriages, births and funerals), traditional festivals and community work, Lotha clans are actually united the least when it comes to elections, with only 16% of his respondents stating that elections are a period of clan-cohesion (ibid: 76). Clearly the rhetoric of clan-wise electoral support and actual electoral practices at times refer to two different things altogether.

THE HOUSEHOLD MODEL

The fourth model, the household model, is most clearly practiced by the Angami and Chakhesang Naga tribes. Here traditional aristocrats are absent, while village councillors and clan leaders have little or no influence over the voting behaviour of 'ordinary villagers.' Instead, individual and household deliberation is more pronounced, and 'social pressure' to vote collectively, except in incidental cases, absent. Comparatively, among the Naga people, the Angami and Chakhesang (formerly eastern Angami) tribes appear to come closest to the elevated democratic principles of free, fair and autonomous individual deliberation. Although it must be instantly qualified that this 'individual deliberation' often culminates into a 'household decision', and that it is only on rare occasions that members of the same household cast their votes differently. 'Shame' is spoken of a household in which different members cast their votes for different candidates, and compared to the breakdown of the family, even to divorce. Exceptions are however there, and I have come across a handful of families who consciously decided to divide their household votes over two candidates equally, as they happened to have close kinship relations with both. In the household model, individual voting might, on polling day, be substituted, by village council order, into a system of 'household voting', in which the head of the household is empowered to cast the votes of all his household members.

The Angami and Chakhesang Naga have a marked 'democratic archaeology', a feature British officers wrote about with a sense of admiration. About the Angami Naga, Butler wrote: 'Every man follows the dictates of his own will, a form of the purest democracy which it is very difficult to conceive of as existing even for a single day and yet that it does exist here is an undeniable fact' (cited in Hutton 1921a: 143). Hutton, in turn, defined the Angami as a 'debating society' with the authority of village leaders, if they existed, being nominal: 'their orders are obeyed so far only as they accord with the wishes and convenience of the community' (ibid: 142–43). Hutton continued: 'disputes, when settled at all, were probably settled by a sort of informal council of elders, who would discuss the matter under dispute with one another, the parties, and the general public at great length, until some sort of agreement was arrived at' (ibid).

What Butler termed as the 'purest democracy' and Hutton called a 'debating society' was in reality more akin to the 'ideal polity' for Socrates and Aristotle, with the 'philosophically minded' and the 'virtuous' responsible for the decision-making process. Among the Angami and Chakhesang it was usually the elders, warriors and wealthy who deliberated decisions, commonly barring women, the physically feeble and the village poor from equal participation. That said, the traditional polity of the Angami and Chakhesang was, on the whole, less hierarchical, people less inclined to obey to authority, and this more egalitarian disposition now appears to show itself in the kind of public 'declarations of support' that filter from the Angami and Chakhesang areas. Here they are not signed by an angh or chief, by the convenor or president of a village's apex body, or by the president of a clan's union, but by a long list of individuals, cutting across clans and villages.

The Congress Committee of Meluri, inhabited predominantly by the Pochury Naga (who were formerly part of the eastern Angami and Chakhesang), declared: 'A total of 72 households hereby resign from the NPF party and joined the INC Party'. The statement was subsequently undersigned by the heads of the 72 households, stretching the 'declaration of support' into an elongated column. In other instances, a single person deems it desirable to publicly declare his alliance, like a former candidate of the RJD who wrote, 'Since the party [RJD] is not in a position to come to power even in near future, I have decided to join Indian National Congress (INC)'. In most cases, however, it is households, cross-cutting villages and clans, which are the units of measurement in the newspaper declarations. Another previous RJD party worker also resigned and publicly declared that he had done so 'along with 31 households ... to support the Indian National Congress Candidate'. And another declared, 'I, Mr...President Khezhakeno Unit (youth wing) and my followers resigned from my post and primary membership of the Congress and join the NPF.' In the household model, every head of the household becomes a political player in its own right, and occasionally confusion arises about a person's political alliance. When three persons from Pfutsero Town found their name mentioned in the newspaper among those who had resigned from the Congress candidate, they instantly wrote a re-joinder, condemning the 'false declaration' made, and asserting that, 'we have not resigned.'

In this model of electoral politics, 'kitchen-politics' (not meant in the conventional gendered sense of household decisions, but as an electoral strategy in which candidates and his party workers visit house to house to attract voters) is the main electoral strategy. Every person, every household, needs to be convinced personally, allotted time and effort to, and while securing the support of a prominent village or clan leader might certainly benefit the candidate's local standing, it hardly suffices in securing majority support. It is this individuality, coupled by the highly personalized nature of 'kitchen-politics', which renders electoral politics in the constituencies in which the household model is in vogue a very intensive and lengthy affair, often commencing many months before the scheduled date of the elections.

CONCLUSION

The above four models, although the most prominent ones, are not the only ways through which Nagaland's democracy is performed. Another variant might be called the 'range model', and holds that, in certain areas, villages located on the same hill range make collective voting decisions. This happened among a section of the Khiamniungan Naga: 'The Noklak NPF party welcomes the Thang Range Public Organisation (TRPO) consisting of five villages ... The TRPO firmly decided to support the NPF candidate.' Another model might be the youth-model, as the following statement indicates, 'We, the undersigned Independent Youth declare wholeheartedly to support the candidature of ....'

This last declaration hails from Dimapur, which is Nagaland's most urbanized and most intermixed area, with Naga tribes and some non-Naga tribes residing there, as well as a sizeable number of immigrants from other parts of the country. It is here, in this amalgam of communities, that the four models above apply the least. The five constituencies in the Dimapur plains and nearby foothills are invariably larger compared to those in the hills, the levels of intimacy between candidates and voters lower, and, in large parts because of this, party-politics more pronounced than 'person-politics.' But in these constituencies too voting is hardly a private and individual matter. While traces of the four models are present, though less conclusively so, new collectives are formed and declare their 'unflinching', 'unconditional', and 'unwavering' support for their preferred candidates. Self-help groups, enacted to uplift the economic status of its members, are one such new collective, and in the wake of the election one self-help group declared that it had lost confidence in one particular candidate 'for showing no concern to Self-Help Groups' and 'unanimously decided to give full support' to his opponent. Also communities as a whole may promise their collective support, like the Rongmei Naga community in a particular area of Dimapur: 'the Rongmei ... extends unconditional support to the NPF', or as the youth of the Kuki community did in another constituency, 'We, the undermentioned Kuki Community Youth have resolved to extend our full support to the Independent Candidate.'

If participating in elections expresses 'the symbolic affirmation of the voters' acceptance of the political system and of their role within in' (Lukes 1975: 304), Nagaland, with a voter turnout of well over 90% during the last election, which is significantly higher than the average turnout in most Indian states, seems to be among the premium Indian states in which the idea of democracy has consolidated.[9] Yet it is also important, argues Khilnani (2009: 5), 'to explore the diverse political imaginations and arguments that sustain (or undermine) democratic politics.' Democracy as a universal set of practices and values is an ideal, and this essay shows that it is just that, an ideal.

While almost universal in its scope and discourse, democracy is performed differently in different places. In a way, this is obvious, American Democracy is not the same as French Democracy, and French Democracy and Indian Democracy are again very different. What this essay has asserted is that local communities, Naga tribes in our case, rather than passive absorbers of modern democratic principles, possess the agency to appropriate, reinterpret and rework the idea of democracy according to their own cultural values and traditional polities. Put differently, modern democracy has locally manifested itself as a new arena to perform 'past politics.' This is not to argue that Nagaland's electoral models may not change over time, or that the practitioners of these models are innately recalcitrant to the modern ideology of democracy. The models presented here are fluid, flexible and open to contestations, and during the 2013 Nagaland state assembly elections certain powerful local voices were raised against the selection of village and clan consensus candidates.

In the upshot, the presence of these four electoral models suggests that Naga tribes are both the repositories and enactors of their own particular versions of democracy, remoulding its institutions and principles into their own traditional polities. It shows how different Naga tribes instead of adjusting themselves to modern democratic ideals, adjusted democracy to themselves. Shah (2010: 185) refers to this indigenous or tribal 'search for alternative, more informed models of political life' as 'arcadian spaces', building upon the 'culturalist critique' of the post-colonial Indian state. These 'arcadian spaces', Shah insists, are not simply 'spaces of utopia', but are based on the political potential of central elements and values of, in her case, the indigenous Munda society in Jharkhand (ibid). However, whereas Shah argues that the Munda attempt to keep modern democracy, as well as the state machinery, at arm's length, the case of the Naga shows that democracy is not so much resisted, as it is actively appropriated, reinterpreted and reworked to suit local political cultures. While ideas of balloting and elections have now firmly etched themselves at the centre of Naga society, the Naga versions of performing democracy suggest that, when seen from a local perspective, the elevated modern democratic principles of individual, impartial, and autonomous deliberation are strange ideas, indeed.

06

DIFFICULT DECOLONIZATION: DEBATES, DIVISIONS, AND DEATHS *WITHIN* THE NAGA UPRISING, 1944–1963

Political conflicts have lifecycles: like persons they go through different stages with each associating with particular behaviours, experiences, emotions and viewpoints. While each stage informs the articulations and acts that become seen as characteristic of the next, these stages do not necessarily follow in a unilinear fashion, nor is it always possible to demarcate different stages in a clear-cut manner. Their points of beginning and ending are often fuzzy, overlapping, and open to interpretation. However, especially as time passes, distinct stages tend to become analytically distinguishable and recognizing these offer heuristic frames to better understand the evolution of political conflicts. Reading stages into a political conflict may not be feasible in the heat of the war, or even during its immediate aftermath, but become the domain of 'second-generation historiography', or the more professional, more detached forms of history writing that emerge after 'those who experienced the war fade away and, with them, the scars, emotions, myths, and self-justifications that were part of their mental make-up' (Van Schendel 2016: 76).

The protracted Indo-Naga war is one such political conflict whose historical trajectory can be deconstructed and analysed in the form of analytically distinguishable stages. At the time of writing, the conflict continues to evade a final political settlement, although since the 1997 Indo-Naga ceasefire the war has increasingly turned into a low-intensity conflict. In this context, it remains 'first-generation historiography', written by stakeholders or veterans of either the Naga Movement or the Indian state and its army, that dominates public discourse and moulds popular understandings of the conflict, its causes and consequences.[1] Gradually, however, space is beginning to open for more detached reflections on the conflict, particularly concerning its origins and early beginnings in the 1940s and 50s.[2] While historians differently portray and theorise the Naga Movement, the moment the actual war breaks out is shrouded in less ambiguity: 'Troops moved into Tuensang by Oct. 1955', B.N. Mullick, then Director of India's Central Intelligence Bureau, recounted, 'and the war with the Nagas started from then' (cited in Vashum 2000: 112).

The outbreak of war occured within the stage of the Indo-Naga conflict I propose to demarcate and discuss here, which is the period roughly between the Battle of Kohima in 1944, which ended Japanese expansionism in the east, and the enactment of Nagaland state in 1963 as an envisaged (but failed) political compromise to the demand by the Naga National Council (NNC) for complete Naga sovereignty. This stage often finds itself subsumed into a larger master narrative of the Naga struggle that reconstructs a relatively straight and uncomplicated historical trajectory that sees the genuine awakening and NNC-led political mobilization of a highland community situated off the beaten track of both Indian civilization and colonial domination, and of Nagas' collective resolve to take up arms to fight for a place on the table of nation-states. Alternatively, if the story is told from the vantage of the Indian state, the dominant narrative apportions blame to a 'misguided' Naga elite that seeks to undermine the territorial and national integrity of the Indian state.

Simplistic historical reconstructions of any war are worrisome enough in themselves. In the case of the Indo-Naga war such readings become particularly constrictive, though, when they make the present and future generations see the armed conflict – and the death, misery and societal destruction havocked in its name – through a reductive lens of historically inevitable and clear-cut fault-lines between India and Nagas that erupted in full force during the difficult process of decolonization. These prevailing views, attractive for their absence of complexity, however, ignore the anguished debates, interpersonal and intertribal differences, contingent histories and events, dissenting voices, political assassinations, and sharp differences within the rank-and-file of the NNC prior to the outbreak of the armed conflict, and whose inner dynamics and sentiments could as well have produced outcomes other than war.

While the Naga Movement is home to a growing body of scholarship, I am not aware of any study that concentrates in detail on the period between 1944 and 1963. This is a lack because the political debates and events that transpired in this period not only led to the outbreak of armed conflict, but also set the stage for later developments and complications that continue to haunt and divide Naga society, including intertribal antagonisms and a broad division into 'underground' and 'overground' Nagas. This essay uses archival histories to challenge and complicate the historiographical certainty apportioned to the early political evolution and outbreak of the Indo-Naga war. I tell the narrative that follows through hitherto scantily used sources, including official statements and memorandums, colonial tour diaries and personal journals, memoires and biographies, and those memories recorded by history. First, however, the next section offers, in much abridged form, a few reflections on the rise of Naga political consciousness and self-assertion during the era of late-colonialism.

ANTECEDENTS OF NAGA NATIONALISM

Modern Naga political history can be read as the product of two mutually constitutive processes – the internal dynamics of clan, *khel* (village ward or sector), village, and tribe and the effects and transformations impelled by systematic contact with external agencies and events such as colonial rule, Christian missions, and the First and Second World Wars. Their conjunction is what first gave rise to an encompassing, though ever fraught and fragile, sense of a pan-Naga political identity that became articulated during the era of late-colonialism. While most Naga nationalists prefer to frame the Naga nation as God-given, rather than man-made, and speak of a perennial, historically immutable Naga essence that was not created but awakened in the 20th century, most historians agree that the Naga nation, in its present form and substance, did not flourish in primordial isolation but emerged and took on significance in relation to particular historical processes and cataclysmic events.

Historians variously theorise the experience of colonial rule – here including 'pacification', administrative unification, the imposition of an Inner-Line regime, and ethnological classification – and Christianity – its universal 'truths', the standardization and Romanization of languages, the advent of mission schools and education – as centripetal forces that established the initial terms for an emergent Naga national identity (see

Thong 2016; Thomas 2016). Other reconstructions are less processual and highlight specific events, such as the recruitment of an estimated 2000 Naga villagers from different clans, villages, and tribes into the Labour Corps that was dispatched to war trenches in France during the First World War. Toiling within the sound of guns, these Naga 'coolies', the argument goes, gained political consciousness as they were introduced, with harsh clarity, to the modern compulsions of nation, nationalism, and patriotism (Chasie 2005).[3] The journey across seas and the war trenches subsequently 'awakened the spunk of the Naga nationalism' (Yonuo 1974: xii) as it led to a rethinking and broadening of Naga identity that began to transcend divisions along tribal, village and clan lines.

The returning home of these Naga labourers is popularly associated with the establishment of the Naga Club in 1918, the first pan-Naga apex body, even as most of its founding members had *not* been part of the Labour Corps but were newly educated and entrepreneurial Nagas, the majority of whom were serving the colonial government. It is under the aegis of the Naga Club that, in 1929, Naga representatives petitioned the Simon Commission, which had come to British India to study constitutional reform. Were the British to depart, as rumour already had it, they pleaded: 'We [the Nagas] should not be thrust to the mercy of other people... but to leave us alone as in ancient times.' While, bar a few, the 21 signatories belonged to the Angami Naga and hailed from Kohima and its immediate surroundings, they nevertheless claimed to represent not only 'those regions to which we [the signatories] belong... but also other regions of Nagaland' (Vashum 2000: 175). This determining influence of the Angami tribe in Naga political expressions was to remain characteristic, as subsequent sections will show, of the beginnings of the Naga uprising. This thesis of Angami 'leadership' or 'domination' (depending on who you ask) is personified by the charisma and activities of Angami Zaphu Phizo, whom was the fourth president of the NNC and the main ideologue and prophet of Naga nationalism, and whose ascend to power and influence I will discuss further below.

While historians debate and disagree about the relative importance of these processes, events, and the political magnetism that emanated from Phizo, they broadly agree that, taken together, they transformed a social fabric that revolved strongly around fragmented and 'primordial givens' into a society progressively preoccupied with constructing a more generic Naga cultural and political identity.

The next two sections show how experiences during the Second World War further emboldened this emergent conception of the Naga in a self-conscious and politically assertive national mould.

THE SECOND WORLD WAR AND THE NAGAS

If Naga labourers travelled frightening journeys on rundown ships to participate in the First World War, the Second World War announced itself at Naga doorsteps. In December 1941, the first Japanese bombs fell on Rangoon, the capital of British Burma. A few months later large swathes of Burma were in Japanese hands. India was to be conquered next and rumours of an imminent invasion spread across the hills and valleys of Assam (Bower 1950: 171). Contrary to expectations, the Japanese advance paused at the foot of the Patkai range, the jungle-clad and upland frontier that separated India and Burma. To prepare for the assault, Allied Forces turned the Naga highlands, and neighbouring hills, into a huge 'military bulwark against Tokyo' (Guyot-Réchard 2017: 7). In 1944, Japanese forces began their by now long anticipated march into India and which resulted in a destructive battle that bogged down to the towns of Imphal and especially Kohima, whose hilltop garrison the Japanese placed under siege.

The Battle of Kohima raged between April 4 and June 22 1944 and witnessed some of the fiercest hand-to-hand combat in the Second World War (see Guyot-Réchard 2017). While thousands of Allied Soldiers lost their lives, victory was nevertheless claimed by them, making Kohima to the Japanese what 'Stalingrad was to Russia and Alemein to the Dessert' (Philipps cited in Horam 1988: 57). What greatly frustrated the Japanese Army, as well as the collaborating Indian National Army (INA) led by Subhas Chandra Bose, is that, at the decisive moment, Nagas sided with Allied Forces, instead of capitalizing on the opportunity to revolt against their colonial rulers. A large literature of military analyses and memoires document how Nagas actively contributed to the Allied Victory by serving as scouts, interpreters, spies, labourers, orderlies, and levies.[4] Wrote John Colvin (1994: 35): 'Irrespective of the tribe or sub-tribe, the record of the Nagas during the Japanese occupation was one of extraordinary loyalty to the British'. General Slim (1956: 341) similarly acknowledged: 'These were the gallant Nagas whose loyalty, even in the most depressing times of the invasion had never faltered'.

But while this official narrative firmly places the Nagas on the 'good side' of history, not all Nagas sided with the Allied Forces. Amongst those who did not was the later NNC president A.Z. Phizo. On the eve of the Japanese invasion of Burma, Phizo was in Rangoon, where he had arrived some years earlier out of a mixture of business interests and 'self-imposed exile' following a series of 'anti-British statements' in Kohima that earned him the reputation of a 'potential troublemaker in the eyes of officialdom' (Steyn 2002: 48). Despite past ill-feelings, Phizo enlisted himself as a volunteer in the British Army. 'I did not hate the British, only their colonialism and what they stood for', he justified his decision many years later (cited in Steyn 2002: 52). However, Phizo's political convictions prevented his actual enrolment:

> At his interview trouble arose when he was told that Asiatics could not be enrolled and he would have to change his nationality to either Anglo-Indian or Anglo-Burmese if he wanted to enlist. Such a suggestion, of course, immediately put his back up in no uncertain way – his uncompromising retort being: 'I am a Naga first, a Naga second, and a Naga last'. An inevitable stalemate ensued. The commanding officer, Major Sample, lost his patience and summarily ordered him to depart. Once again, stubbornly dignified Phizo had his way: 'If you tell me to go, I will go, but for my part I have offered my services' (Steyn 2002: 54).

Following this encounter, Phizo, accompanied in Rangoon by his wife and brother Keviyallay, did not join the large stream of refugees that fled towards India, but stayed put. He now offered his services to the Japanese:

> When war came to Burma in 1942, my brother and I were asked by the Japanese Army to assist them. As they promised to recognize Nagaland as an independent sovereign state, we rendered whatever service we could towards what seemed to us the liberation of our own country (Phizo 1960).[5]

In the end, it was not Phizo but Keviyallay who guided several Japanese patrols into both the Naga 'Control Area'[6] and the Naga Hills District (Steyn 2002: 58). Meanwhile, Subhas Bose arrived in Burma. Phizo met him on several occasions, and became, somewhat informally, associated with the INA, again on the premise that Bose would recognize Naga independence after the British would be routed. While Phizo was inspired by Bose's 'charisma and boundless energy', he is said to have 'refrained from joining the cries of *Jai Hind* whenever and wherever Bose appeared'. Phizo offered to join the INA in their invasion of India, but was 'rebuffed', reportedly because 'he would be needed once Nagaland had been liberated' (Steyn 2002: 60). Phizo subsequently waited out the war in Rangoon (Nibedon 1978: 23).

After Burma fell back in British hands, Phizo and Keviyallay were arrested on charges of collaborating with the enemy. Phizo was jailed and remained so for eight months. Following his release in 1946, he returned to the Naga Hills, and now did so 'with his mind full of unwavering determination and revolutionary ideas to achieve political independence for his homeland' (Yonuo 1974: 199).

FROM RECONSTRUCTION TO POLITICAL ASSERTION: THE MAKING OF THE NAGA NATIONAL COUNCIL

By July 1944, Kohima was reduced to ruins and rubble. 'After the battle I was one of the first to return. The entire place was strewn with corpses, rubble', reflected Langalang (cited in Aram 1974: 18), the Headmaster of the Kohima High School and soon to become an influential NNC member. Villages through which Japanese and Allied Forces had passed too suffered painful destruction and depletion. Fields lay uncultivated, granaries were empty, and most livestock was confiscated and slaughtered. This destruction, however, was also politically productive with the war serving as 'an agent of *ethnicization*' (Guyot-Réchard 2017: 3; emphasis in original). As Fürer-Haimendorf reflected:

> When the Japanese invaded Burma and India during the Second World War the Naga Hills became a battleground. Soldiers of various races passed through, lived, fought and died among the Nagas. Thus new people, new weapons, new attire, new food and above all new ideas were introduced to the Nagas and when the War came to an end they could not go back to the old secluded life (cited in Joshi 2012: 26).

In the aftermath of the war, the Assam Governor constituted an Assam Relief Measures organization that provided relief and reconstruction for war-affected areas. In the Naga Hills District, Charles Pawsey, the District Commissioner, invited Naga government officers and tribal leaders to his bungalow and proposed the formation of the Naga Hills District Tribal Council (NHDTC) 'with the aim of uniting the Nagas and repairing some of the damage done during World War II' (Elwin 1961: 51). While Pawsey saw the NHDTC as a technical, apolitical body, 'once it was formed the council increasingly became a platform for Nagas to express and debate some of their pressing political concerns, ultimately leading to the formation of the NNC in February 1946' (Thomas 2016: 102). As opposed to the NHDTC, which soon dissolved, the NNC was wholly an indigenous creation.

The NNC began with 29 members and was organized around two central councils: Mokokchung and Kohima. Its members represented all Naga tribes located within the Naga Hills District and several of the 'Control Area'. Membership, however, was dominated by the Angami and Ao tribes with 7 and 5 members in the council respectively (Misra 2000: 29). At first, the NNC received 'official patronage' from colonial officials who perceived of the Council as a 'unifying and moderating influence' (Elwin 1961: 51), and who were themselves engaged in discussions on the future administration of the hills.[7] However, as NNC members became more politically assertive, they increasingly began to view the Council with apprehension. 'There is a somewhat nebulous body in existence (more or less self-created) called "the Naga National Council"', J.P. Mills, a veteran administrator among the Naga and then Advisor to the Governor in Shillong, wrote to William Archer upon the latter's posting to Mokokchung. Mills explained: 'It is not "National" at all, of course, though it may be nationalistic. It has to be treated with politeness – rudeness never pays – but I personally don't regard it the mouthpiece of the public'.[8] In his judgment, Mills was to be mistaken as the NNC soon became the catalyst of political developments in the Naga highlands.

THE DEBATE WITHIN: AUTONOMY VERSUS INDEPENDENCE

Dominant Naga national reconstructions tell that immediately after its formation in 1946, the NNC began to prepare itself for complete independence, ultimately resulting in a unilateral declaration of independence based on the general will of the Naga people. This single master narrative highlights the political unity of the Naga people and presents the enactment of the NNC and the declaration of Naga independence as complementary events that followed in linear and relatively uncomplicated fashion. This section unsettles such historical certainties and complicates the proclaimed inevitability of Nagas' claim to independence by focusing on debates, disagreements and divisions within the NNC rank-and-file between its formation in February 1946 and the Naga declaration of independence on August 14 1947, one day before India achieved hers. I am not aware of any surviving minutes of early NNC meetings (if they were kept in the first place), and I therefore rely on official memorandums and statements issued by the NNC as well as on secondary sources, mostly in the form of diaries, notes, and correspondence written unfortunately not by Nagas but by colonial officers (and the spouse of one such officer) then posted in the Naga Hills District. These officers kept themselves abreast of (and also interfered into) political developments through personal discussions with NNC members.

'The Naga future would not be bound by any arbitrary decision of the British Government, and no recommendation would be accepted without consultation' (Lisam 2011: 447), the first NNC memorandum read and was submitted to a British Cabinet Mission that visited Delhi in April 1946. The generality of this statement is not because NNC members lacked concrete political vision, but because, right from the beginning, the NNC was broadly divided into two camps: those in favour of meaningful Naga autonomy within Assam and India and advocates of complete Naga independence. These conflicting political viewpoints revealed themselves along tribal lines with Ao Naga representatives, supported by their Lotha neighbours, arguing for autonomy and Angami delegates making the case for Naga independence.[9] Basing her notes on conversations with Aliba Imti, NNC's first president,[10] and Mayangnokcha, the vice-president (both Ao Nagas), Mildred Archer (the wife of William Archer, then Sub-Divisional Officer of Mokokchung District) detailed the rift between the Mokokchung and Kohima centres of the NNC:

> On the Kohima side of the district, the Angamis and Kacha Nagas began to dream of a fully independent Naga Hills. 'Until the British conquered us, we ruled ourselves. We were never under the Assamese. Why should an Assam Raj be foisted on us now? During the war we saw the plainsman. We know his tricks. We will never be safe without a Naga Raj'. But on the Mokokchung side, the Aos and Lhotas were much less hostile. The Japanese were halted on their boundaries. They have experienced no Indian exploitation, while a few who were educated in Jorhat and Shillong [Assam] had even imbibed some Congress ideas.[11]

In important parts, these conflicting political positions seemed a response to divergent historical experiences, not least in relation to the Second World War. While the war destroyed and depleted Kohima and most Angami villages, Mokokchung district was saved this disaster, witnessed fewer Japanese and Allied soldiers on its soil, and was so spared the exploitation most Angamis experienced. After the war, Angami villagers favourably compared the behaviour of Japanese soldiers to that of 'the "Punjabis"' (Guyot-Réchard 2017: 21) with whom they had sided. Subhas Bose's INA conjured similarly disparaging evaluations. 'They treated us like dirt', an Angami headmaster recalled, then added: 'It will be like that if the plainsmen rule us.' 'I worked as a road contractor', another Angami narrated. 'The Indian officers made me promises but they never kept them. They only wanted bribes. The Pathans and the Sikhs were the worst. How can we stand against the plainsman?' (cited in Guyot-Réchard 2017: 21). But not just differential experiences of war. Divergent trajectories of Christian conversion and pre-existent intertribal animosities, too, shaped Ao and Angami political positions differently:

> Moreover at the back of their [Ao and Lotha] minds was the vague fear that Independence would mean in practice not a Naga Raj but an Angami one. They saw themselves weakened by Christianity [Ao Nagas were the first to convert in large numbers], no longer militant in outlook, and opposed by a vigorous thrusting tribe [Angami] which was still proud of its warriors' traditions and was only recently weaned from head-taking. Mildred Archer Diaries, 18-07-1947. Digital Himalaya, Naga videodisc. Url: http://himalaya.socanth.cam.ac.uk/collections/naga/record/r67023.html

This apprehension of a Naga independence becoming an 'Angami Raj' was to remain an important subtext of NNC debates. While touring the Rengma Naga, neighbouring the Angami, William Archer noticed the strengthening of village defence walls. Villagers told him that they did so for reasons of 'cattle', but when Archer asked poignantly: 'for Angami cattle?', 'they laughed and did not deny it.' Archer wrote: 'Rengmas fear an Angami Raj on the one hand and an Assam Raj on the other, the latter the lesser of the 2 evils'.[12]

Differences between Angami and Ao delegates came to a head during an NNC meeting in Wokha, the Lotha Naga headquarters, in June 1946. Kevichusa, the first Naga graduate and a senior government servant in Kohima, strongly made the case for Naga independence: 'Self-government should mean a government of the Nagas, for the Nagas, by the Nagas. Nothing else means anything to the Nagas. We have to be masters of our own country and be free'. Ao delegates were 'unconvinced' and 'realising that only through a united front would any advance be possible, the Angamis yielded to Mokokchung opinion [and] abandoned the demand for independence'.[13] What resulted was a four-point memorandum, which T. Sakhrie, the Angami NNC Secretary, dispatched to Jawaharlal Nehru. It read:

1. This Naga National Council stands for the solidarity of Naga tribes including those in the un-administrated areas.
2. This Council strongly protests against the grouping of Assam with Bengal.

3. The Naga Hills should be Constitutionally included in autonomous Assam, in a free India, with local autonomy and due safeguards for the interest of the Nagas
4. The Naga tribes should have a separate electorate (Vashum 2000: 69).

In his response, Nehru endorsed the first three points, but rejected the idea of a separate Naga electorate: 'We are against separate electorates as this will limit and injure the small group by keeping it separated from the rest of the nation.' Nehru also informed that an Advisory Committee would soon be enacted to offer recommendations on the constitutional inclusion of the Assam hill tribes, and added that this Committee 'should have representatives of the tribal areas' (Vashum 2000: 69-70).

Once enacted, however, the Committee was primarily made up of Congress politicians from Assam, including Gopinath Bordoloi (Assam's first chief minister) and had only two tribal representatives: Nichols Roy, a Khasi Reverend married to an American and known to favour an integrated Assam, and Mayangnokcha. This immediately irked the NNC: 'Everyone realised that the object of the sub-committee was not to give the Nagas the constitution they wanted but to ensure that Congress ideas of what the Nagas ought to want should prevail'.[14] It reinvigorated the Angami voice for independence, and in the next NNC meeting, in February 1947, Angami delegates proposed that a clause be included in any agreement that allowed for a Naga interim government for a period of ten years, under the protection of either the British or Indian Government, and after which Nagas would freely decide their political future. A furious debate ensued with Ao representatives standing by the Wokha resolution. It was only after the interference of Pawsey, who called the disagreeing NNC members to his bungalow, that the deadlock was resolved. This time Ao delegates yielded to the Angami position and the proposed clause was added to a new memorandum. Pawsey's intervention (and not just in this instance) frustrated Phizo. He reflected later: 'I had seen nationalists at work in Burma. I had witnessed what patriotism could achieve. What I found on my return to Nagaland was nothing — no unity, no ideas. Everybody waited to hear what the District Commissioner wanted' (cited in Steyn 2002: 72).

Mayangnokcha presented the new memorandum to the Advisory Committee in Delhi, but was rebuked by its members: 'Your memorandum is merely history... Who ever heard of a Naga interim government?', they reacted. 'I tried to reason with them', Mayangnokcha recounted, 'but they were all sour. They do not argue straight. They twist your words. There is no love in them. No one of them desired the Nagas' good. They think only of Assam'.[15] A frustrated Mayangnokcha tendered his resignation. A few months on, in May 1947, the Advisory Committee visited Kohima to meet the NNC. Bordoloi proposed several suggestions for Nagas' constitutional inclusion in an independent India. 'Give us a reply to our demands, then we will answer your question', is what NNC members responded. The meeting ended with Bordoloi retorting: 'You are really very obstinate'.[16] In a report of the meeting, the Secretary of the Committee stated: 'It was clearly perceived that the Council was now dominated by certain Angami leaders like Kevichusa and Lungalong and the more reasonable elements were prevented from asserting themselves' (cited in Chaube 1999: 141-2).

Now it was Sir Akbar Hydari's, the Assam Governor, turn to try and resolve the deadlock. Three days of consultations in Kohima resulted in an agreement known variously as the 'nine-point agreement', the 'Hydari agreement', and the 'Governor's agreement'. It proposed measures of executive, judiciary, and legislative autonomy. Its ninth, and soon controversial, clause read:

> The Governor of Assam as the Agent of the Government of the Indian Union will have a special responsibility for a period of 10 years to ensure the observance of the agreement, at the end of this period the Naga Council will be asked whether they require the above agreement to be extended for a further period or a new agreement regarding the future of Naga people arrived at (Nuh 2002: 67-8).

The Hydari agreement divided the NNC. While it was realised that most clauses were 'very loosely worded' and that 'it said nothing of an interim government',[17] it did fulfil the Ao demand for autonomy and Ao representatives, guided by Mayangnokcha and Aliba Imti, were ready to accept it. The Angami response was more complicated and disagreements led to a split between the historically influential Kohima and Khonoma villages, and their respective traditional allies and tributaries. While the Kohima group reluctantly accepted the agreement, the Khonoma group, of which Kevichusa, Sakhrie, and Phizo were part, called upon Hydari to clarify whether clause nine allowed Nagas to declare their independence after ten years if they would so desire. When Hydari explained that it did not, and threatened violent repercussions if Nagas would proclaim independence, the 'Khonoma Nagas' rebuked NNC leaders for having agreed to it, seceded from the NNC, and began a movement of their own under the banner of the People's Independence League (PIL) with headquarters in Khonoma village.

Confusion within the NNC mounted further when, a week after the Hydari agreement, the Advisory Committee met in Shillong. Aliba Imti, who replaced Mayangnokcha as a member, attended, but discovered that the Hydari agreement had been brushed aside by the Committee, whose members insisted: 'We find the recommendations made by us cover in essence the measure of autonomy contemplated by the Nagas and go much further in some respects'.[18] It were these recommendations that ultimately became the basis of the Sixth Schedule to the Indian Constitution that came to apply to selected upland areas (and later also certain territories in the plains) in India's Northeast. Aliba Imti objected against the Committee 'treating the Naga Hills District as part of Assam and not as an independent area',[19] but he was overruled. In the aftermath of the Shillong meeting, Mildred Archer recorded how 'those who never liked the agreement now feel themselves no longer pledged to it, while those who were satisfied are at loss to understand the position'.[20] Another NNC meeting was scheduled. This time in Mokokchung.

On the 21st of July, Mildred Archer wrote in her diary:

> Today there is great excitement as the Naga National Council is beginning to assemble. Kohima is sending Angami, Rengma, and Kacha Naga delegates, while Sema, Lhotas and Aos are coming in from villages all over Mokokchung. Imlong and Hopongki, the Chang and Sangtam members, are putting their shops in order and already the air is full of trade and politics.

The splitting away of the 'Khonoma group' was the first point on the agenda. Mildred Archer wrote down what Aliba Imti told her: 'the Angami split is more serious than was thought. The Khonoma group have denounced the NNC and formed a separate independence party. A delegation has gone to Delhi and he hears that they have met Gandhi and Jinnah. Their action is a challenge to the NNC and the delegates must now decide what counter steps to take'. Mayangnokcha, however, was of the view that 'a little "extremism" will do no harm', reasoning: 'the Congress leaders will be more ready to listen if they had a preliminary shock'.[21] He then proposed that the NNC send a counter-delegation to Delhi. To be noted, here, is that at this stage, less than a month prior to India's independence, the demand for Naga independence was still talked about as 'extremist' within the NNC.

The Hydari agreement was next on the agenda. Once again, Ao and Angami positions clashed with the Angami insisting on the modification of clause nine to allow for the possibility of Nagas seceding from the Indian Union after ten years. Ao delegates, on the other hand, argued in favour of the original agreement and wished to press for its immediate implementation. After three days of discussion, it was the Angami viewpoint that prevailed. This resolution now split the Ao: 'All the morning, excited angry groups of villagers have been standing round and complaining of Mayang[nokcha]'s "treachery." Late last night they angrily abused him. "We stood by the Governor's agreement", they said, "What right had you to change it?"'[22]

Meanwhile, confirmation arrived that the Khonoma delegation had met both Jinnah and Gandhi in Delhi, and it was said that both leaders did not object to political projections of Naga independence. In Assam, Bordoloi reacted with fury: 'The question of the Nagas remaining independent of the Indian Union is absurd. A section of the Angami tribe under the leadership of persons from the village of Khonoma is misguided and their number is small'.[23] The NNC reacted and, apropos Mayangnokcha's suggestion, send a counter-delegation to Delhi.

'The suspense in Mokokchung is electric', Mildred Archer wrote as India's independence was drawing closer. 'Some of the Aos are exasperated, others are bewildered and every day the silence thickens'.[24] On August 12 a cable arrived informing that the NNC delegation had met Nehru and summoned all NNC members to Kohima for an emergency meeting. Mildred Archer pondered: 'Have the Mokokchung demands been granted? Will the meeting be asked to ratify the new terms? Are we on the verge of a Naga revolt? No one can say and no one dares to guess'.[25]

The meeting with Nehru had not gone well. While Nehru listened carefully to the NNC delegation at first, after Longri Ao, an NNC delegate, remarked, somewhat crudely, 'if the clause is not accepted the Nagas will go their own way', Nehru banged the table with his fist: 'India cannot be split into a hundred bits. If you fight we shall resist'.[26] The next day, two press communiqués appeared. The first, on behalf of the Indian Government, said: 'We can give you complete autonomy but never complete independence. You can never hope to be independent. No state, big or small, in India, will be allowed to remain independent. We will use all our influence and power to suppress such tendencies'.[27] In turn, the communiqué the NNC released stated:

> The Naga National Council recently sent a full representative body to Delhi to reach a settlement regarding their future relationship with India. In interviews with some of the Government of India leaders in Delhi, they were given to understand that their demands could not be satisfied in full. Since the people they represent will accept nothing short of their full demands, the members of the various delegations have decided that the Naga National Council is henceforth free to decide the future of the Naga people in the way that suits them best.[28]

The NNC met in Kohima on 13 and 14 August and decided that India's independence celebrations will be boycotted in protest against the government's refusal to revise clause nine of the Hydari agreement. In Khonoma, the People's Independence League took matters in its own hands and on August 14 declared Naga independence. Its leaders drafted a cable to the United Nations. It read:

> Benign excellence,
> Kindly put on record that Nagas will be independent. Discussion with India are being carried on to that effect. Nagas do not accept Indian Constitution. The right of the people must prevail regardless of size (Nuh 2002:115).

The cable, copies of which were addressed to Delhi and Indian newspapers, never left the Naga Hills, however. The postmaster, sensing the sensitivity of the cable's contents, referred them for clearance to Pawsey, who ordered the cables to be withheld. As a result, 'Nothing therefore reaches the press, not a word appeared announcing their tremendous step'.[29]

NAGA RAJ OR KHONOMA RAJ?

'Since 15 August, nothing has happened', Mildred Archer told her diary on August 23. 'The Khonoma group have had a number of meetings but have so far done nothing to set up a rival government. Pawsey thinks that having declared their independence they are now at loss to know what to do next'.[30] In their private correspondence, Pawsey, Archer, and other colonial officials disparagingly referred to the PIL as the Khonoma 'independence racket'[31] and doubted their true motivations: 'In Khonoma it is the Christian clan [khel] which demands complete independence. One is indifferent and the other does not want it — the clan which want it does so because it desires to re-impose Khonoma domination — to terrorize the region — as Khonoma did before'.[32]

To situate their reasoning we need to back up a little. Prior to British annexation, 'pacification', and overrule, 'No Angamis enjoyed such prestige or levied such widespread tribute as 'Khonoma', wrote the colonial officer J.H. Hutton (1921: 11). Several Kacha Naga villages, he observed, 'seem to have been entirely dominated by settlements of Khonoma Angamis who superimposed on them their own customs' (ibid.: 156). And not just Kacha villages. The colonial archive reveals that Khonoma raids and tributary relations extended far and wide. Inside Khonoma, the 'Christian khel', which colonial officers singled out as the forerunner of the independence claim, referred to the Merhü khel. This khel was heir to powerful chiefs and warriors, had earned itself a hardy reputation for subjugating villages (as well as for struggling with the other two Khonoma khels over property and domination within the village), and put up a particularly fiery resistance against British invasions in the 19th century.

'Today I have been reading a number of tour diaries... The most interesting is by Capt. John Butler who was here from 1870 to 1875', wrote Mildred Archer. She continued: 'It is amusing to see how Butler found the Khonoma group a wearisome problem with their unending feuds and "stubborn importunity". It is the same provocative qualities which mark their incursion into politics today'.[33] 'It is not perhaps surprising that Kevichusa himself should come from the Merhü or partially Christian khel of Khonoma', William Archer agreed, referring here to Kevichusa's political argument for Naga independence.[34] Not surprising, too, then, in this line of reasoning, is that A.Z. Phizo hailed from the same village and khel. In this reading, the Khonoma declaration for Naga independence was framed within intra-Naga constellations of power and hierarchy: not only did the independence claim provided a new political arena to struggle over pre-existent rivalries and divisions, it also became the basis for an envisaged regeneration of Khonoma village, and the Merhü khel within it, as the leading political and intellectual Naga bastion.

The Khonoma declaration, for one thing, imbued new tensions between Khonoma and Kohima villages, which shared a long history of feuds and raids. Being attached to the offices of Pawsey, Kevichusa was a long-time Kohima resident, but when his wife hoisted an Angami cloth to a bamboo pole in their yard in support of the Khonoma declaration, her doing so 'immediately revived the old Kohima-Khonoma rivalry of headhunting days'. An angry crowd of Kohima villagers surrounded Kevichusa's house and shouted: 'take it down'. Anticipating a breakdown of law and order, Pawsey personally intervened to have the flag removed. 'Kohima [villagers] are very angry with Khonoma', he subsequently reported to William Archer.[35]

The PIL, meanwhile, sought to defuse apprehensions about a looming 'Khonoma Raj'. In a cyclostyled paper they produced and called 'Our Home News', they wrote: 'Some people said that independence is the voice of Khonoma. What silly talk! How foolish it is! Why is Indonesia fighting today? Is it not for Independence? Why Mahatma Gandhi and Pandit Nehru and all the Indian leaders went to jail? Is it because of their foolishness? Is it not for the independence of India? So, why not say I am not Khonoma, but a Naga'.[36] In the following issue of Our Home News, the PIL both admonished and encouraged the NNC:

> The present situation is very serious. Those members who are and have been in the NNC seem to be feeling down-hearted. There can be no good reason for this lack of enthusiasm. It is true that their old friends [the Khonoma group] have left the NNC because they want something higher than what the NNC is still now fighting for. A nation must move on according to time and circumstances. Those who are still in the NNC must buck up their spirit and face the situation with manly determination.

The statement then continued:

> We are convinced that INDEPENDENCE IS THE BEST SAFEGUARD [sic] and the only salvation for the Nagas to be free from political turmoil... But a few NNC members talk as if they have the fate of the Nagas in their pocket. So we challenge the NNC to take a referendum whether the Nagas want independence or join India. We know definitely that people in the villages are very angry and they will never agree to join India.[37]

It was this challenge to 'take a referendum' that, a few years later, resulted in the Naga plebiscite, which became foundational to the Naga political struggle. I return to this shortly.

THE ABEYANCE OF THE 'HYDARI AGREEMENT'

While the 'Khonoma group' was pushing for independence, the NNC continued to pursue the revision of clause nine of the Hydari agreement. Governor Hydari himself, however, became increasingly wary about the agreement — both in its original and proposed revised form. He now told William Archer:

> The Nagas must learn to fit in. They must shed their insularity. The hills must be integrated with the plains. I look forward to a time when the hillmen will be indistinguishable from the plainsmen. We must modernize the tribes. We must make them citizens of the new India. From this point of view, the

objective must be greater and greater subordination, lesser and lesser independence.[38]

As William Archer communicated Hydari's stance to Aliba Imti, the latter admonished the colonial officer: 'You have also failed us'.[39]

In response, Aliba Imti wrote a letter to all NNC members in which he called for tougher action: 'That the Naga people attach so much importance upon the point no 9 modified and as such as we had anticipated from the very beginning that hardly will there be any government who will recognise it easily without strong opposition and firm stand from the Nagas themselves'. His letter went on:

> I personally have lost confidence that words alone will bring no effect upon the politicians of India. I presume the Nagas mean what they are uttering for it should be our motto now – "Deeds but not words." 1. Decision should be made in favour of non-cooperation with the existing government. 2. One month's ultimatum be given to the Government of India. 3. From the beginning of Nov. '47, the government servants of Naga people should be ready to lay down their pens. Naga Hills must show worthy of the CALL [sic].[40]

Imti's letter exacerbated intra-Naga political divisions. 'Perhaps the Angami will favour civil disobedience, but if the Aos stay true to type, I am sure no one in Mokokchung will',[41] Mildred Archer predicted. Imti's political shift, from autonomy into the direction of the Khonoma position, indeed upset the other Ao NNC members, who now decided to boycott the NNC meeting scheduled for September. Mildred Archer wrote: 'They [the Aos] are all angry with Aliba and his pompous announcements. They are opposed to civil disobedience and they are tired of being dragged along by the Angamis. The Aos are prepared to accept the Governor's agreement, although they are still not happy about Clause 9, and are anxious that a committee should start to work out the details'.[42] But while civil disobedience was discussed during the September meeting, no consensus was reached and instead a committee was enacted to work out the original Hydari agreement.

Clause 2 of this agreement read: 'Executive – The general principle is accepted that what the Naga Council is prepared to pay for, the Naga Council should control'. As the Committee tried to work out what departments the NNC could reasonably manage on its own, the problem of finances immediately arose. Increasing the house-tax by 'four or five times' appeared the only option. This, however, was a contentious matter. Mayangnokcha opined: 'The villagers will pay anything for complete independence, but what will they pay for this? If we double the house-tax they will grudge it... If we treble it they will refuse to pay any tax at all'. Representing the Kohima circle, Krusihu added: 'The Independence party will laugh at us. They will tell the villagers, "You have not got independence. You have only got taxes"'.[43]

Despite difficulties of finance, the committee fleshed out a draft constitution and another NNC meeting was called to deliberate on it. In this meeting several ambitious alterations and additions were proposed and incorporated, to the extent that, William Archer adjudged, they 'completely nullify the Governor's [Hydari] "agreement" and amounted to a new constitution for an independent state'. 'The same people [of the NNC] speak without stopping', Mayangnokcha lamented after the meeting concluded. 'At the end a vote is taken and everyone agrees without knowing what is really being decided'. Amongst those overruled were Hopongki and Imlong, the Sangtam and Chang delegates of the 'Control Area'. They wished for the 'Control Area' to remain under Assam as the NNC did not have the finances to develop it. Mayangnokcha blamed Governor Hydari for his failure to expedite the initial agreement: 'This delay has given the Nagas time to talk and talk. If he had acted quickly, none of these present difficulties would have arisen'.[44]

Aliba Imti led an NNC delegation to Shillong to meet Governor Hydari with the proposed constitution. Hydari, however, refused to meet them unless they withdrew the ultimatum, which the NNC was not prepared to do. On the 2nd of December, Mildred Archer wrote: 'At the bungalow, we found a typed notice from Aliba announcing that at 12PM on 5 December, the Naga Hills would leave the Indian Union'.[45] Pawsey successfully pressed the NNC to have the ultimatum postponed to 31 December, but this too did not prompt a response from either Hydari or Nehru. The ultimatum passed. However, divisions within the NNC prevented a declaration of Naga independence or large-scale civil disobedience and records available suggest that the first months of 1948 passed in an uneasy calm.

Then A.Z. Phizo stepped up.

THE ASCENDANCY OF A.Z. PHIZO

In the spring of 1948, the draft Indian Constitution was published and proposed the Sixth Schedule as the legal basis and machinery to safeguard measures of autonomy for all Assam hill tribes, including Nagas. By now, however, the NNC had moved beyond their initial political demand for autonomy and its members refused to see the Sixth Schedule as the constitutional translation of the Hydari agreement. Sentiments were now changing fast in the Naga uplands. If, early in 1948, Hydari could tell Pawsey that 'Kevichusa has arrived in Shillong, but I am told he and his party [the PIL] have little following in the hills' (cited in Steyn 2002: 77), the continued abeyance of the Hydari agreement progressively strengthened the position of the 'Khonoma group', of which Phizo was rapidly turning into its most prolific and influential leader.

Phizo began the touring of villages and in fiery speeches decried the timidity and servility of the NNC, lambasted Akbar Hydari, and warned villagers about the taxes and restrictions the Indian state would soon and surely impose upon them if they would not actively resist the enclosure of their hills. Phizo was persuasive and the theory and voice of Naga independence was gaining ground. While stirring up popular support, Phizo also followed a constitutional line and repeatedly called upon authorities in Kohima, Shillong, and elsewhere to seek clarification on the government's position. 'What struck me about Phizo at my first meeting was his extraordinary thoroughness and pertinacity', Nari Rustomji, Advisor to the Governor, recalled, then continued:

> He was armed with neatly typed, systematically serialized copies of all documents relevant to the Naga problem and he gave the impression of carrying, in his little briefcase, the destinies of the entire Naga people. Everything had to be documented, nothing left to chance, and as soon as the discussions were concluded, he insisted on having the minutes drawn up while the proceedings were still fresh in mind, and taking copies certified personally by the Governor and Chief Minister... The next I heard of him was when I received monumental letters addressed by him from a jail in Calcutta to the Governor General, Rajagopalachari.

In June 1948, Phizo was arrested for stirring trouble in the Naga highlands. From his prison cell, he appealed to the India's Governor-General: 'I, A.Z. Phizo, Naga, your state prisoner, address this letter to you as one of the spokesmen of the Naga people', he began a series of letters. He then wrote:

> Since we endured a life together as the British conquered subjects along with the Indians, we sincerely believed India not to interfere in our liberty and freedom now the British had [sic] left and India is politically free. But the possibility of India's annexation of Nagaland and domination over the unwilling Nagas, have become more a fearful problem than

the British Imperialism whose home country was at least several thousand miles away... (see Nuh 2002: 51-62 for the complete letter).

An answer Phizo did not receive.

While incarcerated, the vehicle in which Phizo's wife and infant son travelled met with an accident, instantly killing his son and grievously injuring his wife. Phizo appealed for release on compassionate grounds. His plea was successful and he was conditionally released in December 1948. Jwanna, his wife, made a slow but successful recovery in the Welsh mission hospital in Shillong, with Phizo at her side. In August 1948, Phizo was permanently released, reportedly 'in recognition of a bond of good behaviour' (Steyn 2002: 79).

Meanwhile, Hydari passed away (as did Bordoloi soon after). His successor, Jairamdas Daulatram declared the Naga Hills as an unambiguous and integral part of Assam and India, a political position he impressed upon NNC delegations that called on him. When he subsequently visited Mokokchung he was greeted with 'Go Back' placards. Humiliated, Daulatram dispatched armed police into the Ao region. It was an action that further strained relations and in a follow-up NNC meeting Ao and Sema Naga leaders publicly, and for the first time, 'cry for complete sovereign independence' (Steyn 2002: 80).

It is amidst these political developments that Phizo returned midway 1949. His spell in prison for advocating Naga freedom now added to his name an charisma, and he resumed, ever more vigorously, his touring 'from one village to another in the Naga inhabited areas to mobilise support for Naga freedom' (Yonuo 1974: 200). His popularity soared and ultimately resulted, in 1950, into his election as NNC president. In analysing the beginnings of the Naga Movement it is nearly impossible to overstate the influence of Phizo. Literature that exists on him indeed typifies him as a 'Moses of his people' (Horam 1988: 45) and 'father of Naga nation' (Ao 2002: 21). Even an Indian General conceded how, from the late 1940s onward, Phizo 'operated his strings to skilfully that one by one all tribes were caught in his net, which he cast far and wide and with speed' (Anand 1980: 70).

VIOLENCE OR NON-VIOLENCE: THE NNC DIVIDED (AGAIN)

Phizo's ascendency to NNC president signalled the definite replacement of the initial Ao stance for autonomy with the Angami, but especially

Khonoma, demand for independence. However, it did not take long for new divisions to emerge within the NNC over the preferred strategy to achieve this political end. This divide, which turned deadly, was between those who sought to metamorphose the NNC into a militant organisation and advocates of a Gandhian strategy of nonviolence. The main protagonists, here, were Phizo and Sakhrie, the NNC president and secretary, who turned from 'friends' into 'foes'. Both leaders hailed from Khonoma. But whereas Phizo's election to NNC president reinvigorated Khonoma's longstanding political supremacy in the hills, the Sakhrie-Phizo fallout simultaneously created a wedge within the village, and was to stir inter-clan tensions that blemished its social fabric for long decades following.

As president, Phizo immediately 'put the house of the NNC in order and filled its executive with his own chosen men from the People's Independence League [which is subsequently disbanded], purged all his opponents who were determined to remain in India [from the ranks of the NNC]... and strove to make it a militant political organization pledged to fight for the sovereignty of Nagaland' (Yonuo 1974: 201). In response, Governor Daulatram severed all communication with the NNC, insisting that 'no useful purpose would be served by having personal discussion with NNC representatives unless they made it clear that they would enter into talks with an open mind to discuss the place of the Nagas within the framework of the constitution of India' (cited in Steyn 2002: 80–81). At this increasingly tense juncture, the NNC formally followed the path of nonviolence. While a new NNC memorandum, adopted in 1950, declared that 'anything that is autonomous in character will not be accepted by Nagas', it simultaneously asserted: 'The aspiration and inspiration of the Nagas is to fight for freedom through peace and goodwill, not through bloodshed. The Nagas are strongly determined to fight constitutionally for the liberation of their motherland – Nagaland' (Steyn 2002: 81).

It was in this spirit of struggling 'constitutionally' that Phizo announced the plebiscite the PIL had wanted to carry out as early as 1947. But if, back then, the plebiscite was envisaged as a tactic to silence the Ao voice for autonomy, in 1951, with the official NNC policy already shifted to independence, the plebiscite was conducted to dispel, once and for all, claims from the Indian government that the independence demand was the handiwork of a few 'misguided' Nagas. Bishnuram Medhi, who succeeded Gopinath Bordoloi as Assam's chief minister, personalized this view: 'I cannot think', he said, 'of any demand for independent sovereign Naga state raised by a few handful of leaders, mostly Christians' (cited in Maitra 2011: 22). Phizo wrote yet another letter to India's president in which he explained that a Naga plebiscite was to be held 'with the view of furnishing the people and the Government of India with evidential and conclusive proof of their national aspiration and for independence'. In the same letter he regretted 'the scant attention paid to the case of the Naga people by the Government of India despite very fervent and earnest pleadings', and concluded by inviting the Government of India to 'send their observers to witness the whole processing of the plebiscite from beginning to the end' (Nuh 2002: 92-3).

At this stage, Phizo and Sakhrie still worked in tandem. Not only had Sakhrie actively campaigned for Phizo's election as NNC president, he now led the organizing of the plebiscite. He printed the papers in Imphal and transported them by truck to Khonoma, from where he saw to it that they were rolled in bamboo cylinders and dispatched to Naga villages (Sakhrie 2006: 11). One the eve of the plebiscite, Phizo addressed a large crowd in Kohima:

> We are here to commence our voluntary plebiscite to put on record and to express our mind, our national policy, in the form of thumb impression. It is five months now that our nation has been given time to discuss about this plebiscite voluntarily offered by us to prove our unity and our spontaneous willingness to continue to live on as a distinct nation. In the past five months I have visited every region of our area and met everyone of you. What we do now will go down in our history (see Nuh 2002: 116-133 for the complete speech).

The plebiscite's result, as declared by the NNC, was an overwhelming 99% of thumb prints in favour of independence. An NNC delegation subsequently carried the plebiscite papers to Delhi, but where, to their dismay, the plebiscite was derided as illegitimate and non-consequential. And when several subsequent meetings between Phizo, or NNC delegations sent by him, and Nehru (variously held in Delhi, Assam, and Manipur) also proved futile, as well as turned increasingly frosty, Phizo departed from his earlier commitment to struggling through constitutional means. He called for civil disobedience. This time civil disobedience was actively participated in: 'School teachers resigned, children left their studies and village headmen returned their blankets [that signalled their authority and alliance to the government]' (Nibedon 1978: 39). In addition, and crucially, the NNC boycotted independent India's first general elections in 1952 and 'not a single vote is cast' (Sema 1986: 92).

Things came to a head in 1953, when Nehru, accompanied by the Burmese Prime Minister U Nu, visited Kohima with the aim of persuading the Nagas into accepting the Sixth Schedule. The NNC prepared to meet Nehru, but Deputy Commissioner Barkataki denied them the opportunity.

Instead he instructed NNC leaders 'to listen what the two Prime Ministers would say' (Yonuo 1974: 204). The Nagas gathered in Kohima responded in style and 'as Nehru and his cavalcade started moving towards the podium, the Naga assemblage started moving out... The Nagas left in full purview smacking their bottoms' (Nibedon 1978: 45). What followed this Naga walkout were repressive police measures that included raids on the houses of top NNC leaders, including Sakhrie's, the establishment of nine additional police posts, and the enactment of the Assam Maintenance of Public Order (Autonomous Districts) Act, which bestowed extra-constitutional powers on the armed police to decisively and swiftly quell any Naga 'disturbance'.

Anticipating arrest, Phizo slipped into Tuensang, the formerly 'Control Area', and from where he began organising a guerrilla force. According to one reading: 'The adamant posture of the Assam authorities, perhaps natural in those given circumstances, forced Phizo and his men to pledge for a war that would not admit of truces, retreats or compromises' (Nibedon 1978: 57). In a highly symbolic move, Phizo declared the formation of the Hongking Government in 1954 as the government of all Nagas, so formally undercutting the authority and jurisdiction of the Indian government. The next year, in 1955, the Indian Army moved into Tuensang, which was soon followed by reports of encounters, scuffles, attacks, and burning villages. The war began.

Experiencing new levels of insecurity and violence, voices within the NNC raised objections to Phizo's turn to armed resistance. Amongst these were Sakhrie and Jasokie. While subscribing to the thesis of Naga independence, Sakhrie preached passive resistance. In a letter to Purwar, a Ghandian activist, he wrote:

> [there] are developments such as the NNC has so far worked to keep in check. The idea is gaining popular favour and momentum. The situation is getting out of control... After the first strike it will not stop until it exhausts itself. We must therefore prevent the first strike from being ever struck. This must be attempted by peaceful methods (cited in Sakhrie 2006: 13-14).

Phizo disapproved strongly of, what he saw as, Sakhrie's softening stance. In several meetings in Kohima and Khonoma, the two debated furiously. 'You are placing your opponent in a position where he feels morally wrong to oppose you', Sakhrie countered Phizo. 'Fight rather than be oppressed... Die rather than lose your honour' (cited in Sakhrie 2006: 13), Phizo returned. Sakhrie not only took on Phizo verbally, but also began 'blazing his own trail with the message of peace and non-violence... touring the countryside in a bid to dismantle Phizo's guerrilla machine' (Nibedon

1978: 64). It fragmented the NNC and followers of Phizo and Sakhrie now convened separately. Sakhrie's influence was growing and he called for a NNC meeting on the 31st of January in which, it was rumoured, he planned to table a no-confidence motion against Phizo's presidency. It infuriated Phizo as 'Sakhrie's vehement opposition to Phizo's theme of violence made the threat to his preeminent position in the NNC too real' (Anand 1980: 96). Followers of Phizo arrested Sakhrie, took him into the jungle, tortured him for two days, then killed him. The gruesomeness with which this was done made it not just a murder, but a 'crucifixion' (Nibedon 1978: 71). Sakhrie's assassination was the first in a series of attacks by, what press reports soon called, Naga 'extremists' on 'liberals.'

The scheduled NNC meeting and the no-confidence motion never took place.

VIOLENCE AND THE RETURN OF THE 'LIBERALS'

'They have killed Sakhrie! The balloon has gone up', Carvalho, the District Commissioner, exclaimed upon receiving the news (cited in Stracey 1960: 79). While Phizo was seen mourning Sakhrie's death, and termed the murder a great tragedy, all leads pointed to his personal involvement. A police warrant (and a bounty of 5000 rupees) was issued against his name on charges of 'rioting, abduction, trespass, murder, and conspiracy to commit murder of T. Sakhrie'.[46] Sakhrie's rising influence in the rank-and-file of the NNC had been the Indian Government's last hope of seeing Phizo's guerrilla army contained organically. It now reacted strongly: 'Full Army operations in the Naga Hills', *The Statesman* reported on 31 March 1956.[47]

In the aftermath of Sakhrie's murder it was not just arrest Phizo needed to dodge. Sakhrie's clan cried for revenge and Khonoma split into rivaling camps. What colonial officers dubbed as the 'Christian khel' and 'forerunner' of the Naga independence claim turned into a site of internal division and violent tension. Once again Phizo disappeared. His loyalists, now referred to as 'Phizoites', followed suit, and in February 1956 it was reported that 'All top leaders of the Naga National Council led by its president A.Z. Phizo have gone underground and are directing lawless activities in isolated areas'.[48]

The armed conflict was multisided, and while the Indian Army hunted after NNC members, Phizo and his men pursued the 'liberals' within the NNC and word had it that they were working their way down a hit-list (of which Sakhrie had been on top). 'Official confirmation is lacking', *The Statesman* reported, 'about the latest rumour that another Naga young man belonging to the liberal group has been shot dead'.[49] The Phizo-led armed uprising also pitched, what the Indian Army called, 'hostile' against 'loyal' Naga villages (or what the NNC called 'national' and 'anti-national' villages). In June 1956, for instance, seven Ao Naga villages publicly pledged to 'break completely with Phizo and his associates and to abstain from violence'.[50] Another report read: 'Naga rebels kidnapped seven loyal Naga leaders in the Mokokchung [Ao Naga] sub-division of the Naga Hills District and beheaded at least four of them'.[51]

Amidst this engulfing crisis and chaos, Phizo enacted the Federal Government of Nagaland (FGN) as the Naga government, replacing the earlier Hongking government that operated from the formerly 'Control Area.' By now, two guerrilla wings were fully operative and called the Home Guards and the Safe Guards, both of which specialized in classic 'hit and run' attacks on Indian police posts and army convoys, as well as assaulted 'anti-national' Naga villages. The Indian Army stepped up its 'operations' even further, often exerting force at Naga guerrillas and villagers alike. A European tea-planter in the Assam foothills wrote to Pawsey in August 1956:

> The Indian Army is in full occupation of every section of the Naga Hills. 60% of the Ao villages have been burnt... 70% of the Sema villages have been burnt, and 30% of the Angami. The army uses incendiaries. Worse still: the Nagas are not allowed to rebuild them so they are living in the jungles as best they can. Their crops are being deliberately destroyed and any Naga seen is apt to be shot on sight so that they cannot enter their fields anyway.[52]

On February 5 1957, Pawsey received another letter from the same tea-planter: 'Conditions in the Naga Hills seem to go from bad to worse. No one ventures to predict what the outcome will be. There is so much wrong now on both sides and so much pig-headedness to go with it'.[53] Violence continued to escalate, and began to draw voices of protest from elsewhere. On the floor of the Assam Assembly, an elected member accused the Indian Army of 'excesses' and declared: 'I cannot support the steamroller of police rule in the Naga Hills'.[54] In the Indian Parliament, Rishang Keishing, a Tangkhul Naga MP from Manipur, blamed the Indian Army of orchestrating 'an orgy of murder'.[55] Nehru, on his part, defended his armed forces and stated that no talks would take place until Phizo and his men surrendered their demand for independence. As for Phizo himself, he slipped out of the Naga Hills and into East Pakistan towards the end of 1956. In the year 1960 he arrived in London – officially to internationalise the Naga issue – but where he soon adopted British citizenship and died in 'self-exile' roughly three decades later, still in the armor of NNC president. But I am getting ahead of myself.

While the Naga Army was outnumbered by Indian armed forces many times over, it put up a daring fight: 'Naga tribes hold down 30.000 men [Indian soldiers], *The Telegraph* reported on March 20, 1957.[56] Here and there, Naga guerrillas won battles. 'Naga rebels... have scored their first spectacular triumph by sending a platoon of Indian soldiers home naked', *The Statesman* reported on August 5, 1957. The article went on:

> The platoon was stripped of rifles, ammunition, and every stich of clothing in the steaming Naga hills near the Burma frontier. They surrendered after another platoon of the same regiment — the Garhwal Rifles from the Indian plains — had been massacred. The tribesmen, who have a headhunting tradition, let them go after stripping them. As the naked soldiers ran away, the Nagas jeered after them.[57]

Even more Indian armed forces were dispatched into the hills, and violence flared from one village to the next. From London, Phizo (1960) called it 'genocide', while Indian commentators began to speak of 'India's little Vietnam' (Nibedon 1978: 75).

The grim violence exacerbated the crisis within the NNC, to the extent that the *Assam Tribune* reported its 'dissolution' following 'a rift between the leader of the council, Phizo, and its members'.[58] 'Dissolution', however, was too strong a wording for the resurrection of Sakhrie-inspired 'liberal' NNC voices, despite continued threats to their lives. In September 1956, Jasokie, Sakhrie's former right-hand and fellow Khonoma villager, led a delegation of 'liberal' NNC members to Delhi where they told Nehru that they were 'convinced of the futility of the so-called demand for independence' and condemned 'the use of violence by some misguided sentiments of their people [read: Phizo and his followers]'.[59] On returning to the Naga Hills, they pursued internal NNC reforms through the enactment of a 'Reforming Committee'. However, with Phizo resisting these reforms, and him ruling the day, the group of NNC liberals resolved to break away from the NNC and proposed an all tribes Naga People's Convention (NPC) to deliberate the political situation.

Came August 1957. A reported 1765 tribal representatives of both the Tuensang Area and the Naga Hills District convened in Kohima.[60] The Convention explained its coming together as a response to the 'killings and widespread suffering' and their desire to 'end the infinite sufferings and bloodshed'. Five days of discussions resulted in three demands that were communicated to Delhi: 1) to come to a 'satisfactory political settlement', 2) to amalgamate the Naga Hills District and the Tuensang Area of NEFA into a single administrative unit, and 3) a 'genuine, general amnesty' for Naga rebels. The Convention also called on Phizo and his guerrilla army to renounce 'the cult of violence' (Yonuo 1974: 232). Imkongliba Ao was selected as the Convention's president and entrusted to head a delegation to meet Nehru in Delhi for political negotiations. Nehru applauded the NPC's efforts, consented to the demands, and acted promptly: a general amnesty was declared immediately, Naga political prisoners were released, and the Naga Hills and Tuensang Area merged into a single district within Assam in December 1957.

To further deliberate the nature of a definite political settlement a second NPC was scheduled for May 1958. The NNC, however, took exception to this 'overground' political process and warned that NPC activities should 'not pose any obstruction on the way of independence of Nagaland' (Yonuo 1974: 228). Warnings and threats were issued to the villagers of Ungma, who offered to host the NPC meet. Within the NNC views on the NPC were not unanimous, however. S.C. Jamir, a later Nagaland chief minister and organizing member of the Ungma Convention, recalled: 'To clarify the real stand of the underground, Dr. Imkongliba and I met Mr. Jakrenkokba, Advisor to the Home Guard in the village at Sungratsue. He gave us verbal assurance and clearance to go ahead with the preparations for the Convention' (Jamir 2016: 125).

Attended by an estimated 2700 delegates, the Ungma Convention condemned violence of any source and sort, appealed to the Indian government to extend the period of amnesty, and envisaged the political and administrative elevation of the Naga Hills and Tuensang Area from a district into a state within the Indian Union, but with special provisions for autonomy. Significantly, the Convention also enacted a Liaison Committee with the task of contacting the NNC/FGN and to persuade 'underground' Nagas into joining the 'overground' political process. The Committee was chaired by Kevichusa, an early advocate of Naga independence and former confidant of Phizo (as well as his immediate relative), but who disassociated himself from the NNC after its turn to armed struggle. Naga underground leaders rejected the Liaison Committee's overtures and instead asked Kevichusa 'to inform the Government of India to confirm recognition of the Naga Federal Government first as the basis of negotiation for a political settlement' (Yonuo 1974: 229). For the NNC/ FGN, the Indian Government communicating with the NPC was an affront to the Naga plebiscite, from which they derived the legitimacy to represent the Nagas politically. The NPC, they insisted, carried no such legitimacy. A disillusioned Kevichusa reported:

> I have to report after meeting different leaders that up to this time the Naga Political Party [NNC] does not desire to have any negotiation except on the issue of Independence... So the stalemate continues, and will, I am afraid continue for some time longer. I do believe in the good sense of our people, and I earnestly believe that change in the mind of the people will also come and there will be a settlement on practical lines. But I and my colleagues [of the Liaison Committee] feel that a forced settlement will not bring about any permanent solution (cited in Nibedon 1978: 117-118).

Kevichusa's message that Nagaland statehood will not bring a political solution, but only produce further divisions was not heeded to by the NPC, which instead enacted another Committee to work out a draft constitution. In a public meeting, Kevichusa made his dissent known: 'I was the originator of the resolutions of the NPC in 1957. But, friends, I had not the slightest suspicion that a political settlement was going to be made behind the back of those who had their difference with the Government. It was, therefore, a surprise to me that a second NPC was held in Ungma in May, 1958 and the question of a political settlement was raised' (cited in Nibedon 1978: 117). 'I hold no brief for the rebels', Kevichusa clarified (ibid.: 120), but then insisted that the NPC was to act as 'a bridge between the Government of India and the underground people', not to push for a settlement of its own (ibid.: 117).

A third (and final) NPC met in Mokokchung in October 1959 to discuss the draft constitution that was prepared. This meeting culminated into 16 concrete demands to the Indian Government, core among which was the creation of Nagaland state (Nibedon 1978: 88). This demand was accepted by Nehru, who subsequently ushered the Nagaland statehood bill through parliament. From London, Phizo reacted with dismay: he reiterated that the Naga struggle was for complete independence, called the NPC a 'puppet assembly' (Yonuo 1974: 236), and stated that 'No agreement can be recognized regarding the future of Nagaland except with the people who are truly representative of the Naga people', which Phizo insisted was not the NPC but the NNC/FGN (Stracey 1960: 93).

To waylay these political developments, the NNC stepped up its guerrilla attacks, bombed a train in Assam, and shot down a Dakota plane of the Indian Army, capturing its four crewmen (Yonuo 1974: 237). Phizo's stance did not dissuade the NPC from enacting an 'Interim Body' to prepare the grounds for statehood. In this, Jasokie became a prominent leader and was seen as the carrier of Sakhrie's legacy. Jasokie's leadership had repercussions in Khonoma that was 'now split by a deep hatred between the two khels of Phizo and Jasokie' (Stracey 1960: 103). While the Interim Body and the NNC were now at loggerheads, 'only a handful [of the Interim Body] had never come under Phizo's revolutionary doctrines' (Nibedon 1978: 85). With Nagaland statehood drawing closer, Imkongliba appealed, once again, to the NNC/FGN:

> I, as the President of the Naga People's Convention, appeal to all the Nagas, including the underground people to join hands with the members of the Interim Body in building up a strong and progressive state of our Nagaland. For the last six years, beginning from 1956, there had been killings, bloodshed and burning of villages causing great suffering to the people on account of widespread armed hostile activities followed by military operations throughout Nagaland. It is high time, therefore that all the sensible citizens of Nagaland should devote wholeheartedly to bring peace to the land doing away with the mutual suspicions and hatred amongst us (reproduced in Jamir 2016: 132).

The NNC/FGN refused to heed. Instead, in a final attempt to obstruct 'overground' political developments, it targeted the Interim Body; [Its members are] the inevitable targets in the shape of verbal abuse [by the NNC], which included such words as 'traitors' and worse... words, which for a Naga were harder to bear than the bullets which were also flung at them' (Stracey 1960: 94). In August 1961 Imkongliba was assassinated by the NNC. Another member of the Interim Body, Phanting Phom, was killed the next year, while several other members made narrow escapes. Many decades later, S.C. Jamir reflected on this period: 'I would also like to keep it on record that the underground's aim was to eliminate all leaders and functionaries of the Interim Body; but they were not successful in their efforts' (Jamir 2016: 134). The reason the Naga Army was not successful in carrying out these assassinations was because Interim Body members were guarded day and night by Indian security forces, an observation which further indicates that it does not serve to look at the Naga uprising in terms of a clear-cut Naga-India binary.

On the 1st of December 1963, Dr. S. Radhakrishnan, India's president, flew to Kohima to inaugurate the state of Nagaland. He spoke:

> Friends, I have great pleasure in inaugurating the new state of Nagaland. It takes an honoured place today as the Sixteenth State of the Indian Union... [Our] attempts to secure you the fullest freedom to manage your own affairs have culminated in

the creation of Nagaland State... May I also express the hope that, now that the wishes of the Nagas have been fully met, normal conditions will rapidly return to the State, and those who are still unreconciled will come forward to participate in the development of Nagaland (reproduced in Sharma and Sharma 2006: 253).

Coming 'forward' the NNC/FGN did not. To the contrary: 'All those wishfully expecting the collapse of the Underground after the granting of statehood found themselves to be wrong' (Horam 1988: 12). As predicted by Kevichusa, Nagaland statehood worked to divide Naga society more definitely into two – the people of the new state and the people supporting the NNC/FGN – although the boundaries between them soon had very many crossings, so further complicating the Naga struggle, and the Indian state's response to it, in ways that, five decades on, continue to impede a permanent political solution of the Indo-Naga conflict.

07

GENEALOGIES OF NAGALAND'S 'TRIBAL DEMOCRACY'

What do democratic institutions and procedures consist of, if not socially meaningful arrangements between persons concerning governance and power? What is Indian democracy specifically if not a 'human democracy' (Piliavsky 2015) at once animated and agitated by social relations? The form and substance these social relations take often vary from one state to another, but the particular mode and meaning democratic politics and representation take is everywhere formed out of historically evolved political socialities, social subjectivities, and cultural proclivities and penchants, or what anthropologists have begun to call democracy's inevitable 'vernacularisation' (Michelutti 2007).

Most liberal political theorists, and their ventriloquists, find this vernacularisation of democracy difficult to accept, even perceive, and their theories – the one more abstract than the other – often end up eliminating democracy of the sociality that, in fact, shapes it (Piliavsky 2014: 29). Empirically, democratic life in the United States (US) and Europe does not differ from Indian democracy (in the ways they so markedly do) because democratic institutions and formal procedures significantly differ, but because the social inhabitations of these democracies vary vastly. Postulating thus is not to undermine the importance of democratic institutions, laws and procedures, political parties, and ideologies for the functioning of any democratic regime, but to criticise prevailing views that essentialise democratic institutions as quintessentially formal, rational-legal, and detached 'things', rather than approaching them for what they actually are and do: real human beings pursuing meaningful social relations and goals.

Take political parties in India. Commenting on the mushrooming of parties and party-splits, André Béteille (2017: 23) notes how, across India, loyalties to family, kin, and communities frequently override party ideologies to the extent that 'the shifting alliances among political parties that are a conspicuous feature of the Indian political scene are often governed by the personal loyalties of leaders and their followers.' In these decisions, political ideology, in terms of a clear-cut left-centre-right political spectrum, may only play second fiddle. Relatedly, voting preferences and patterns are often connected with pre-existent societal structures, sentiments, and struggles, which remapped themselves unto the democratic arena where they found new expressions in a language of politics, parties, and elections. As such, political and party allegiances are often no more than a 'mask' behind which real social struggles operate. Formal democratic institutions, in this way, did not so much give birth to modern Indian politics as postcolonial India birthed its own distinctive versions of what democratic politics and elections are about.

Various scholars have noted how Indian democratic politics is often performative, more than ideological (Banerjee 2011); a competition between collectivities, more than an exercise of individual autonomy (Chandra 2007); a tournament between generous patrons and providers, more than a place of equality and impartial governance (Piliavsky 2014); an agitated contest between castes and communities over local territorial dominance and subordination (Witsoe 2013); and, pertinently, 'substantially about access to state resources' (Prasad 2010: 142; Khilnani 1997).

As opposed to most political theorists and theories, anthropologists and sociologists have long agreed that Indian politics and its elections are deeply immersed in historically and culturally specific social processes and divisions; most prominently the fragmentations and fault – lines of castes. Initially, in the aftermath of India's independence, it was envisaged that forcing the caste system 'to face and to enter politics' (Khilnani 1997: 5) would slowly but surely obliterate caste hierarchies and foster social equality driven by the great political equalizer that is universal (adult) franchise. Elsewhere, particularly in the US, the introduction of universal franchise – the political equality and individual autonomy it projects – worked to 'dispose each citizen to isolate himself from the mass of his fellows', and, in deliberating his vote, 'gladly leaves the greater society to look after itself' (De Tocqueville 1969: 506). But, such individualisation and detached judgment is not what came to characterise the Indian electorate.

True, democracy and elections offered unprecedented political participation and opportunities for upward mobility for the poor, lower castes, and other oppressed sections of the society, but this did not rust pre-existent 'primordial' social attachments, divisions, and boundaries. Instead, democratic politics solidified and politicised these. India's democratic machinery, while upsetting some social and political hierarchies and cutting through certain old inequalities, everywhere emboldened and politicised social relations, particularly between castes and communities, rather than transforming Indian society into a nation of autonomous and equal citizens. Béteille (2017: 137) reflects thus:

> with the advantage of hindsight one can see that it would have been impossible to exclude altogether the operation of caste in the political arena. But the extent to which it has penetrated that arena and become a consideration in all political calculations is unsettling.

Oftentimes, caste and community equations drive electoral politics: 'politicians are obsessed with caste... Candidate selections in Uttar Pradesh are most of the time based on caste arithmetic', observes Lucia Michelutti (2007: 645). This persistence of caste in Indian political life has been theorised – with varying degrees of celebration (as exemplifying emancipatory politics), criticism, and condemnation – as evidence of the socially enmeshed, 'vernacular' character of Indian democratic life.

The history and contemporary presence of caste in Indian politics is of course widely acknowledged, and its changing modes, modalities, and moralities have been widely debated over the past decades (Béteille 1965; Jaffrelot 2003; Michelutti 2007; Kothari 2009, to name just a few). Entire library shelves, indeed, are today filled with books that link caste, politics, and democracy. But, India is not just a country of castes. It is also a place of tribes, a large and disparate number of them. However, compared to the bulky literature on caste and democracy, we still know precariously little about the form and functioning of democratic politics amongst tribes. This makes for a serious comparative lacuna, one which, at the level of sociology, impedes the kind of careful comparison that has long proven fruitful to capture the intricacies of social life. If caste is deemed central to any understanding of contemporary Indian politics, what about those states and constituencies in which tribes preponderate numerically? What shape does its democratic politics take? Has democratic politics similarly worked to politicise tribal identities? Do collectivities of tribe, too, regularly, override the normative ideal of individual and autonomous political deliberation? These are important questions to explore in order to gain a fuller and richer understanding of the societal complexities that shape Indian democracy.

The remainder of this essay invites its readers to start reflecting on these questions in the context of the Naga highlands in Northeast India. In the colloquial, Nagaland is referred to as a 'tribal state', inhabited, as it is, by sixteen state-recognised tribes. These tribes, while collectively identifying as Naga, also manifest themselves as self-directed political communities that today variously compete, contest, and conflict over territory, belonging, and (especially) access to and ownership of the state and its resources. Oftentimes, the term 'tribalism' is applied locally to capture the inter-tribal competition and the occasional communalism that has turned into a distinctive, modern feature of Nagaland's political life. 'The prevalence of tribalism', a Nagaland Minister remarked a few years ago, 'is destroying the social fabric of Naga society... This monster of tribalism overshadows us and curbs all minds' (*Nagaland Post* 2010). A caveat before proceeding. As much as inter- (but also intra-) caste relations take on different political shapes in different parts of India, 'tribe', too, is inherently plural in its local manifestations, and the following discussion on the political genealogies of Naga tribes in relation to modern democratic life may, therefore, not necessarily be illustrative for 'tribal India' as a whole.

Despite popular views of tribe as antique and unchanging social groups, among the Nagas, tribes are not historically stable units, nor do they represent a 'natural way' of political organisation and articulation. Further, most certainly, they – I will illustrate – were traditionally not the politically loaded entities they appear today with Naga tribes vying for power and control of Nagaland state and its institutions. Their contemporary politicisation, I pose, must be understood in relation to modern effects of state and democracy. To trace and place the current politicisation of these tribal identities, the section that follows first takes a step back to explore, in much abridged form, the ethno-genesis of distinct Naga tribes. Next, I discuss the colonial state-driven process of 'particularising tribes', which set the stage for the subsequent postcolonial, post-statehood, politicisation of tribal identities among Nagas as they came face-to-face with democratic institutions and competitive elections. I end with a few reflections on, what we might call, Nagaland's 'tribal democracy.'

WHERE DO NAGA TRIBES COME FROM?

Where do Naga tribes come from? Are their long-forgotten homes located in China and Mongolia, from where they travelled, with lengthy stops in Burma, to their present hills, as oral history tells? Village elders often narrate such stories. Some of them insist on more precision and detail how Nagas were amongst those conscripted to construct the Great Wall of China, but managed to escape and flee southwards. Several Naga folktales, on the other hand, speak not of migration, but of an *emergence* of specific tribes from stones, caves, or holes in the ground. Either way, Naga tribes are represented as historically stable entities that either migrated or originated as preset communities. In contemporary parlance and politics, such notions are reified through the verse 'since time-immemorial', which Naga tribal leaders and scholars habitually invoke when they discuss their tribe's past. Yet other reconstructions rely on pseudoscience and trace Naga origins to Borneo, and other islands in the southern seas – were Nagas originally a 'sea-faring people?' Nuh (2002) asks – with whose peoples, British colonialists and several postcolonial scholars observed, Nagas share strong physical and cultural affinities (Hutton 1921a: 8). While steering clear of reducing these local histories to mere fancies and misconceptions (the past, after all, is wide and deep enough to accommodate multiple narratives), here I propose that, rather than antique origins, important tribal-genetic processes took place during the colonial era.

Popular historical perspectives reconstruct that the Naga highlands were made up of disparate tribes which, prior to their (partial) enclosure into the British Empire, were political communities with a history of fierce self-governance. In actual practice, however, it was seldom that separate Naga villages asserted themselves as a tribal entity that in its form and functioning was considerably constant, corporate, and cohesive. During the pre-British times, both the locus and ethos of Naga political structures and sentiments were vested not in the tribe, but in the prototypical Naga 'village republic' (Wouters 2017a). In fact, as a vernacular term, the idea and idiom of tribe did not exist. 'Tribe', indeed, is an exogenous category 'originally used in African contexts and was transferred to British India' (Berger and Heidemann 2013: 6). 'Prior to the colonial era the use of a generic term to describe tribal peoples was, on the whole, absent', thus rendering the formation of tribal identities a 'process from without' (Xaxa 2005: 1363). Little wonder, then, that most Naga tribes do not have an indigenous term that denotes 'tribe' in its contemporary sense.

Their semiotic non-existence apart, the historical absence of the idea of Naga tribes can also be deduced from centuries-old Ahom *Buranjis*, or court chronicles, kept by Ahom littérateurs in the adjacent Brahmaputra Valley. Occasional entries concerning Nagas do not refer to generic Naga tribes, but mention specific Naga villages and village-clusters, or classify Nagas by the *duars* (gateways between hills and plains) they frequented. In their references to upland Nagas, usually in relation to raids and retaliations, the Buranjis used ethnonyms such as Itania, Lakma, Tirulia, Banfera, Mithonia, and Joboka Nagas (Baruah 1980). These nomenclatures have long fallen into oblivion, making it hard, though not always impossible, to reconstruct to which Naga villages, or village-clusters, they referred. What they did not refer to, to be sure, were politically unified Naga tribes.

After the British ousted Ahom kings and nobles from the Assam plains in the 1820s, and colonial officers first climbed the Naga uplands, they, too, did not encounter a set of distinct and clearly demarcated Naga tribes. What they found instead was a kaleidoscope of 'ethnographic chaos' (Jabobs et al 1990: 23), linguistic fragmentation down to village levels (Hutton 1965), and complex and cross-cutting political allegiances between villages, clans, and *khels* (wards). Such observations further indicate that, back then, there was little sign of there being clear-cut tribes, certainly not in the sense of territorially demarcated, historically stable, culturally homogenous, and linguistically uniform political entities that Naga tribes nowadays like to introduce themselves as. What, then, catalysed the social formation of such contemporary, much more rigid, tribes?

It is here that we need to account for the orientation and impact of colonial rule among Nagas. From the middle of the 19th century onwards, but especially after the creation of the Naga Hills District in 1866, colonial officers began to arrive in the Naga highlands. Their duty was primarily to enforce 'law and order' and extract revenues, but while doing so they also engaged in the observation and analysis of the subjects under their control. The first generation of colonial officers often expressed profound confusion and frustration about Nagas' seemingly disjointed social and political set-up, the different languages spoken in every other village (at times even within a single village), the divisions and rivalries between villages and clans, and the vastly varying cultural expressions, customs, and religious predispositions. In their desire to nevertheless create an unambiguous social map of the Naga highlands, colonial officers resorted to the concept of tribe and sought to pigeonhole clans and villages into larger, reasonably well-defined groups.

SELF-PERCEPTION

For India more widely, and in the context of caste, an animated body of postcolonial scholarship argues how this colonial fascination with defining and listing communities gradually changed not only the way Indian society was represented, but also how it came to perceive of itself. An influential argument holds that the colonial regime increasingly felt the need to classify, chart, and categorise Indians into distinct and hierarchically linked social groups (Inden 1990; Cohn 1997). In the process they may not have invented castes, but certainly promoted a pan-Indian caste paradigm of social life, or what Louis Dumont (2004: 222) calls the 'substantialisation of caste.' To illustrate this argument, scholars have variously highlighted the role of census, laws, and arbitrary ethnological classifications in the colonial re-imagination of Indian society, the upshot of which was the creation of a new way of 'seeing' social life that ultimately Indians themselves were infatuated with.

This debate is yet to be definitely settled, but can we imagine a similar process that lies behind the making of Naga tribes? If we can speak of *Castes of Mind* (Dirks 2001), can we also speak of 'tribes of mind?' While postcolonial theorists have criticised the mismatch between colonial, or Western ideas, concepts, institutions, and thought, and the traditional flow of Indian social life (Chatterjee 1986; Nandy 2002; Chakrabarty 2007), they uniformly agree that colonial imaginaries and categories stayed after the withdrawal of imperial forces in 1947. Is 'tribe' one such category; a fiction and figment manufactured into a political reality? A new mainstream in critical anthropology and postcolonial studies of Northeast India recognises that postcolonial scholarship, rather than criticizing and rethinking colonial categories, reified the borrowed category of tribe. 'Contemporary anthropology', Ramirez (2014: 5) duly notes, 'relies strongly on the categories provided by colonial depictions.'

Do discourse, administrative categories, and colonial imagination, then, wield sufficient power to definitely restructure social formations? Must the origins of Naga tribes, in their contemporary sense, in short, be located in the experience of colonialism? The following reflection of a former district commissioner of the Naga Hills district, 30 years after his retirement, points into this direction: 'The present [postcolonial, post-statehood] administration of the [Naga] area, for one thing, have gone still further than we did in my time in *particularising* tribes' (Hutton 1965: 16; emphasis mine).

PARTICULARISING TRIBES

If we adopt a wide historical lens, it is this state-led process of classifying and 'particularising' tribes that, I argue, came to provide the social and political undergrowth for the contemporary tribal essentialism and tribalism that marks Naga society today.

To be sure, it would be rather presumptuous to bestow the colonial regime with sufficient power to invent Naga tribes out of thin air, or to forever fix tribal identities (Subba and Wouters 2013: 204). For one, important ethno-genetic processes preceded colonialism. For instance, before the advent of British rule, the Chang Naga village of Tuensang began conquering neighbouring and nearby villages, and culturally and linguistically 'converted' its inhabitants into Changs (Hutton 1987: ii-iv), thus laying the rudimentary framework for the later Chang tribe to emerge. Historical conjecture, moreover, suggests that the present-day Ao and Angami Naga tribes first started to appear as unified tribe-like entities – albeit crudely so at first – in strategic response to marauding Ahom and Manipuri (followed by the British) armies. British arrival in the Naga highlands thus coincided with several endogenous ethno-genetic processes towards political entities that began to transcend clans and villages. In the postcolonial era, such ethnogenetic processes continued – 'the tribal groups of Nagaland are forming new affiliations and using names hitherto unknown to Anthropology', Elwin (1961: 5) observed in the early 1960s – while several older tribes have over time split, or are currently on the verge of splitting. As such, tribal social formations did not begin or end with the colonial experience.

What the colonial administration did work to effectuate, however, was both the wider institutionalisation of tribe as an official category and the rise of 'tribal consciousness;' an increasing cognisance of tribe as both the base of social identity and a 'strategic efficacy' (Tambiah 1989: 343) for political mobilisation. As the British set out to administer the Naga highlands, they began to methodically survey the land and its people, and sought to reduce 'ethnographic chaos' into a neat compendium of tribes. This was an ambitious and counter-intuitive exercise, but persisted in for purposes of simplifying administration and to enumerate and classify subjects into orderly categories; a process undoubtedly grounded in the modern state's imperative towards standardising 'any social hieroglyph into a legible and administratively more convenient format' (Scott 1998: 3). It was ambitious because of the dazzling diversity internal to the Naga populace, and counter-intuitive in view of Nagas' acute political fragmentation on the basis of clans and villages. Among the Sema (now Sumi) Naga, 'the tribe', Hutton (1921b: 121) acknowledged, 'is not an organized community at all.' About the Lotha Naga, Mills (1922: 96) similarly observed how 'every village is an independent unit in the tribe.' 'As with all Nagas', Mills (1926: 176) postulated more broadly, 'the real political unit of the tribe is the village.' However, administrating and reckoning individual villages seemed – to the colonial government – a great deal more tedious, confusing, expensive, and, on the whole, less efficient compared to an image of the Naga highlands as a composite of neatly demarcated tribes.

This classification of Naga social groups into distinct tribes was never easy or unambiguous. Note, for instance, the following remark by Mills (1922: 2):

> Yacham and their small neighbour, Yong... speak a dialect resembling Chongli [and Ao Naga language] but follow Phom or Konyak customs to a great extent. Yacham recently told me that they really did not know what they were — Aos would not recognize them as Aos and their trans-Dikhu neighbour [Chang Naga] would not accept them as kinsmen.

A critical question, here, is precisely when and why it became problematic for the Yacham and Yong villagers to not belong to any tribe? The answer would tell us a few things about the materialisation, institutionalisation, and ultimately the local fascination of 'the tribe' among Nagas.

Despite such and similar ambiguities, colonial officers were to pursue in their tribe-wise reckoning of the Naga uplands over the following decades, and gradually clans, villages, districts, and administrative zones came to be based on imagined tribal territories and identities. Colonial administrators also began to conjure tribe-wise ethnological descriptions, which allowed them to single out and compare Naga tribes. Monographs, for instance, were commissioned and written tribe-wise. Even as its writers usually acknowledged the difficulties they faced in defining and delimitating the particular tribe they wrote about, the titles of these books always particularised individual tribes, for example, *The Angami Nagas* (Hutton 1921a), *The Lhota Nagas* (Mills 1922), *The Ao Nagas* (Mills 1926), and *The Sema Nagas* (Hutton 1921b), a trend later followed by postcolonial scholars.

In this process of ethnological classification, British administrators-cum-ethnographers also 'discovered' tribe-specific behavioural traits. The Angami, for instance, became known for their 'hospitality', 'geniality', and 'bouts of deep melancholy' (Hutton 1921a: 39). Of the Sema Naga, Hutton (1921b: 26) wrote: 'In his good characteristics he is to some extent the Irishman of the Naga tribes, generous, hospitable, and frequently improvident (in which he differs markedly from the canny Lhota).' J P Mills (1922: 19), in turn, offered a comparative analysis of fidelity between Naga tribes: 'The Lhota husband does not imitate the habitual unfaithfulness of the Ao, nor does he, like the Sema, boast of his immoralities and decorate the grave of a deceased Don Juan with a tally of his liaisons.' It was through this dual process — the one administrative, the other ethnological — that notions of distinct, discrete, and politically organized Naga tribes became more and more institutionalised.

Colonial officers were not the sole creators of this new social map of the Naga highlands, however. Missionaries, too, contributed to its drafting. In the wake of colonial rule, mission-stations were established in, what the colonial administration had identified as, 'tribal headquarters.' The Bible was translated in the language missionaries perceived was most widely spoken in a particular region (in the process often elevating a particular dialect into a tribe's official language), while during annual meetings, and in progress reports, missionary activities and future plans were deliberated tribe-wise, making missionaries speak about the Ao, Lotha, Sema, and Angami mission fields. Curators and travelers also followed this trend, and museum-collections and travelogues soon distinguished between different tribes, often comparing and contrasting them in terms of material culture, social organization, and customs.

But if the British wanted clearly separable tribes for purposes of administrative convenience, Nagas, crucially, appeared ready to construct them. As Nagas became more cognisant of the British interest in 'tribe', local leaders, while approaching the colonial government, increasingly often articulated their interests and grievances on the basis of tribe. Local leaders also began to enact tribal associations committed to bringing education and development to their parts of the hills, so beginning to unite clans and villages and instilling in them a sense of common belonging and purpose.

Meet Imlong Chang, an influential *Dobashi* (interpreter, which was an official post during colonial times,), businessman, and church leader during the colonial era. In 1945, on 1 April, he invited 10 elders to his residence and formed a committee called the Chang Tribal Committee. Of his motivations, S Takam (1988: 24–25), his biographer, writes:

> Although he was a brave warrior, he despised war. His main concern was to ensure that the head and body were buried as one and not in separate villages (as the result of, then still occurring, headhunting episodes).

Besides effectuating pacification, Imlong Chang envisaged the committee to work towards 'the advancement of the [Chang] tribe', which included the promotion of missionary activities and education. The first important task this committee faced, however, as it was narrated to me by its current president, was to demarcate the length and breadth of the Chang tribe, which had hitherto been a fluctuating, somewhat elusive, entity. The subsequent process of 'Chang-making' was haphazard and complicated by a great deal of confusion regarding which villages could be considered culturally and customarily Chang. That this was a haphazard process is revealed in that over the following years various villages initially classified as Chang changed their mind and opted out of the Chang fold to join another tribe. In politically organising and defining itself, the Chang tribe was not unique but part of a wider pattern in the 1940s and 50s that saw the emergence of tribal apex bodies.

A process that began due to colonial policies was thus adopted and elaborated upon by Nagas themselves. We must not underestimate how, through the establishment of these tribe-wise apex bodies – as a response and reaction to the colonial emphasis on tribe – Nagas applied their agency in this process of 'particularising' tribal groups and identities.

THE POLITICIZATION OF NAGA TRIBES

A process of 'particularising', or indeed 'tribalising', Naga society that began in the colonial era accelerated after the retreat of imperial powers from the Naga highlands. The Naga National Movement, which insisted on Naga independence, for instance, adopted the concept of tribe to arrange its rank-and-file, promised far-going tribe-wise autonomy in an envisaged sovereign Naga-land, while over time tribalism and tribal splits became the prime reason for the Naga movement's fragmentation into rivalling factions (Shimray 2005; Panwar 2017). But, this dimension of the politicisation of Naga tribes is not the story I will trace here.

In the postcolonial era, but particularly after Nagaland attained statehood in 1963, the role of tribes in both the political process and public domain was enlarged. To begin with, constituencies were by and large delimited based on tribal territories (with the exception of the urban areas of Kohima and Dimapur, whose populace represents a mixture of tribes), resulting in tribe-wise political representation with elected politicians belonging to the same tribe regularly aligning into distinct political blocks. Development allocations and other state resources, too, became increasingly arbitrated tribe-wise, as were reservations for government jobs and university seats. It was from the mid-1970s onward that the Nagaland Government added an additional local layer to the pan-Indian reservation system by classifying each Nagaland tribe as either 'forward' or 'backward', offering special quotas to the latter. No sooner that this official categorization of Naga tribes based on their perceived levels of material development etched itself at the center of Nagaland politics and governance did it transform into a source of strife, litigation, and contentious politics. More than anything else, it pitched tribes against each other as they competed over access to the state and its development resources.

In hindsight, it was such administrative measures that turned 'the tribe' into a definite political machinery for articulating and levying demands on the state. Quite suddenly, tribe was everywhere. Tribe was everything: government jobs, university admissions and scholarships, development schemes and subsidies, political representation, identity and identification, social life itself. Along the way, tribal apex bodies, first conceived in the late colonial era, assumed more powers and proclaimed themselves to be the sole representative voice of its members. Tribe-wise youth, student, and church organisations grew out of the ground, political mobilization followed tribal lines, outbursts of tribalism turned more frequent and ferocious, and 'the tribe' became a modern way of governance and living.

This post-statehood tribal competition in the democratic arena had wide ramifications, including Nagaland's notoriously skewed population censuses. Ankush Agrawal and Vikas Kumar (2013) showed convincingly how vastly inflated population censuses, but especially the 2001 census, resulted from Naga tribes deliberately exaggerating their population numbers in view of an impending (but later postponed) delimitation of electoral seats, which are demarcated based on demographic figures. As different Naga tribes sought to protect and enlarge the numbers of electoral seats in their 'possession', numbers were manufactured and made-up, resulting in a superficial increase of Nagaland's population with roughly 64% between 1991 and 2001. Nagaland's vastly skewed census figures, in short, resulted from an inter-tribal contest over political representation.

In terms of democracy and elections, what emerged were, what Witsoe (2013: 68) aptly calls for Bihar, 'democratic networks of governance.' Such networks, Witsoe explains, are not democratic in a liberal sense, but refer to 'networks of influence based above all on electoral considerations.' At the state level, such electoral considerations often played themselves out on tribal lines. And, for Naga politicians, the easiest and simplest way to expand their political clouts was to whip up tribal loyalties and sentiments to their support. Modern democracy met the 'tribal psyche', if there was indeed such a thing, and, in Nagaland's post-statehood history, it were often educated politicians who proved to be amongst the worst merchants of tribalism.

The distribution of ministerial berths and portfolios particularly manifested itself as a tournament between tribes. Political power, as it is currently understood in Naga society, is not measured in the sense of ruling parties or coalitions, but in terms of the tribes that successfully appropriate influential political (and administrative) offices and portfolios inside the government. And those Naga tribes who 'fail' to secure such posts readily resort to the language of 'tribal discrimination' to express their grievances. It is here that we encounter the fundamentally 'sectional' nature of democracy and governance in Nagaland. Elected politicians are expected by their electors to privilege 'their own.' Even as Nagaland politicians became known and criticised for deriving personal wealth out of their privileged access to the state, they also became known and praised for redirecting state resources to their clan, village, and tribe. Across Nagaland, Jimomi (2009: 399) writes, '[A Minister forget[s] that he is the Minister of Nagaland, and he becomes the minister of his own tribe, becomes the minister of his own clan.'

The Ao Naga, for instance, are today thought of as materially advanced in large parts because one among their own ruled the state as a chief minister for nearly two decades, and during his rule bequeathed Ao Naga constituencies with manifold privileges, resources, and opportunities. The Angami Naga are said to be catching up given that, more recently, an Angami chief minister ruled the state for two consecutive terms, while 'eastern' Naga tribes partially describe their experienced economic 'backwardness' to the feat that no chief minister has ever hailed from among them. This inter-tribal competition, which is my focus here, manifests itself at the terrain of state-level politics, not, I must qualify, at the micro-level, inside constituencies, in which inter-tribal contests descend into intra-tribal competition with politicians and electors belonging to the same social group fragmenting into rivaling political allegiances.

Thus, if much noted 'miasma of tribalism' (Horam 1988: 23) among Nagas has been framed in terms of past headhunting feuds, communal antagonisms, linguistic incommensurability, as well as seen as a volatile source of recurrent splits in the Naga movement, in the post-statehood Nagaland democratic arena tribalism reproduced and revealed itself through tribe-wise competition over discretionary allocations of political offices, government employment, and state resources.

NAGALAND'S 'TRIBAL DEMOCRACY'

When one take a closer look at the modus operandi of democracy in Nagaland, concepts like political parties and ideology turn out to be deceptive, if not outright inaccurate to analyse local democratic politics. In their functioning, Nagaland political parties have been depicted as staunchly 'non-ideological in character' (Amer 2014: 6). Evidence for this is galore: frequent cross-carpeting and party-hopping by politicians, pervasive politics of defection, unlikely coalitions (Nagaland has the distinction of recently having had, if only briefly, a coalition that included both the Bharatiya Janata Party and the Congress Party), and a near cyclical rise and fall of political parties. But, while political ideology, in its conventional sense, indeed offers little to understand the inner-logic and workings of democracy in Nagaland, this might also indicate the complex cultural transitivity of the concept of ideology as, amongst Nagas, a great deal of ideology is invested in protecting and promoting the needs and interests of 'the tribe.' This reveals itself in demotic political judgments that praise those politicians successful in appropriating and redistributing government positions and state funds to 'their own people' and condemn those who fail to privilege their own tribe while in political office as 'ideologically misguided.'

To be sure, the contemporary proclivities of Nagaland's tribal democracy were never natural or inevitable, but, as this essay has shown, the product of particular social and political conditions that trace back to the colonial rule. Today's enlarged role of 'the tribe' in Nagaland's political processes, therefore, remains best understood as a (likely unintended) effect of state and democracy. The politicisation of tribal identities that resulted from this is viewed with apprehension by liberal political theorists and proponents of 'good governance' who insist that collectivities and loyalties of tribe are incompatible with the values of modern democracy. It is also viewed with apprehension by those Naga nationalists and intellectuals who want to see Naga society rise above divisions of tribe and develop in unison. The Naga historian Horam (1988: 26) laments thus: 'those Naga individuals who rise above tribal considerations... are considered to be renegades by their own tribes.'

While carrying out prolonged fieldwork in Nagaland, I found that acts and articulations of tribalism were also bemoaned by several of my friends and interlocutors. They spoke about tribalism as a form of societal corruption, as endangering peaceful coexistence, and for sowing suspicion, misgivings, and disunity. Yet, rather than adjudging present-day tribalism in Naga political life as the final spasms of 'primordial', 'pre-modern' affections and affinities — now on the verge of being replaced through an 'integrative revolution' (Geertz 1973) by the emergence of a modern Naga society steered by civic values and unity — they insist that tribal loyalties and tribalism are not just persisting in public and political life, but are actually on the rise and saturating democracy and society.

■ ■ ■ ■ ■

08

LAND TAX, RESERVATION FOR WOMEN, AND CUSTOMARY LAW IN NAGALAND

Influenced by Verrier Elwin's views on tribal lifeworlds, Jawaharlal Nehru wrote, in his foreword to Elwin's *A Philosophy for NEFA* (1959), that tribal communities in India's Northeast 'should develop along the lines of their own genius and [that] we should avoid imposing anything on them. We should try to encourage in every way their own traditional arts and culture.' It was in part a follow-up on this philosophy, but primarily as an envisaged (but failed) political compromise in relation to the Naga demand for independence that Nehru assented not only to the enactment of Nagaland state in 1963, but also the crafting of Article 371A of the Constitution, which reads:

> Notwithstanding anything in this Constitution, no Act of parliament in respect of religious or social practices of the Nagas, Naga customary law and procedure, administration of civil and criminal justice involving decisions according to Naga customary law, ownership and transfer of land and its resources, shall apply to the State of Nagaland unless the Legislative Assembly of Nagaland by a resolution so decides.

More than five decades later, the legal implications of this amendment continue to be debated with some insisting that, to the letter, Article 371A almost makes of Nagaland a 'foreign country within the Indian Union', as no laws or policies designed in Delhi apply to Nagaland unless Nagas — here represented by the state legislature — adjudge it as appropriate to Naga traditions, customs, and cultural proclivities. Interpreted thus, Nagas, truly, were allowed to develop themselves 'along the lines of their own genius.'

However, the benevolence of this Naga genius, as reflected here through its customary laws and practices, is now contested by (female) voices within Naga society, claiming that, deep down, Naga customary law is shaped by a culture of subjugation and gender-inequality. Such sentiments are hardly new, but recently erupted in full force in relation to the proposed implementation of (an amended version of) the 'Nagaland Municipal Act 2001.' At issue, are taxes on land and 33% women reservation, as proposed by the 2001 Act (which itself was a much delayed response to the 74th amendment to the Constitution, which came into force in 1993 to provide a common framework for the mandate and structure of urban local bodies). The question is whether these provisions do or do not contravene and encroach on the spirit and jurisdiction of Naga customary law, as safeguarded by Article 371A.

While the battle lines are not always so clearly drawn, the fault-line, broadly, is between the Nagaland government and the Naga Mothers Association, which both desire the implementation of the municipal act because central funds flow in for urban development (the release of which remains conditional to the holding of municipal elections, and which, because of these controversies, have been several years overdue) and the broader issue of women's empowerment. The opposition benches are made up of a host of tribal apex bodies, which staunchly oppose the Municipal Act for infringing on Naga customary law, which does not recognize both taxes on land and a reservation system for political representation.

The pages that follow do not engage hands-on with the public protests and violence that recently took place in Nagaland, the bandhs imposed by tribal bodies, the subsequent deferral of the scheduled municipal elections, and the political aftermath of this crisis. Many journalists and commentators have already done so. What I aim to do instead is to sketch the wider socio-historical context against which the current controversy unfolds.

LAND AND TAXES

'Taxes', the Naga writer Charles Chasie explains, 'has always been an abhorrent issue where Nagas are concerned. It led to the killing of the first

British Political Officer in the Naga Hills in 1879 and the war against the British that followed... Taxation was again a large part of the reason for the rise, and sustenance, of Naga nationalism although other reasons were there' (cited in *Morung Express*, 05-02-2017). Today, taxes, once more, are at the forefront of societal unrest. While most people hate taxes (who likes giving away part of one's income and assets?), Nagas seem to hate these more than most. They hate taxes in the fear that the imposition of taxes on land signals the beginning of the end of Nagas' absolute control over their land and its resources.[1]

For A.Z. Phizo, who captained the Naga National Council (NNC) into its struggle for independence, the idea of sovereignty itself was always less about state, courts, and a Weberian monopoly on violence, but crucially hinged on Nagas' unconditional ownership over their land and its resources, cattle and other possessions, and communitarian ethics (Wouters 2015: 103–107). Phizo (1951) spoke thus:

> [Among Nagas] land belongs to the people as private property, and every family possesses land. We uphold every person as sovereign: man and women alike. Every family is a landlord; but, there is no landlordism in Nagaland... land being so owned by the people who are in their person sovereign... We do not pay even land tax, which is always a crushing burden to the mass citizens in many other countries.

This 'taxless' Naga customary arrangement Phizo contrasted with the position of farmers in places across India. 'What is the lot of Indian cultivators?', he asked, then answering himself: 'They are mere tenants in their own soil and not the sovereign owners of their own land as in our [Naga] country.' It was the urgency for Nagas to protect their age-old landholding system — as shown in the popular local axiom *Ura Uvie!* ('our land is ours') — that Phizo preached as he moved from one Naga village to the next rallying people behind his political movement. An elder in a Chakhesang Naga village recalled Phizo's visit to his village as follows:

> He spoke about socialism, the Naga Nation and that we had been an independent people since time-immemorial. I did not understand all of what he said that time, but we of course supported that all our land, cattle and possession should remain ours, and ours alone. Phizo explained that the Indians, if we would not resist them, would count our land and cattle and make us pay taxes over them, and that we would so lose our freedom.

While the sonority of Phizo's voice has now dwindled, treatises detailing Nagas' intimate connections with their ancestral land have flourished since. Authorities on the set-up of Naga society variously detail their relationship with their land in terms of 'stewardship' and 'reciprocal co-dependency' (Vamuzo 2012: 9), as 'the core of culture', 'origin of ethnic identity' (Varah 2013: 249), and 'symbol of identity' (Longchar 1996: 22), as based on a 'triune concept of God-Land-People' (Imsong 2011: 14), and, in general, as shaped by 'a deep sense of supernatural, spiritual and ancestral attachment' (T. Jamir 2015: 108). What is emphasized too is that whereas in places across the country 'all land belongs to the government', in Nagaland 'land belongs to landowners and the community' (Imkongmeren 2015: 61). In fact, the history of post-statehood governance in Nagaland can be read as a history of tussles between the state government, which requires land to effectuate development, and Naga landowners who hesitate to give up any inch of their land.

But while land and identity are everywhere intimately connected, not every Naga, under customary law, has equal access to land. To begin with, roughly half of the Naga populace comprising women are proscribed from inheriting ancestral land. They are now calling for change and 'gender justice' within the Naga landholding system (T. Jamir 2015: 112–114). But not only are women landless, so-called 'late-comers' in several villages, that is, those Naga villagers and clans thought to have settled in the village after its initial establishment, may be restricted in owning land (George and Yhome 2008: 7). Moreover, some Naga villages were traditionally ruled by hereditary and aristocratic chiefs who were the 'Lord of the manor' (Hutton 1921b: 150) and presided over a 'feudal mode of production' (George and Yhome 2008: 8).

But if such qualifications undermine the singular notion that every Naga is a landowner, they do not negate the deep triangular connection between Nagas, land, and identity, as well as longstanding apprehensions over taxes on land. True, the Nagaland Municipal Act only applies to urban settlements, of which traditionally Nagas had none, but where exactly the urban ends and the rural begins is not always clear. It is further feared that once taxes on urban lands are in place, this system might gradually find its extension into Naga villages, in the process forever altering Nagas' absolute ownership over their land and its resources. The Nagaland government has now recognized this sentiment and in the Nagaland Municipal (third Amendment) Bill (2016) omitted the clause on taxes. The government stated:

> all references and operative provisions relating to 'tax on lands and buildings', wherever these occur in the Nagaland Municipal Act 2001, shall be deemed to have been omitted.

Among many Nagas, however, the worry of a legal loophole remains, and they wonder whether 'shall be deemed' means the same as 'actually removed' and whether 'omitted' implies 'deleted.' 'Nagas are not legally minded', Phizo (cited in Nuh 1986: 89) once explained, but statesmen and politicians, he warned, are: '[They] search for a flaw in the legal system and try to produce one when there is none.' While Phizo spoke these words long ago, the fear of such a 'legal ambiguity' ran against the proposed implementation of the municipal act.

GENDER AND WOMEN EMPOWERMENT

While the issue of taxes on land has seemingly been resolved, at least according to the government, the question of women's reservation has turned ever more volatile. What is advocated by Naga women's organisations, in brief, is the view that customary law not just privileges Naga males, but is deeply patriarchal in its outlook, and so prevents women from receiving their dues. For them, it is the dark side of customary law that restricts and restrains women from inheriting land and from acquiring positions of public and political leadership.

Gender is of course a multidimensional concept, and the status and standing of women in any society can, and should, be measured along multiple axes, at times making gender comparisons between different communities and cultures a problematic undertaking. What can nevertheless be argued is that in various domains Naga women outdo their counterparts across India. If the safety of women can be interpreted, or at least in parts, as a reflection of their social status, *The Hindu*, basing itself on data from the National Crime Records Bureau, declared Nagaland as the safest state for women in India: 'With an estimated female population of over 11 lakhs (in 2014), the rate per lakh population comes to six. In fact, it is the only State in our country to have rates of crime against women in a single digit' (cited in *The Hindu* 22-08-2015).[2] Nagaland also enjoys a female literacy rate that is well above the national average, while the female workforce participation rate is 'fairly better than the National average' (Sashimatsung 2015: 31).

Statistics, however, can conceal as much as they reveal; female literacy, after all, does not necessarily equate empowerment, while the female workforce participation rate does not tell us about levels of job-seniority, equal pay, and prevailing gender divisions on the work floor. That said, as early as the 1960s Verrier Elwin (1961: 104) commended the status Naga society bestows on women:

> Although there is no matriarchy among the Nagas, women hold a high and honourable position. They work on equal terms with men in the fields, and make their influence felt in the tribal councils.

If, in the past, Naga women, while not actually part of customary bodies, at least possessed the agency to 'influence' decisions, present views that Naga women are wholly excluded from decision-making bodies would suggest that, in recent decades, patriarchy has strengthened. Dolly Kikon (2002) offers a partial explanation for this. The marginalisation of women, she argues, has deepened due to the particularistic 'socio-legal interaction between the Naga people and the State apparatus' (2002: 174) in the context of protracted political conflict. It was amidst the Indo-Naga conflict, the spiralling violence, and the militarization of the hills, that, Kikon writes, women became 'the main targets of State oppression.' This led to the 'shrinking of the social space' for women and impelled a 'significant transformation' within the 'internal dynamics of Naga society, where women have had to engage with the strengthening of patriarchal modes of control', resulting 'in the legitimising of processes of exclusion or marginalisation of women from decision-making and political power' (ibid.: 176–177). While Kikon is upfront in identifying the patriarchal hierarchies at the base of Naga customary law, she cautions against 'any piecemeal attempt at segregating the status of women in Naga society from the political and militaristic development within society itself' (ibid.: 181).

What remains evidently clear is that in the post-statehood era, Naga women have had little to no role to play in Nagaland's political arena. Amer (2013: 93) writes:

> While improvements in women's educational and professional status [as the statistics cited above indicate] may be a stimulus for women's empowerment this is clearly not sufficient to win elected office. In the electoral history of Nagaland, spanning a period of more than four [five] decades, fifteen women candidates have contested, but all were repeatedly defeated.

Of all political contestants in Nagaland, Amer calculates, only 0.76% were female with a zero success rate. Democratic politics across Nagaland, plainly, has been a men's game. Given that roughly half of Nagaland's voters are female, this would also imply that females themselves do not wish to vote for other females or, alternatively, that they are stripped from the autonomy to adjudicate on their own votes. For Amer (2013: 94) the absence of women in Nagaland's political arena remains best understood as a reflection of the patriarchal set-up of Naga customary law: 'The traditional institutions around which Naga social and political life revolves have never recognized the rights of women as primary decision makers.'

Across India, and in multiple domains of social life, reservations have been applied — with varying degrees of success and with countless side-effects — to transform the society in ways that did not grow organically. Female voices within Naga society insist that reservation for women is now the only way to improve women's public and political power and standing as the spirit of Naga customary law is unlikely to adapt to modern times. This view is understandable. Another angle to this debate, however, is that, if anything, history shows that Naga customary law is not necessarily rigid and conservative, but adapt and change — albeit only gradually so — over time.

NAGA CUSTOMARY LAW

Perhaps contrary to popular knowledge, Naga customary law is not an ancient fossil or commandments hewn in stone. Customary law permits a certain drift in form, content, and emphasis, and when moral values, religious beliefs, ideas of justice, and the political context changed, Naga customary law usually followed suit. Notwithstanding the regular rhetorical invocation of 'since time-immemorial' to explain and justify the status-quo, a closer look reveals that much of what is now considered traditional Naga customary law and procedures has its genesis in Nagas' modern history, a history strongly shaped by colonialism, massive conversions to Christianity, and enclosure into the Indian nation-state.

While, for instance, *dobashi* courts are today (rightly) celebrated as the personification and repository of Naga customary law, the institution of dobashi (whose literal translation is that of 'interpreter') is, technically speaking, not a Naga tradition, but was created by the colonial government in its political scheme to extend colonial authority and control deep into the Naga uplands. Dobashis were bequeathed with power and privileges, but conditional on them assisting colonial offices and officers in upholding law and order, communicating colonial decrees to villagers, and in settling disputes. And if, at village levels, *gaonburas* (village headmen) are nowadays an intrinsic part of customary proceedings, they too were initially village-wise British appointees roped in to effectuate the collection of 'house-tax', and for which they received a commission and a red woollen shawl that signalled their standing and loyalty to the colonial government. While British colonialism transformed the workings of Naga customary law, the entrance of Christianity, from the late 19th century onward, altered its character and substance. Christianity's influence is seen not just in the prayers that nowadays precede and conclude most customary proceedings, but can also be read in the ideas of 'forgiveness', 'compromise', and 'divine judgment' that seemingly have become hallmark values of Naga customary law.

That such values are modern alterations is not always recognized. Shimray (2011: 12) characterizes Naga customary conceptions of justice as 'a means of building amity and unity through consultations and mentoring [in which] the arbiter takes the role of a mediator between the parties in dispute in order to reconcile them and encourage a healing in their social relations.' Naga customary law, Shimray concludes, 'clearly prioritizes reconciliation and social harmony over redress and punishment.' While this might be an apt reading of the spirit of *contemporary* Naga customary law, it is nevertheless one far removed from the customary laws colonial officers encountered and wrote about in detail when they first climbed the Naga inhabited hills.

Back then, it was the rule of retribution that reigned supreme. Colonial officers, for instance, observed how thieves were 'customarily beaten by the kindred of the victim' (Hutton 1921a 148) or 'trussed up like a pig... [and laid] on a bed of nettle-leaves' (Mills 1926: 194). In other parts of the hills, not only was 'the thief killed on the third offence (he is let off twice), but his wife and children are killed as well, an effective way of stopping hereditary tendencies in crime' (Hutton 1921a 148). Female thieves, however, were dealt with less 'harshly'; they 'were rolled in a mud-hole and stamped upon in the mud' (ibid.: 149). Yet other Naga villages and tribes allowed both thieves and debtors to be sold as 'slaves' (Mills 1922: 111).

Before proceeding, it must be qualified here that Naga customary law is inherently plural. It differs not only from tribe to tribe, but also from village to village, and, as such, Naga customary law, as a singular body of law, does not exist. However, any suggestion today of having a culprit beaten, killed, stamped upon in the mud, or sold as a slave would be immediately objected to by village and tribal bodies, precisely because this would contravene the spirit of Naga customary law. Clearly something has changed, and, most would agree, for the better. What drove these alterations were changing perceptions of the cosmos, and of what constitutes the good moral and social life.

Naga customary law, then, was never frozen in time. Contrary to state laws, which, once written down and ratified, make a sort of orthodoxy possible – hence the concept of 'archaic laws' – customary laws are processual and potentially flexible. It is for this reason that the Justice D.M. Sen (1976: v) spoke with profound wisdom when he objected, in the mid-1970s, against a proposal by the Nagaland government to codify Naga customary law, arguing:

> I am very much against codification. The moment your codify you make it final and firm and rigid. The societies, the tribal societies are developing much faster than any other societies and you yourself do not know what you are going to retain and what are you not. So codification means binding yourself.

To be sure, while the form and substance of Naga customary law adapted and reinvented itself in the passing from the pre-colonial to the post-colonial and post-statehood era, it always did so in ways that remained distinctively Naga in custom and culture. In fact, it seems its very capacity to adapt and change that explains Naga customary law's remarkable resilience as well as reveals its genius. At the present juncture, with the call for inclusion of women in public and political life, Nagas have been given yet another opportunity to invoke their genius in deciding the present and future outlook of customary law.

09

FEASTS OF MERIT, ELECTION FEASTS, OR NO FEASTS?

On the Politics of Wining and Dining in Nagaland

One of the small joys the election season offers ordinary villagers in Nagaland is the inevitable feasts hosted by politicians. In the Chakhesang Naga village I shall call Phugwumi, and where I was carrying out research when the 2013 State Legislative Elections ensued, election feasts became twice-daily events from roughly two weeks prior to Polling Day. Meals were partaken in five political camps – usually a part of an open compound cordoned off by wood and bamboo, set around an open fire, and decorated with party posters and flags – presided over by three rivalling politicians who supplied the camp(s) of their followers with a steady inflow of rice, vegetables and meat. Of these ingredients meat was the one crucial, and some days an entire pig or buffalo was walloped towards a camp, then cut, cooked and eaten. Supplied too, albeit less openly, was liquor; cans of beer and cheap, and sometimes not so cheap, rums and whiskies. Less openly because Nagaland is designated a 'dry state', the outcome of a persistent lobby by the locally influential Nagaland Baptist Church Council (NBCC), which construes the intake of alcohol as an abomination before God. Politicians fear being caught contravening the law and church endowed morality, and therefore entrust the task of distributing liquor, which is invariably demanded, to one of their aides.[1] This wining and dining was crucial during the election period, and its historical imprints, intricacies, and its contested moralities today, the subject of this essay.

In the run up to the 2013 elections, the standard of generous politicians and feasting villagers came under heightened scrutiny and criticism in Nagaland. The NBCC, in its self-assigned task to morally and spiritually guide the Nagaland populace, launched a state-wide Clean Election Campaign, and, among a host of other things, sought to impress on local electors that accepting food and drinks from politicians amounted to being bribed and deceived. In a booklet the NBCC published and distributed through their many associated churches, they asserted: 'if somebody makes any offer of alcohol or other intoxicant or give you dinner to vote or not to vote for a particular candidate it is bribery and punishable' (NBCC 2012: 10). By reasoning thus, the NBCC's stance only subscribed to the ethics, guidelines, and rules set by India's Election Commission, which prohibits election feasts for they offer electors undue inducements – or even perceive of them as outright attempt by politicians to procure votes – so belying the spirit of free and independent judgments on part of India's voters. It is despite this proscription that election feasts are reported in places across the country, and in an effort to waylay the Election Commission's inspecting gaze some politicians reportedly try to garb election feasts as religious or social functions (Piliavsky 2014b: 161-168). For the state of Karnataka, for instance, this led the Election Commission to remark:

> A doubt has been raised with regard to participation of candidates in the community kitchen (langar, bhoj, etc.) organised by religious communities in their religious institutions as a matter of customary practice and the bhoj/feast, etc. offered as a matter of social practice following a ritual ceremony, like marriage, death, etc (Indian Election Commission 2013: 26).

The doubt, obviously, was about who paid the food bills, or even stood behind organizing the event. Piliavsky (2014b) noted an increasing ingenuity among politicians across North-India to organise the election feasts their supporters expected – and which the politicians themselves saw as the most convincing and effective way to promise and symbolize the largesse voters sought in their political representatives – without attracting attention from the Election Commission, and risking its wrath. They feasted electors, for instance, in events camouflaged as wedding ceremonies or birthday parties, but ones without any brides, grooms, or birthday boys and girls to be found (ibid.: 165-66). In comparison, most of Nagaland's politicians ostensibly saw no reason to cover-up their election feasts, certainly not in Phugwumi where such feasts took place for everybody to see, and for every supporter to enjoy.

When Bayart captivatingly characterized democratic politics across Sub-Saharan Africa as a 'politics of the belly', he qualified that this figurative metaphor did not carry any normative judgment, but that it was informed by a 'system of historic action whose origins must if possible be understood in the Braudelian *longue durée*' (1993: ix; emphasis in original). In line with Bayart's reasoning, the pages that follow seek to illustrate that rather than the moral abomination and electoral fraud the NBCC and the Election Commission perceive of the eating and drinking chapters of elections, in Nagaland such feasts are also informed by a particularistic set of age-old practices and principles that socially elevated those capable to act as 'providers', and in which the throwing of feasts near-mechanically amplified a feast-giver's social status, standing, and sway – a practice known in anthropological annals as the Naga feast of merit. Crucially, then and now, I pose, it was not just a wealthy and ambitious villager's gesture to host a feast, or indeed feasts, but it was morally and socially expected of him to do so, as intrinsic to a wider moral economy and order of social stratification in which the less prosperous could count on the village rich to now and then showcase their largesse.[2]

In what follows I will start with a historical perspective and discuss the traditional practice and morals that underlay the Naga feast of merit, common to most – though not all – Naga tribes, that is until Christian missionaries sought and succeeded to (by and large) abolish it. Then we return to the ethnographic present as it unfolded in Phugwumi and witness how, despite the NBCC and the Election Commission ruling against them, election feasts became regular and lavish displays in the run up to Polling Day. Exploring their inner-logic, significances and complexities, we will hear from those with their bellies stuffed to find out the values, reasoning, and meanings they attached to being fed during the election period. But we will also hear from local critics, among them mostly those closely engaged with the church. But besides church-workers alone, some Phugwumi elders are also critical of today's election feasts, albeit for different reasons. What they allege, as I will discuss, is that elections feasts are but a flawed imitation of erstwhile feasts of merit. To be clear, the relationship between traditional feasts of merit and contemporary election feasts may not be deterministic (we cannot know, for instance, whether election feasts would have taken place in Nagaland if there had been no historical antecedent in lavish feasting), yet I do postulate the presence of salient similarities in the inner social and moral logic that guide and inform both types of feasting. Before proceeding, the next section briefly sketches the historical and ethnographic context in which democratic institutions, ideas, and practices unfolded in Nagaland.

THE SETTING

Nagaland's experience with modern, procedural democracy, Chasie (2001: 247) evaluates as 'complex, difficult and painful.' It was complex because it caught Naga society 'in a transition from tradition to modernity' (ibid), difficult because of the 'disparate nature of the [Naga] tribes', and painful because democratic institutions were introduced amidst 'the unresolved Naga political issue, with simultaneous "insurgency" operating during the entire period' (ibid.). It is the still lingering demand for Naga independence – albeit today often framed (and toned down) to an 'alternative arrangement' of sorts – and the challenge this poses to the authority and legitimacy of the local state machinery that admittedly makes Nagaland hardly a straightforward place for ventures into the substance of India's democratic life.

It was in its quest for independence that the Naga National Council (NNC), which under the presidency of A.Z. Phizo spearheaded the Naga Movement, boycotted the country's general elections of 1952 and 1957.[3] In 1963, after nearly a decade of devastating clashes between Naga and Indian Armies, Jawaharlal Nehru changed gear and carved Nagaland out of Assam, as a state within the Indian Union. Although this move was rejected by the NNC, which immediately condemned as 'traitors' and 'reactionaries' any Naga who pledged allegiance to the new state, statehood, and the jobs, schemes and subsidies it brought, it was hailed by a section of Naga leaders who turned themselves into a first generation of politicians and bureaucrats. The first state elections were conducted in 1964, after which elections became both regular and gradually also participatory (Amer 2014), even though the NNC and nascent Naga nationalist groups continue to condemn them as 'Indian elections imposed on Naga soil.' After multiple dissensions, splits, and rivalries within, the Naga cause today is primarily represented by contending factions of the National Socialist Council of Nagalim (NSCN), which is currently in a long-drawn ceasefire with the Central Government. But even as negotiations are taking place, and have taken place for two decades, this has not led to a permanent solution, keeping Nagaland's political landscape both multi-layered and volatile.[4]

Within Nagaland, my ethnography is drawn from the Chakhesang Naga, one of the state's sixteen state-recognized tribes and the inhabitants of Phek District to the east of Kohima, Nagaland's state capital. The

Chakhesang is a new tribe. New in the sense of first seeing daylight in 1946 when several village clusters hitherto part of other tribes resolved to breakaway and fuse into a tribe of their own making, to be called Chakhesang. Among the Chakhesang Naga, Phugwumi constitutes the largest village. Akin to many Naga villages, Phugwumi sits perched high on a hilltop from where it stands guard over its neatly excavated paddy fields below. As polling day drew closer electoral politics came to dominate most conversations and actions of the villagers, most of whom openly associated themselves with one or another candidate.

State-wise, the Naga Peoples' Front (NPF), which had been the ruling government since 2003 after ousting a nearly two decade rule by the Congress Party, sought a hat-trick of electoral victories, and most opined that the party stood good chances of achieving this. However, with besides the sitting MLA (NPF Party), also two former Ministers and a promising newcomer contesting the election fray, Phugwumi's constituency was thought of as an especially competitive one, and in the wake of the election supporters of all four candidates had reasons to believe they were in the driving seat.

The quest for votes was locally often ferocious, at times tense, and while voters based their decision on whom to give their votes on complex and multiple reasons, the throwing of feasts for supporters was a strategy followed by all four candidates, and is the sole focus of the remainder of this essay.[5] To start discussing this, the next section adopts the ethnographic *longue durée* to historically and culturally situate the local principles, merits, and moralities of feasting.

THE MORALS AND MERITS OF FEASTING AMONG THE NAGA

Election feasts, we noted, are hardly unique to Nagaland but occur in places across the Subcontinent. For Rajasthan, and North-India more widely, Piliavsky (2014b) evocatively traced their practice to age-old patron-client relationships and the vintage Jajmani system to which they were intrinsic. If in the past '"feeding' and "eating" – both the act and the metaphor – was the crucial link between donors and servants' (ibid.: 160), a similar logic and cultural idiom, Piliavsky writes, exists between politicians and voters today:

> the language of feeding is the key moral idiom in which people evaluate politicians and conceive of the ways in which politicians relate, or ought to relate, to their constituents... [they title of] feeder express the conception of patron as

> genitor and provider, as a source of both sustenance and personal substance for his clientele (ibid.: 163–164).

But while across North-India the inner-logic of politics as patronage (see Piliavsky 2014a) may be informed by long-standing patron-client relationships, expressed through an evocative cultural idiom of feeding and eating, and culminating into a set of values and expectations thence symbolized through politicians' hosting election feasts, no traditional patron-client system, or an otherwise hierarchical and ritual division of labour, ever had much prominence among the Naga. And yet, if anything, election feasts in Nagaland tend not to be the single-day events reported elsewhere, but usually last for days and weeks prior to polling day.[6] Hence if not a remnant or remapping of patron-client relationships and Jajmani structures and sentiments, what, then, might election feasts among the Naga be a 'changing continuity' of? To start exploring this, the writings of Von Fürer-Haimendorf, the first trained anthropologist to study the Naga through prolonged participant observation, appear to provide us with an important clue.

Researching the Naga in the 1930s, Fürer-Haimendorf witnessed 'hundreds and thousands of megalithic monuments' with each of them erected to commemorate the 'fame and generosity' of a particular feast-giver (1976[1939]: 19) in whose name the megalith had been erected. On further inquiry, he found that, among the Naga, one's social status an standing did not rely on the accumulation of wealth, but that social ascendance could be achieved through a person dispensing his wealth by throwing lavish feast, an elaborate social institution popularized as a feast of merit. Haimendorf had hardly been the first visitor to the (then) Naga Hills District to notice this local custom and the moral and social principles it relied on. Half a century earlier, Colonel Woodthorpe, travelling far and wide in the area, put to paper his sheer astonishment about the long rows of monoliths he observed in villages across the Naga Hills. He commented: '[these monoliths] are either monumental or simply commemorative of some big feast given by a rich man.' He also noticed how a great deal of effort and sweat went into pulling and erecting such stones:

> These stones are often of great size, and are dragged up into place on wooden sledges shaped like the prow of a boat, the keel curving upwards. On this sledge the stone is levered, and carefully lashed with canes and creepers, and to this the men, sometimes to the number of several hundreds, attached themselves in a long line, and putting rollers beneath the sledge, they pull it along until it has been brought to the spot where the stone is to be erected (Woodthorpe 1881: 53–4).

The monolith, once erected, came, in a way, to inhabit the virtues and achievements of the feast-giver in whose honour it was erected, and continues to enshrine them today. While joining *Athe* for village walks, as I did often, I noticed how he was able to relate each of Phugwumi's many monoliths to a particular feast-giver, even if the feasts had taken place several generations ago. For an aspirant villager to climb the social ladder, to expand his sway and have his voice heard more loudly, a single feast would hardly do the trick. In the course of his life an ambitious person was expected to provide a series of feasts (locally called *zhotho müza*). Such feasts were ritually sanctioned with each of them allowing the feast-giver a further display that denoted his social ascendancy. In Phugwumi, the symbolic index of social stratification would start with a feast-giver's right to wear a specifically embroidered shawl, followed by the permission to decorate his house with X-shaped boards and carvings, to ultimately large monoliths being erected in his name. Put differently, by performing the feast of merit the feast-giver in a way absolved material wealth, but accumulated material symbols. As a social institution, the feast of merit therefore is both an equalizing force in economic terms, and one fostering a certain social hierarchy.

On a tour through the Eastern Angami area, now Chakhesang, Fürer-Haimendorf stumbled onto a large open compound with houses on two sides:

> Cross barge-boards rose from the gables of one of the houses, like the enormous antlers of some proud stag. Proud, too, must have been the owner of these wooden horns, for they showed that he had given several of those expensive Feasts of Merits whereby the Naga rises in social prestige and in the esteem of his neighbours (1976 [1939]: 9).

In Phugwumi, a complete series would involve nine feasts, after which a row of nine monoliths would have been erected in the feast-giver's name, a life-long exercise that involved such grandiose expenses that only three villagers are remembered to have ever accomplished this. In fact, most villagers would never find themselves in the position to throw a single feast, and instead relied on the village wealthy to, now and then, enable them to lavish on meat and rice-beer. Fürer-Haimendorf explained:

> The wealth of the ambitious was employed to provide food and enjoyment for the less prosperous members of the community, for at a Feast of Merit there was meat, rice and rice-beer for every man, woman and child in the village (1976 [1939]: 47).

While few villagers were able, everyone aspired to be a feast-giver, and this ambition, the colonial officer J.P. Mills wrote, had a stimulating impact on local agriculture. It is worth quoting him at some length:

> the essence of this system [Feast of Merit] is that every male Naga, if he is to acquire merit and status in this world and the next, must give a series of feasts, every detail of which is strictly prescribed... they begin with the sacrifice of a pig and end with that of at least one domestic bison garnished, so to speak, with quantities of cattle and pigs. An immense amount of rice and rice beer is consumed, and more rice than money goes to the buying of the animals. The Feasts therefore directly simulate agriculture. More important sill are the privileges they win for the giver. At stated stages in the series he and his wife gain the right to wear special cloths, which increase in splendour and in the elaborateness of their embroidery the further he advances. He is also entitled to embellish his house with carved posts and beams. It is important to remember that, no matter how rich a man may be, he can win the rights to these cloths and carvings only by giving feasts (1935: 134).

Seen as a historical social institution, the feast of merit thus seemingly invoked contradictory principles, combining tendencies of economic redistribution and social differentiation, of both socialism and snobbery, but crucially it vested social eminence in a person's ability to act as a provider, not, say, in mere accruing.

Unfortunately, the feast of merit was among the first sacrifices mostly American and Welsh missionaries demanded from new Naga converts, interpreting them as an ostentatious wastage of wealth and its free-flowing rice-beer as inducing immoralities of sorts. Its gradual abolishment had wide ramifications: the same J.P. Mills commented: 'a great number of very fine embroidery patterns and carvings designs owe their existence entirely to this system of Feast of Merit and will continue to exist only as long as the system does' (1935: 134), then lamenting: 'one has only to stroll through a Christian village. There may be many rich men with granaries bursting with rice, but not a fine cloth or carving you will see' (ibid.).

If Mills lamented the missionaries' abolishment in terms of the fine clothes and carvings no longer embroidered and engraved, for ordinary villagers it also punctured a core aspect of a moral economy that benefitted and entertained them. In Phugwumi some village elders still vividly recall, and sometimes feel nostalgic to, the feasts of merit they witnessed in their youth. A number of houses continue to flaunt the meticulously carved wooden walls and cross barge boards distinctive of the house of a feast-giver, but these decorations are of no recent manufacture. After the majority of villagers took to the new religion from the late 1950s onward, feasts of merit saw a steep decline in Phugwumi, then died out completely.[7] Except perhaps, somewhat paradoxically, on Christmas Day when a Christianised version — that is a feast of merit without rice-beer — is invariably organised for the congregation by a wealthy villager, usually a politician, contractor, or a high-ranking government officer, and who, in return for his generosity, is offered a shawl, and is collectively prayed for during the church service.

But even if now abolished, as a traditional social institution the feast of merit provides a valuable window into values, norms and expectations that informed social differentiations, a moral economy, as well as local notions that surrounded village leadership. To emphasize, the decision to throw a feast was hardly optional on part of the rich and ruling, but morally expected of them. Summing up the pre-state qualities expected of village rulers among the pre-state Naga, Hokishe Sema, a former Nagaland Chief-Minister, reflected in his memoirs:

> These [village] rulers have some person distinction acquired by them through their performances of sacrifices and good judgments. They also have a great economic power and their capacity to help the poor and the needy in the village is greatly appreciated. They provide food, shelter, and clothing for the needy in an emergency. It is a great shame for the rulers if their subjects go to other villages for food. It is the duty of these rulers to ensure the security and welfare of their subjects (1986: 168).

While in Phugwumi there existed no mechanical linkage between becoming a feast-giver and becoming a village leader as, then and now, the wealth and wisdom needed to guide the villagers are known to be two different domains altogether, while village elders were invariably ascribed more wisdom than others. However, village leaders were often, though not always, also known as feast-givers, and, in any case, were expected to be capable to act as providers and guarantors, as Hokishe Sema's quote well captures. The next sections attempts to show that it is in this traditional feast of merit, the practices, principles, and morals that lied beneath them, that the inner-logic of today's election feasts is vested, even though, as will become clear, such feasts are no straightforward remapping of the feast of merit and today draw contentious judgments.

THE CONFLICTING MORALITIES OF ELECTION FEASTS

The first episode of food entering the election domain in Phugwumi was about five months prior to Election Day when a pair of trucks pulled into the village. Both were stacked with fifty-kilogram bags of rice, one for each Phugwumi household. The rice had been arranged and paid for by an aspiring politician. 'In compensation for the year's bad harvest', the generous politician had explained as his aides went about distributing the heavy bags. 'An electoral strategy', most in the village understood.

But sacks of paddy is hardly the kind of feeding associated with election feasts, which started in fullness in the weeks and days preceding Polling Day. Three out of the four candidates opened camps in the village (with two of them maintaining two each — a general and a youth camp). It was in these camps that supporters came together and discussed the latest political developments, digested facts and rumours, devised new strategies, but most of all to eat lunches and dinners, and to enjoy a good time with friends and neighbours. The food prepared was always lavish, and never without meat, which for most in the village remained too scarce for everyday use in ordinary times. Such excessive feasting was also part and parcel to elections in the Naga inhabited hills of adjacent Manipur, and in the run up to the 2012 Manipur state elections an article in a local daily read:

> Election fever has gripped the hill district of Manipur in spite of the social impasse triggered by several issues with the latest being the new district creation demand boom. However, these issues are not the common worry for the intending candidates. With speculations doing the round that assembly election in Manipur is likely to be held in five months' time, election related programmes are underway. However, most of the intending candidates are finding it hard to satiate their followers when [it] comes to feasting. Feasting is the all-time favourite of all the election-related occasions in the hill districts... With pork being the all-time favourite, the difficulty in finding pigs has become a great headache for the tribal politicians... Knowing the situation, butchers and those farmers are set to do brisk business. A matured pig costs now anything between Rs 25.000 to 30.000 in most parts of hill districts (Newmai News Network, 08-09-2012)

Securing sufficient meat posed an organisational challenge to politicians in and around Phugwumi, and it was still many months before the elections that rumours spread conveying that a certain politician had approached 'this or that person' with the request to fatten his pig(s) with the promise to procure its meat during the election period. To satisfy demand, politicians also imported meat from neighbouring Assam, but electors invariably preferred meat from animals locally reared, and a politician supplying 'Assam meat' ran the risk of causing both grouchy bellies and tongues.

Akin to the past feast of merit, this element of provisioning on part of politicians was not just a voluntary gesture. To the contrary, electors expected to be fed during the election season. Throwing feasts was seen as a candidate's moral obligation, as a bondage that came with his ambitions and aspirations to find acceptance as a leader (and shame on those aspirant leaders stingy in their supplies!). Most 'eaters' in Phugwumi testified to this logic; 'he wants to be our leader, so he must feast us', or simply 'it is his duty to feed us' Some others, especially youths, appeared to reason less in traditional but more in transactional terms: 'I am helping in his campaign, he must feed me.' But if the moral obligation on part of leaders to feed, and the expectation of ordinary villagers to be feasted, shows clear parallels to practices and principles of past feasts of merit, today's election feasts have also become sites of conflicting judgments and moralities, to which we will now turn.

If election feasts were morally denunciated and configured as distorted electoral practice by the NBCC and the Election Commission, in Phugwumi there was a clear moral reasoning to such feasts. We already saw how 'eaters' relied on a pre-existing moral framework, derived from the traditional feasts of merit and perennial notions of good leadership, to explain and justify their eating at the invitation of an aspiring leader. However, little could draw as vicious moral disapproval than witnessing the same person allowing himself to be feasted in camps belonging to rivalling candidates. In fact, no self-respecting villager would fill his stomach from two camps. Paradoxically, it is in such restrictions that we might find a deeper moral critique. This is so because in a traditional feast of merit all villagers would eat, irrespective of the rivalries and divisions that existed within the village — in fact, not showing up for a feast could draw instant moral disapproval. Elections feasts, in contrast, do not exhibit such a sense of community and inclusiveness as they are meant for political followers only, and it is this exclusivity in feasting which, some Phugwumi elders tell, only exemplifies the disunity and discord electoral politics has brought to the village.

There were other controversies and convulsions. Election feasts are excessively lavish and certainly a great deal lengthier compared to the nine feasts that closed the traditional cycle of the feasts of merit, which moreover an ambitious feast-giver would take his entire life-time to arrange, and even then often hardly managed more than a few. Such excessive feasting is in parts, I pose, because the wealth politicians are thought to accrue during their tenures has become locally thought of as excessive too, and feasts continue to serve as a method and expectation for its dispensing, or at least so for those seeking to enter the political realm. A prime (and related) critique is the ambiguous source of today's wealth. If past feasts of merit were thrown as the result of a feast-giver's many years of toil and sweat exerted in cultivating his fields, election feasts today are thought to be (indirectly) financed by state monies, thus not out of his 'real' and hard labour (most villagers assert that only cultivating fields amounts to 'real labour', as opposed to those who 'sit' in government offices). This difference is crucial, and the notion that election feasts are (indirectly) paid by state monies, rather than through personal drudgery – while not changing villagers' expectations to be feasted by their leaders – metaphorically changes the taste of the meat, and reduces the veneration and esteem bestowed on today's feast-givers.

There also exists a growing realisation that politicians, once elected in office, waste little time on reimbursing themselves on past expenses, plus the additional expenses needed for the throwing of feasts during the next election.[8] 'The more we eat now', as one Phugwumi villager explained, 'the more he [the politician] will eat later.'[9] Such a sequence goes against the grain of the moral economy that stirred feasts of merit, which although created social differentiation, simultaneously worked as an economic equalizer, while, back then, it would take a feast giver many years and hard labour to regain his previous position of wealth (only to be expected to feast it away again). Electors understand this, and if Nagaland politicians have been accused of abusing democracy to 'an industry to earn through malpractice' (Kiewhuo 2002: 61), during election seasons 'campaign inducements [of which feasts make only one dimension] becomes a sort of industry' (Amer 2014: 4).[10] Voters can be as cunning as their politicians, and in the run up to polling day the youth president of one of the candidates, and whose duties included presiding over and supplying the youth camp, complained about the countless troubles and demands he had to face on a daily basis.

'This is the biggest headache to manage', he pointed to a half-empty bottle of whiskey that stood between us and then refilled mine and his glass:

> They [the party youth] demand to be given drinks every night. First we gave them simple rums and whiskies [the cheapest locally available] but now with Polling Day coming closer they insist on beer [which is more expensive locally]. If we don't give them what they want, they will become very difficult to control. They might even shift camps [join another political

party]. All the time I need to call my boss [the politician] to ask for more money to be able to satisfy them.[11]

While rice-beer had long been part of the local diet, and crucial to a successful feast of merit, missionaries had ferociously preached against its intake, and it is therefore perhaps not surprising that it is the free flow of liquor during election periods that especially worried today's church leaders. It was the very abolishment of political camps, in which liquor was often partaken, that was preached by the NBCC, which qualified those camps as 'breeding grounds of all kinds of malpractices such as [the] use of alcohol, drugs, gambling, sexual immoralities, violence... [and other] unfavourable and abominable activities before God' (NBCC 2012: 6–7).

Responding to the NBCC's call, some 'godly' Village Councils in Nagaland prohibited politicians to wine and dine electors, and notified their decision in local dailies, for instance: 'Public Information: the Diphupar Village Council... has unanimously resolved to ban [the] opening of mess for all political parties' (cited in *Morung Express*, 18-2-2013). Phugwumi's village pastor, too, thought little good came from political camps and election feasts, but the Village Council Chairperson saw no possibility to restrict these practices – 'we can't stop it. It has become part of every election', he explained. He himself however avoided to be seen near any political camp, and so did Phugwumi church-workers and others who rated NBCC's divinely-inspired guidelines above he earthly pleasures of eating and drinking.[12]

While the pulpit was the NBCC's chosen platform to counter the wining and dining dimensions of elections, some local (church) organisations went further, and in the wake of Polling Day a local daily reported how in Phek District:

> several surveillance groups have been formed and check posts are set up in almost all villages spearheaded by the CPO [Chakhesang Public Organisation] and CBCC [Chakhesang Baptist Church Council]... the frisking of vehicles started from February 9 [Polling Day was scheduled for the 23rd that month] and so far 1021 bottles of various brands have been seized and were destroyed in the presence of the administration and the police (cited in *Morung Express* 13-02-2013).

A handful of those 1021 seized bottles came from the trunk of the vehicle I happened to be traveling in to witness a political rally in the nearby administrative town, to which I had been invited that morning by the party-worker who sat behind the wheel. Nearing the town, our vehicle had been stopped by volunteers of the Women Wing of the Chakhesang Baptist

Church Council (CBCC) who duly frisked the vehicle. Little did I know of the whiskies present in the trunk, which were solemnly confiscated and subsequently stalled out on the road-side as a display of the party-worker's 'immorality.' As we drove on, the party-worker grumbled about his loss. 'The Church should confine itself to praying and feasting for the election, not checking vehicles.'

In sum: what was taking place in Phugwumi, and in places across Nagaland, was not a simple exchange of meals and liquor for votes, the obtaining of which required a politician a great deal more effort. Instead, providing meaty feasts and liquor answered time-honoured local practices and principles, informed by a moral economy in which the village rich and ruling were expected to be generous. And yet, if the practices and principles surrounding election feasts show multiple parallels with past feasts of merit, its practice today simultaneously diverges from it in crucial aspects, as this section too has sought to illustrate, and which shroud present-day electoral feasts in an aura of moral ambivalence. This critique, with at its core that election feasts do not showcase the inclusiveness and sense of community central to feast of merits, as well as the morally ambiguous origins of the monies used to finance them, remains however of a different nature from the critique levied by the NBCC and the Election Commission, whose disposition remains short and simple: 'No feasts!'

CONCLUSION

If the NBCC and India's Election Commission look upon election feasts as distorted and dissolute electoral practice unbecoming of India's deepening (Heller 2009) and flourishing democracy (Guha 2009; Khilnani 2007), when evaluated in the ethnographic *longue durée* election feasts among the Naga acquire a significance of their own. Rather than undue attempts to woo and buy votes, to most in Phugwumi the principle of provisioning – in the very literal sense of being occasionally wined and dined – has always been integral to their understandings of social differentiation and leadership, to the extent that a leader unable to feed others was often no leader at all.

While it must be emphasized that, certainly in Phugwumi, there existed no mechanical linkage between a feast-giver and a village leader given that seniority and wisdom were evaluated in their own right, the jump from a position of social pre-eminence achieved through the throwing of feasts to one of political sway and prominence was invariably easier to accomplish compared to an ambitious villager without the track-record of a feast-giver. It is akin to traditional feasts of merit that during today's election feasts both feeders and eaters gain, the former in uplifting their local standing, which certainly helps their election bid, and the latter in being able to lavish on meat otherwise scarce, and for some to drink the liquor they otherwise find hard to obtain or afford. Emphasizing the similarities in inner-logic, moral values, and past practices that underlie both feasts of merit and election feasts, however, is far from arguing that election feasts are a direct and uncomplicated recasting of feasts of merit. If anything, as some Phugwumi elders insist, contemporary election feasts — the way they are funded and their exclusivist character — are but a flawed imitation of past feasts of merit.

As noted, election feasts are reported not only in Nagaland but in places across the Indian polity. It would however be wrong to assert that such feasts rely everywhere on a same inner-logic and cultural idiom, and if they have been linked to a resurgence of patron-client relationships, and a cultural idiom derived from Jajmani systems of sorts in Rajasthan and Northern India more widely (Piliavsky 2014), it is in the absence of such pre-existing social patterns that election feasts in Nagaland are not just held, but perhaps well outdo those in most other parts of the India.

On a final note; Nagaland's spectrum of political parties has been criticized for its staunchly 'non-ideological character' (Amer 2014: 6), evidence of which commentators find in the frequent cross-carpeting and party hopping on part of politicians. While Nagaland's electoral politics is indeed not a politics of manifestos, party visions, and public platforms,[13] this might not justify characterizing the substance of Nagaland's democracy as non-ideological. If anything, the cultural transitivity of the concept of party and political ideology is complex, and, among the Naga, as this essay has shown, a great deal of ideology was in fact vested in an aspirant politician's ability to throw lavish feasts.

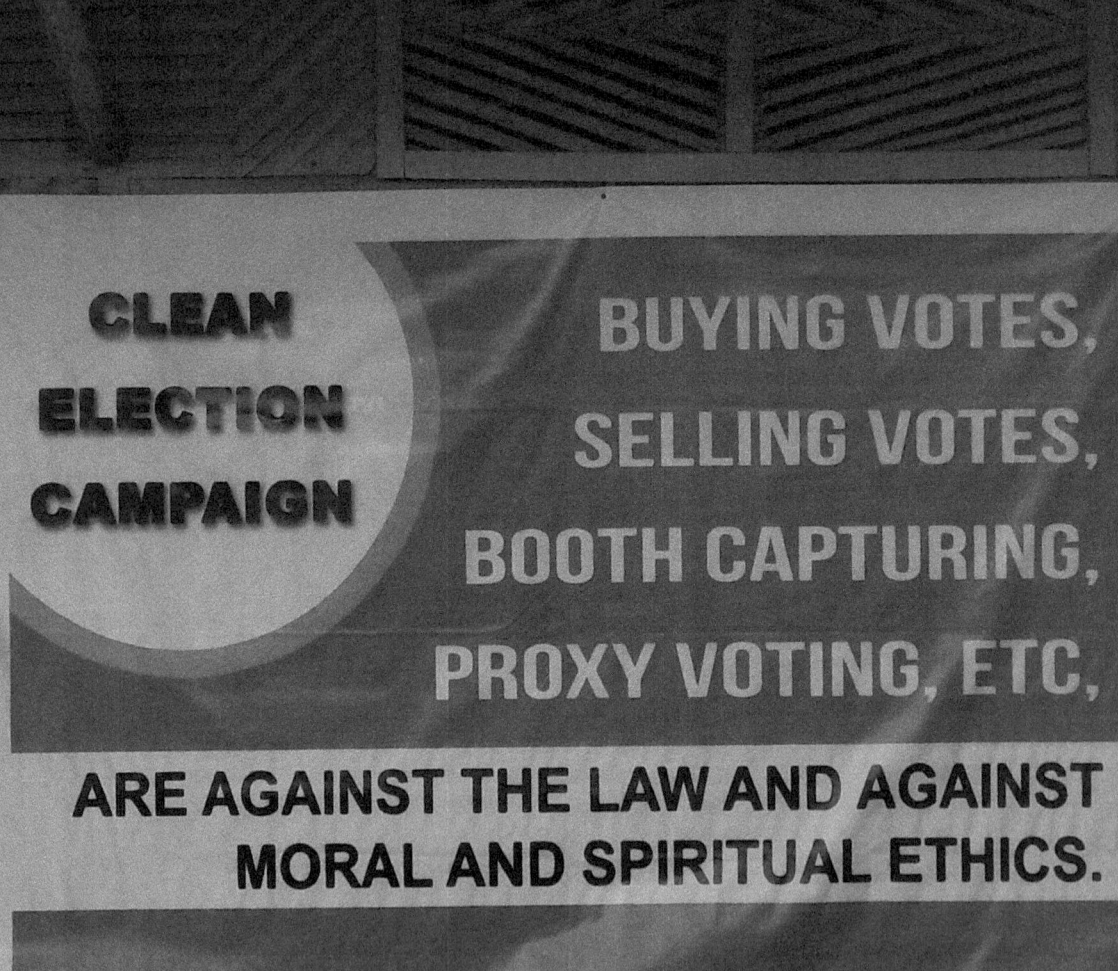

10

WHAT MAKES A GOOD POLITICIAN?

Democratic Representation, 'Vote-Buying', and the MLA Handbook in Nagaland

In the two years I carried out ethnographic research in the tribal and politically-volatile upland state of Nagaland in India's northeast, I occasionally spent a few days in a minister's residence located in the bustling town of Dimapur, perched on the Nagaland–Assam border. The minister is a proverbial 'big shot', a seasoned politician, well known both inside and outside the state, and in charge of a 'plump' portfolio. His residence comprises two storeys, but while the minister and his family reside upstairs, my impromptu ethnography took place in the chambers downstairs.

The ground floor is always cramped with villagers who hail from the minister's faraway constituency (a rough twelve hours' drive away), and who trail down to Dimapur for business, 'government work' (i.e. to apply for a job, subsidy, or development scheme, and for which they anticipate the minister's 'recommendation'), medical treatment, their children's admission into schools or colleges, or as a stop-over on travels into Assam and beyond. But whatever the purpose, once in Dimapur it is certain that they will stay and eat (and complain loudly when meat is not on the menu!) in the house of their democratic representative. During their stay, they usually receive 'pocket-money' to get around town, while those sufficiently bold leave behind educational and medical bills for the minister to settle. At night, the young and intrepid may accost one of the minister's adult children to solicit alcohol, which is locally difficult and expensive to come by given Nagaland's official status as a 'dry state'.

The minister himself – when he is not in his office or on the road – always spares time for his constituents. He listens to their mostly purely personal problems and aspirations attentively, jots down notes, doles out money to some, offers assurances to others, and always impresses upon both his children and servants to look after their everyday needs. 'This is what politics in Nagaland is about', the minister tells me late one evening, visibly exhausted. 'Small or big matters, villagers expect my advice and help. If I refuse their requests they get annoyed, or, worse, campaign against me during the next election. I do my best to help each of them, but they don't understand that I have my limitations also.'

For a Naga politician to witness his residence transform into a hotel, restaurant, and service centre of sorts is hardly a recent 'add-on' to local democratic life, but traces back to the onset of participatory elections in the 1960s. Temsula Ao (2013: 181), a Naga writer of repute, recalls her life transforming after her husband contested elections midway through the 1960s:

> And suddenly from a placid existence, the campaign took us by storm…. The house was turned into a free-for-all arena, where all kinds of people came and went at all times of the day and night. All our resources went into feeding and pleasing these so-called supporters…. Success only made things worse; our life was not our own any more and there was no end to the 'demands' of the so-called 'supporters' as we pawned our souls to the great fraud of our times called electoral politics.

Given the particular form democratic representation takes in Nagaland, it is no coincidence that in a Chakhesang Naga village that I call Phugwumi, where I carried out fieldwork in the wake of the 2013 state Legislative Assembly elections, Athe could articulate the following political judgment about a local politician:

> I don't appreciate his ideology. For several times, I campaigned on his behalf. But what has he done for my family when he was in power? What has he done for our village? He held such big portfolios but see the condition of my house. See the shape of our village! He has hardly helped anyone.

Against the expectations of 'normative democracy' (Nugent 2008: 21-62) voters beseech their democratic representatives, expecting to be wined, dined, and given personal favours –in the form of 'political ideology' measured by a politician's skill in rewarding his voters individually, and (ab)using the state as his chief resource. In conventional political science analyses, this can only be understood through stereotypes: a deceptive auctioning of votes, politically perverse patronage or pernicious 'machine politics' (Scott 1969), jointly indicating a politics that is morally depraved and deluded.

Indeed, scholars and pundits of democratic institutions and elections in Nagaland paint them as a morass of political corruption, clientelism and pervasive vote-buying (Ezung 2012; Dev 2006; Singh 2004), allegedly making elections in Nagaland per capita the costliest in the country (U. Misra 1987). They not only accuse politicians of abusing democracy by turning it into 'an industry to earn through malpractice' (Kiewhuo 2002: 61), but also blame Naga villagers for turning 'campaign inducements [into] a sort of industry' (amer 2014: 4), leading to a politics of reciprocal deceit.

Such readings of democratic representation and politics in Nagaland are derivative of *la pensée unique* of 'liberal democracy', as it is now called.[1] Though the theoretical traditions of political liberalism influence democratic life in Nagaland (and South Asia more widely), drawing the conclusion that democratic politics in Nagaland deviate from liberal benchmarks is reductionist and, ultimately, too easy to be useful. Stressing the distinctiveness of South Asian political life more broadly, some theorists note how popular political styles resemble those of 'Bosses, Captains, and Lords' (Price and Ruud 2009); that political bonds revolve strongly around social networks of patronage and 'ethnic head counts' (Chandra 2004); that democratic politics is 'substantially about access to state resources' (Prasad 2010: 142); and that 'generosity' constitutes the past and present 'cornerstone-value' of political life (Piliavsky 2014: 9). Jointly, they argue for a '"positive" theorization' of democratic difference (Witsoe 2011).[2]

Answering the call for grounded, 'positive' theory, and extending the discussion to the comparatively less-studied tribal periphery of India's northeast, this essay uses ethnography to ask how we may best understand the particular expectations and relations that connect Naga villagers with those they elect to political office, and what this might mean for the ways in which democratic representation is imagined and evaluated. I seek to show that, among tribal Nagas, contemporary democratic politics, and the role of politicians in it, is reflective both of the ethos and ethics of 'traditional' Naga politics and the specificities of Nagaland state and governance.

The (liberalist) image of an elected politician serving the public good in a modern, Weberian notion of detached, rational–legal governance clashes with the local cultural projections of political leaders as (normatively) generous providers to their people, as well as with a centre-led, politically-driven policy of post-statehood largesse — adopted as a counter-measure to the protracted Naga insurgency (see below) — in terms of government employment and state benefits (Nagaland tops Indian charts in both). In Nagaland, it is the moral logic of personally-directed generosity, I argue, that is the bedrock of democratic representation – it is the basis of political judgement, actions and legitimacy. These two radically divergent modes of governance – one liberalist, the other at once culturalist and circumstantial – reflect very different ways of imagining democratic representation derived from alternative historical trajectories and forms of political sociality.

While both liberal political theory and India's statutory laws define (and confine) the institutional and legal relationships, roles, and responsibilities (a list of political do's and don'ts) between politicians and electors, recent political ethnography shows that the cultural and moral (and cosmic) content of the values and relations that bind them – the ways in which voters relate to their performance in office – can hardly be defined in the abstract, but is here, there and everywhere enmeshed in historically-evolved socio-cultural circumstances and conventions (Michelutti 2008; Piliavsky 2014ab). This makes 'democratic representation' not just a hallmark of political modernity, but also – and herein lies this essays's main contention – a reflection of historically-evolved relations and the way a society conceptualises and normatively imagines its political self and sociality.

By approaching democratic representation ethnographically, this essay contributes to fresh anthropological theorising that illustrates the 'vernacular' (Michelutti 2008), 'multivalent' (Guttman 2002: xviii) and 'polythetic' (Wouters 2015) nature of actually existing democracies. In what follows, I pursue the simple (but far from simplistic) question: 'What makes a good politician?' This question, I pose, is an empirical and situated one, innately antithetical to liberalist abstractions. To most liberal political theorists, and their many mimics, the micro-politics I report from Phugwumi will appear as corrupt, nepotistic, clientelistic, venal, and unjust. But this is not necessarily how Naga villagers themselves frame their political expectations and actions. An account of democratic representation that focuses not on postulated liberal models and values, but on political sociality and moral commensality, and the situated social relationships that emerge from this, leads, I will show, to fresh insights about vote buying, clientelism, and corruption.

CONCEPTUALISING DEMOCRATIC REPRESENTATION

In this period of political liberalism, and owing to the far-reaching individualisation characteristic of 'Western' cosmopolitan theory, the act of voting is now equated with personal autonomy (De Tocqueville 1969). It conjures up a historical process through which a liberated 'man the voter' became increasingly imagined as an isolated being whose relationship to democracy was defined by liberal values of personal freedom, freedom of choice and the right to self-expression, as an 'enchanted individual' who stands 'apart from society's constitutive social and political bonds' (Gilmartin 2012: 413).

Against this normative predisposition towards liberal values, a sociological understanding of democratic representation in South Asia (but not just there) reveals that, when stripped back to its bare essentials, democratic representation constitutes a socially meaningful arrangement between 'the people' (however defined) and a politician who represents 'their' voices, needs and interests. Piliavsky puts it this way: 'What is democratic representation if not a social relation?' (Piliavky 2014a: 29). The idea of representative democracy, indeed, expresses the desire for some kind of social relationship. There must necessarily be some form of 'relatedness' between electors and 'the elected' for democratic representation to function and be meaningful.[3]

In South Asia, it is widely observed that the idea of democratic representation is rendered meaningful through social relations (attachments and loyalties to family, kin and community), rather than through notions of individual autonomy or through political ideology (in conventional terms of a Left-Centre-Right political spectrum) (Béteille 2017). Holmberg writes: 'party ideology is more often than not trumped by social relations' (cited in Gellner 2009: 127).[4] The reason that (the still few) anthropologists studying democracy in South Asia are so dissatisfied and disillusioned with contemporary political theory lies precisely in its hegemonic, indeed ontological, elimination of sociality from democratic life-worlds.

Yet the fading prospect, not just in South Asia, but in places across the world, of ever achieving normative variants of democracy, and democratic representation in particular, now challenges and undermines most liberal political theory and thought. Governance in sub-Saharan Africa is now interpreted as a ravenous 'politics of the belly' (Bayart 1993), notable for its prebendalism (Joseph 1987). China is associated with pervasive political clientelism (Gouhui 2014), while politics in the Andes is shot through with vulgar populism and authoritarianism (Levitsky and Loxton 2013). In the subcontinent, politicians behave, and are widely seen, as masters and kings (Price 1989); they introduce themselves as the rightful heirs to Hindu gods and deities (Michelutti 2008), or go about like movie stars (some in certain cases were actually Bollywood or Kollywood heroes and heroines before taking to politics) (Dickey 1993). Others are known as *goondas*, trading in 'muscular politics' (Berenshot 2011), or as mafia dons (with not a few politicians contesting and winning elections while incarcerated in jail) (Verma 2005). The ethnographic complexities and richness such accounts reveal suggest the need to unravel different philosophies, or 'moral teleologies' (Piliavsky and Sbriccoli 2016), of democratic representation, governance and modern political life.

That democratic representation, as a heuristic device, has long been a trope of political science, rather than a theme anthropologists might, or should, study, seems striking, given that, as a discipline, we know a great deal about other political structures and sentiments, be they between 'big men' and their followers (Sahlins 1963), patrons and clients (Gellner and Waterbury 1977), kings and subjects (Gluckman 1954), or between leaders of bands, village headmen, tribal chiefs and those notionally under their control. However, the moment such political arrangements change from chiefs collecting, stocking, and redistributing yams (Malinowsky 1932), or amassing and publicly giving away (or destroying) possessions in great potlatches (Mauss 1966), or competitive feasting, or the ritual slaying and re-enactment of kings, and traditional kings, chiefs, headmen and their subjects transform into politicians and electors, we seem to lose interest in their political dealings, or revert to theories of ethnicity, identity, and nationalism to explain their political life-worlds, perhaps assuming that they turned themselves into the standardised, culturally-cleansed protagonists of what Badiou calls sarcastically 'the good little democrat's handbook' (Badiou 2010: 7).

To analyse democratic representation anthropologically, I begin with Naga 'traditional' political theory and practice; its sociality and political morals shape, in a transformed and contested way, the contemporary form and meaning of democratic representation in Nagaland. I then argue that the particular history and manifestation of Nagaland state, which is made up of small but richly-endowed constituencies, enables the fertile reinvigoration of a pre-existing politics of 'providing'. In subsequent sections, I illustrate these changing continuities ethnographically by detailing and discussing what I variously call 'kitchen politics', 'the MLA (member of the Legislative Assembly) handbook', 'chief-guest culture', and a vigorous 'politics of portfolios'. In all this, I note a dialectical relationship between post-statehood democracy and governance, and the predispositions, penchants and prejudices of home-grown Naga formulations of 'the political'. The upshot is a contemporary democratic sociality and structure of political morals and expectations that are at once historically traceable and culturally contested, but also scripted and evaluated afresh.

THE MORALS AND MERITS OF LEADERSHIP IN THE PRE-STATE NAGA 'VILLAGE REPUBLIC'

'This is Z. Yhobu', Athe explains, pointing towards a monolith, one among many erected in and around Phugwumi. Z. Yhobu is long deceased, but

Athe knows of him because he was a feast-giver in his time: 'He was a successful farmer. A man of wealth. For several times he feasted our villagers. His voice was heard loudly'. During the feast-giver's lifetime, the monolith had been 'pulled' as a testimony to his generosity and the elevated social standing that came with dispensing one's wealth in the form of successive feasts (*zhotho müza*), an elaborate and ritualised social institution known in anthropological annals as the Naga 'feast of merit.'

Traditionally among Nagas, wealth by and of itself had little value; one absolved or exonerated oneself of being rich by distributing one's moveable wealth (derived from a person's skill and stamina in agriculture) through feasting others; in that way, a person accumulated 'merit and status in this world and the next' (Mills 1935: 134). Besides monoliths, specifically embroidered shawls (*thüpükhü*) and house decorations materially symbolised a person's increasing eminence. Touring an Eastern Angami (now Chakhesang) village in the 1930s,[5] Fürer-Haimendorf (1939: 9) observed:

> Crossed barge boards rose from the gables of one of the houses, like the enormous antlers of some proud stag. Proud, too, must have been the owner of these wooden horns, for they showed that he had given several of those expensive Feasts of Merit whereby the Naga rises in social prestige and in the esteem of his neighbours.

In its functioning and values, the Naga feast of merit offers a view into the substance of Naga 'moral society',[6] and the place of social hierarchy in it. While Naga political structures and sentiments varied in form and in the details of their social institutions, two dominant features of their political organisation and ideology were often highlighted by colonial officials: 1) the village is the locus of 'the political'; and 2) most of these 'village republics' operate without a permanent political hierarchy. In the 1920s, the British colonial official Mills wrote: 'The commonest system of traditional governance is that there are no real chiefs at all, and the tendency is for the villagers to be run by such people as have wealth and influence and can shout loudly' (Mills 1926: 28). This was evidently more true of the Angami and Chakhesang tribes, which early colonial officers described as possessing the 'purest democracy' (Butler cited in Hutton 1921a: 143) compared to the more hierarchically inclined Sema and Konyak Nagas.

Phugwumi was a political community without a permanent headman or chief. What this meant, in practice, is that every villager was allowed to 'shout' his opinions and propose political resolutions. That said, the resonance of a man's political voice (women remained largely 'politically domesticated') was conditional on the virtues and merits he had accumulated during his lifetime. The dispensing of wealth through becoming a feast-giver was a prime path to amplify one's political voice, although acts of bravery carried out by protecting and ritually fertilising the village by bringing in the 'soul matter' (Hutton 1928: 403) that resides in decapitated enemy heads, and the wisdom that comes with age,[7] could also augment one's standing. It must be noted here that, regardless of how 'loud' a person's political voice was inside the village, it became considerably muted outside village territory as one's 'own people' usually ended at the 'village gates'.

This culturalist link between wealth and political voice remained subject to the wealthy individual acting as a repostiry of generosity and a material provider of social life. For an ambitious villager, spreading generosity was not just a moral imperative; it was a foundational act that produced and communicated social and political hierarchies. This normative logic also permeated the otherwise hereditary kingship system of the Konyak Nagas:

> At a ritual level, if a village did not prosper, the Ang (king) might be held to blame, just as he was also held responsible for the village's prosperity. If his crops failed he would be unable to give the feasts that symbolized, and to some extent brought about, his power (Jacobs et al 1990: 70).

This working and inner-logic of leadership in the village polity – at once communitarian and transactional – was emphasised by Hokishe Sema (1986: 168), Nagaland's third chief minister, who characterised village leaders thus:

> The rulers have some personal distinction acquired by them through their performances of sacrifices and good judgments. They also have great economic power and their capacity to help the poor and the needy in the village is greatly appreciated. They provide food, shelter, and clothing for the needy in an emergency. It is a great shame for the rulers if their subjects go to other villages for food. It is the duty of these rulers to ensure the security and welfare of their subjects.

Such cultural proclivities to provide were reiterated in the aftermath of British rule by A.Z. Phizo, president of the Naga National Council (NNC), which resisted the Nagas being enfolded into independent India: 'We consider as a privilege to be of service to others which our culture has given the expression we call *mhoso*–to excel (*mho*, overhead; *so*, touch)' (Phizo 1951).

The next section discusses the specificities of Nagaland state and governance, which has worked to enable (albeit unintentionally so) the re-enactment of 'traditional' Naga political practices and principles in a new democratic arena.

POST-STATEHOOD GOVERNANCE IN NAGALAND

What sets democratic institutions in Nagaland apart from those in most of India is the armed conflict that resulted from the NNC, and later the National Socialist Council of Nagalim (NSCN), resisting and then rebelling against the Nagas' incorporation into post-colonial India from the 1950s onwards. As part of this struggle, India's first two general elections (1952 and 1957) were boycotted locally. It was only after the (albeit contested) creation of Nagaland state in 1963 that elections became regular and participatory. Since then, insurgency and counter-insurgency, and, later, from 1997 onwards, a volatile ceasefire, have coexisted with the 'democratic process'. Much still needs to be understood about the interplay between Indian democracy and the politics of Naga insurgency, but here I confine my discussion to two corollaries of the Indo–Naga conflict that have shaped democratic politics and ideas of democratic representation locally, namely comparatively small constituencies and a lucrative political economy of state largesse.

After several devastating years of violent, but inconclusive, clashes between the Indian army and Naga insurgents, and immense suffering (Iralu 2000), India's central government enacted Nagaland state in 1963, envisaged as a political compromise to the Naga demand for independence. In size and institutional and material profile, this new state departed from Indian standards. As a former governor of Assam recalled:

> There were many efforts to pacify the Nagas and through concessions in 1963, the state of Nagaland was created. This state was for a population of barely 500,000—less than the population of many colonies in Delhi, and yet all the trappings that go with full statehood, a legislature, a cabinet, Chief-Minister and later even Governor, went with this new status (Sinha 2001).

The already undersized state (India's smallest at the time) was divided into sixty constituencies, making Nagaland constituencies miniscule compared to most in India; in fact, they are so small that politicians know most of their voters (and opponents) personally.[8] Nagaland constituencies actually shrank further because the local unit of voting is seldom the 'autonomous individual', but strongly revolves around social networks of households, clans, and villages. Consequently, constituencies in Nagaland have been won and lost by a few handfuls of votes, making electoral politics at the fringe of the world's largest democracy a politics of small numbers.

But while Nagaland constituencies are small, they are exceptionally richly endowed. With Naga militants rejecting the legitimacy of Nagaland state, and with the struggle for Naga independence escalating (Dev 1988:9), the central government resorted to offering state largesse, almost instantly elevating Nagaland to the highest recipient of 'per capita expenditure of federal funds for any state in India' (Means 1971: 1016), a status it retained for decades (1993: 176), as well as accumulating 'India's highest ratio of government servants to population' (*Nagaland Post* 22-04-2016). Rather than a technical response to Nagaland's purported economic 'backwardness', this largesse was first and foremost a politically-driven process aimed at expanding state infrastructure in, and the 'nationalizing' (Baruah 2003) of, contested space by tying local livelihoods and social imagination to the Indian state. As Misra notes: 'The Centre started pumping in massive sums of money in a clear effort to wean away sections of the Naga people from the politics of insurgency' (Misra 2004: 53).

The 'overflow of cash and funds' (Nibedon 1978: 201), the 'floodgate of money' (singh 2004: 85) available via the Indian state's commitment to take 'upon itself to provide everything, including employment' (Jamir 2002: 4), means that most Nagas can imagine accessing and influencing their state's many resources. The political imperative behind these post-statehood 'frequently floating easy monies', however, came at the expense of accountability (Sanyu 2003: 442) and, with popular support for Naga independence continuing, government employment and state largesse were soon clouded by a certain ambivalence, making them things to be exploited (see Jamir 2000; Hazarika 2011; Maitra 2011) rather than something that represents the 'public good' and that should benefit the people.[9]

While these 'excess monies' co-opted many, they 'disturbed the rhythm of Naga tribal production' (Sanyu 2013: 442) and created a 'highly corrupt politician-bureaucrat combine' (Misra 2004: 54). They also vastly inflated the clout of elected politicians who, after Nagaland statehood, presided over and capitalised on these state resources. Following the habits of India's political class (Wade 1985), they regularly overruled and politicised bureaucratic programmes and procedures for electoral purposes. But while post-statehood governance was soon mired in narratives of corruption, Naga politicians became simultaneously known – and praised by their electors – for appropriating and redirecting government employment and state resources to their respective clans, villages, and tribes (usually in that order of priority). The arrival of formal democratic institutions, then, did not result, in Geertzian parlance, in an 'integrative revolution' that replaced the affective pull of 'primordial' attachments and loyalties with the virtues of 'civil sentiments' (Geertz 1973). According to Jimomi: '[A minister] forget[s] that he is the minister of Nagaland, and he becomes the minister of his own constituency, minister of his own tribe, becomes the minister of his own clan' (Jimomi 2009: 399).

What do these factors combined – a politics of small numbers, sustained state largesse, and the reinvigoration of 'primordial pulls' – mean for the form democratic representation takes locally? For one thing, it means animated competition between elected politicians over their discretionary allocation of government employment and state resources to their own kin, followers, and constituents. To be sure, Naga electors have a very sectional understanding of the state and expect their politicians to substitute the 'public good' (the idea that one *must* work for the common good, Shah (2009: 295) remarks in a different context, is, of course, itself part of a specific moral agenda) with personally-directed generosity, the very possibility of which is enabled by the small numbers of voters in each constituency. The result is that democratic representation in Nagaland is something of a lucrative 'politics of the belly' (Bayart 1993), tailored to a 'moral society' (Tanabe 2007) that, as discussed in the previous section, has long associated munificence with social ascendency and 'political voice'.

The next sections will illustrate ethnographically what this fusion of past political norms with the particularities of post-statehood governance means for the local form and meaning of democratic representation.

'KITCHEN POLITICS' AND THE MORAL MARKET FOR VOTES

In the weeks leading up to polling day, Phugwumi is a flurry of political activity. Talk about politics inundates the village's social landscape, while the constituency's four rival candidates (two of whom hail from Phugwumi) open camps and supply meat, rice, vegetables, and (more discreetly) liquor. In line with past practice, the ability to feast villagers, and lavishly at that, produces merit, social pre-eminence, and political voice, cultural ingredients of leadership adjuged so crucial that even decrees against 'feeding voters' by India's Election Commission cannot banish these election feasts.[10]

However, in Phugwumi's communitarian ethos, the sum of one's wealth is closely tied to the amount of generosity one is expected to dispense. If, earlier, feasting was the ultimate embodiment of both wealth and generosity, the founding of Nagaland state, its longstanding political economy of largesse, and the widely-suspected self-enrichment of politicians altered and inflated sources of wealth, so that in the new democratic arena the social redistribution of monies and material goods are also plugged into the equation.

Contrary to the noisy bustle of India's urban politics, its massive, sweaty rallies, agitated processions, brash sloganeering, and its tens of thousands voters per constituency, in Pugwumi, and rural Nagaland more widely, electoral politics assumes a much more intimate character. Party workers I spoke to in the wake of polling day calculated that securing the votes of roughly four hundred households sufficed to capture a constituency, a number small enough for politicians, assisted by their aides, to meet personally through 'house-visits'. Given that members of the same household rarely cast their votes differently, among Chakhesang Nagas 'the household' is both the unit and focus of electoral politics. As polling day drew closer, the politicians' expensive vehicles could often be seen parked in Phugwumi. Politicians and their aides went door to door, and in the relative seclusion of (usually) the kitchen, they cemented social bonds and offered incentives in return for the household's exclusive political loyalty. Phugwumi households, in turn, looked to the visiting politicians for the material salvation they associate with access to, and ownership of, Nagaland state, knowing well that it is ultimately elected politicians – not career bureaucrats, or impersonal rational-legal policies – who arbitrate the distribution of state resources.

But even as most villagers readily put their votes 'up for sale', for a household to receive a politician was not just a pretext for vulgar material gratification; a house-visit also connoted a social ritual in which politicians recognised social bonds, listened attentively to the household's trials and tribulations, and discussed ways in which they could help. Proposals were always tailor-made (votes are usually not sold at a fixed price), and variously included the promise of government employment for a household member, gifts, the settling of pending bills, the assurance of a subsidy or (a personalised) development scheme, and often instant cash. Put differently, it was 'kitchen-politics', or the link between a household's collective vote and a politician's ability to satisfy the material needs and desires of its members, not, say, party politics, ideology or state-wide political visions, that etched itself into the core of village electoral politics. Whatever the amount paid, or future promises made, a successful house-visit functioned as a prototypical political contract, and no household wanted to be known for 'trading' its votes to more than one politician.

The deals agreed upon were not just 'transactional', but the outcome of lengthy and empathethic conversations. A politician in a hurry, dismissive of the household's problems, lacking modesty ('being simple'), or ignoring cultural etiquette, was readily ridiculed as self-absorbed and proud, and criticised for his lack of 'ideology'. For instance, when Athe's son died prematurely in hospital, a politician, on whose behalf Athe had campaigned, offered to pay the medical bills, and asked Athe to travel to the state capital of Kohima to collect the money. The sum offered was substantial, but Athe never went to collect it. 'I am an old man', he said. 'He may be a minister, but in age he has to address me as his "father". How can I go to his house to collect money from him as though I am his son?'

The pricing of votes was, in part, the outcome of supply and demand, yet several (non-market) factors operated in determining the cost of votes. For one thing, social proximity mattered, and while no aspirant MLA could escape his test of political worth through a display of generosity, if a candidate was a clan member or fellow villager, the household was expected — and certainly morally appealed to — to trust the candidate's future capacity to provide, rather than insisting on hefty 'pre-paid' incentives. This telecom-style language of 'pre-paid' and 'post-paid' incentives was adopted by party workers when discussing the kinds of deals struck with particular households. However, it also operated as a critique of villagers' (excessive) demands. Nebo, an aide to a candidate from Phugwumi, expressed his disappointment over the many 'pre-paid' demands the villagers made. He told me:

> Of course, it is their right to expect some pre-paid, but they should consider him 'the politician' as a fellow villager. If our villagers demand less, he can spend more in other villages, where votes are more expensive (the absence of close social bonds inflating the price of votes). But once he is elected he will surely bring many government jobs and development schemes to our villagers. In that case, post-paid benefits will be very high.

So far, the popular expectation that aspiring politicians would provide and be responsible for the material welfare of people who were 'their own' appeared to be a rather straightforward re-mapping of Nagas' 'traditional' village-based political theory and practice. However, many Nagas also insisted that the arrival of formal democratic institutions and competitive elections had been corrosive of past conceptions of community and its communitarian essence, while unfavourable comparisons were regularly drawn between the perceived sacrificial and selfless character of past village leaders and the unscrupulous and self-seeking motivations of present-day politicians, who many in Phugwumi accused of privileging their personal material welfare and political survival over the needs of the village community. Such evaluations complicated the relationships between villagers and politicians.

Akho was a political aide to the sitting MLA who entrusted him with conducting house-visits in Phugwumi. This both stressed and exhausted Akho. 'Our villagers are becoming greedier and stubborn', he often lamented. 'They hand me lists of expenditures: medical treatment, admission fees, the repayment of loans, and what not, and expect my boss (as he refers to his politician) to settle these'. It frustrated Akho:

> I try to make them understand that my boss contests on an NPF ticket 'Naga People's Front, the ruling party', and that if we vote him in once again his seniority will guarantee him a plump portfolio. During his previous tenure my boss could not help many villagers because he was not given his own department, but if he wins again this is certain to change. But it is hard to convince villagers nowadays. They say: 'How I am going to feed my children with a party-ticket? A piece of paper won't fill their stomachs. If you give us something now, then we will support you again'.

In Akho's view, things have changed in recent years:

> Democracy has made our villagers individualistic. Everyone wants to be a political player during elections, even poor farmers become stubborn and have many demands. Since democracy is all about numbers, we must give them equal importance. We must make them feel that their votes carry value. If we offer them money, they feel respected.

Akho's narrative resonated with that of Vezo, who resided in the same *khel* (village ward) as I did. 'Perhaps they think my votes are not important', he told me when I inquired into his household's political leanings. 'Polling Day is just a few days away but not a single politician has come to my house yet. Whoever visits my house now, I will give him my votes'. Bypassed by a politician, a 'swing household' like Vezo's resented not only the prospect of missing out on material inducements, but also their lack of social recognition.

In private, Akho explained the swelling demands of villagers as evidence of their rising insularity and as being counter-productive to 'good governance'. He painted a vicious cycle in which his 'boss', once in office, had to make good on his election expenses, leading to both corruption and an inability to keep his 'post-paid' promises. Most Phugwumi villagers adopted a different stance, however; to them, feasts, gifts, and generosity have long been culturalist synonyms for political leadership. At the same time, post-statehood experience told them that – unlike past village leaders – elected politicians regularly forgot their commitments and broke their promises; once in office, they reserved state benefits for their voters alone (as opposed to the 'community-mindset' pre-state village leaders were remembered for). In this context, villagers' insistence on 'pre-paid', or immediate, gratification, even if culturally endorsed, was also a circumstantial response in order to eliminate the risk of a politician defaulting on his 'post-paid' assurances, and to secure material benefits irrespective of whether the politician they aligned themselves with won or lost on polling day.

The next section elaborates this final point by shifting the focus from electoral politics to post-election modalities of governance.

THE MLA'S 'HANDBOOK OF GOVERNANCE'

According to Abrams (1988: 82), the state is 'the mask which prevents our seeing political practice as it is'. In Nagaland, it is the discourse and praxis of state-led development that masks what Witsoe (2013: 68) aptly called in Bihar 'democratic networks of governance'. Such networks are not democratic in a liberal sense, but refer to 'networks of influence based above all on electoral considerations'. Witsoe explains that in densely-populated Bihar, these networks revolve around politicians, party workers, 'musclemen', and political brokers with a proven record in securing votes. In Nagaland's significantly smaller constituencies, such democratic networks are more intimate and extend deep into villages and households.

Nagaland's state machinery, a retired Naga bureaucrat reflected, is fundamentally 'politically driven', with 'political bosses' interfering in all 'government processes' (K. Sema 2015: 227). Government offices and officers act on what is locally and euphemistically known as politicians' 'recommendations', and in Phugwumi, everyone knows that it is hard, often impossible, to secure government employment, a development scheme, or a state contract without the backing of the constituency's MLA.

It is this political principle that explains the actively non-secret nature of local voting. Not only are Phugwumi villagers never secretive about who they voted for, but some preferred to publish their political loyalties in local dailies for posterity and for everyone to know (Wouters 2014). In

Nagaland's often informal, grey, or black markets for state resources, it is one's vote that is the currency for 'recommendations' and so a ticket to future generosity. Not disclosing one's vote, thus, amounts to not voting at all. For their part, politicians in the Phugwumi constituency instruct their aides to maintain village-wise registers that list the households that pledged their votes. It is these lists that, after elections, transform into the MLA's 'handbook of governance'. If, according to Weber (1978: 22), 'bureaucratic administration means fundamentally domination through knowledge', across Nagaland, this knowledge is rarely a reflection of any standardised, rational–legal, or impersonal gathering of data concerning the citizenry, but is based on an MLA's knowledge of who voted for or against him.

While classic anthropology teaches the cohesive force of reciprocity (Mauss 1966), in Nagaland norms of political reciprocity also appear divisive. In the aftermath of the 2013 state elections, in a constituency close to Phugwumi, a victorious politician reportedly promised – during a thanksgiving feast he hosted for his supporters – that 'he would not accept any member from other political parties for the next four years but [would] purchase them in the fifth [election] year if needed' (cited in K. Hoshi 2014). In the local political lexicon, this promise was easily understood by his voters as his pledge to reserve state benefits for his supporters alone. Whoever had voted against him, he now made clear, would have not just lost on polling day, but would have to prepare themselves for a prolonged spell of state marginalisation.

But whereas the denial of state resources communicated 'political punishment', acts of post-electoral generosity and the fulfilment of personal promises amplified a politician's reputation (Piliavsky 2014a: 19). Nagaland politicians, however, often defaulted on the personal promises they made during the election period, and these failures stirred emotions of resentment and revenge on the part of Naga villagers. When Alem learned that he had been shortlisted for a final interview for induction into the Nagaland police, he contacted the constituency's MLA, in whose support he had rallied during the previous election, anticipating his 'recommendation'. But the MLA only said: 'May God bless you in your endeavours'. Alem failed the interview and subsequently accused the MLA of corruption and of being ideologically misguided, and was seen campaigning against him during the 2013 elections. If, across India, moods of 'anti-incumbency' are explained as one of the costs of ruling, in the micro-politics of Nagaland's small constituencies, frequently-fluctuating political allegiances do not reflect political or ideological turnarounds, but often result from personal promises and expectations going unfulfilled.

AN INTERLUDE: 'CHIEF GUEST CULTURE'

In January 2013, Phugwumi hosted a week-long sports meeting in which nearby villages competed. Organising it, and organising it well, was a matter of village prestige. Of all the preparations – including accommodation for visiting teams, food and clearing the playing-field – most energy went into the opening ceremony, for which invitations were dispatched to a number of dignitaries. The most anticipated guest, referred to by the honorific 'chief guest', was a local MLA who was invited to ceremonially declare the games open. On the opening day, villagers and participating teams welcomed the MLA with great fanfare, adorning him with a shawl and a traditional spear, and led him to an elevated platform from where he could enjoy cultural performances, songs, and dances performed in his honour. No sooner had the MLA left, however, than news spread about the monetary donation he had made to both the organising committee and the individual teams. The organisers had counted on this donation (even including it in their budget for the event) and received it thankfully. The MLA had been generous.

Across Nagaland, the inclusion of a 'chief guest' is integral to public functions, be they jubilees, cultural shows or sports events. I attended many such events, and each time, the adorning and praising of the chief guest (most often a politician) was accompanied by the expectation of a generous donation towards the financing of the event. One Nagaland MLA disclosed to a newspaper, on the condition of anonymity, that every year he spent not less than '50 lakh (5 million rupees) in such donations'. The same report described how the (then) chief minister 'has been extremely generous to his district and his constituency, where he had contributes crores (tens of millions) of rupees as chief guest in the past nine years' (*The Telegraph*, 30-01-2012).

Crusaders for 'good governance' object and link the thriving 'chief guest culture' to political corruption because no elected politician has an budget earmarked for such donations. Phugwumi villagers reasoned differently, however. To them, the MLA's generous contribution towards the sports meeting was evidence of his upright ideology and demonstrated his capacity to provide. Here we enter a liminal space between so-called corruption and popular politics, in which universalistic and normative projections of 'transparent' democratic representatives exerting 'good governance' meet their opposite in the moral expectations voters have of them. Moreover, in staging an event in which a politician absolved himself of some of his material riches through public redistribution, and in doing so was adorned and witnessed a rise in his social status, do we not discern the reappearance of some of the merit and morals that shaped the earlier 'feast of merit'?

WHO WANTS TO BE THE SPEAKER?

A few hours after the swearing-in ceremony of Nagaland's new government in 2013, led by the NPF, its central party office was vandalised. The perpetuators were some of the NPF's own party workers. They then marched to the residence of the chief minister, whose gates they barricaded, promising to stay put until their demands for a more 'plump' portfolio for their constituency's MLA was honoured. 'Plump', a term locally used, refers to a government department that generates plenty of job placements, state contracts, development schemes, subsidies and other possible state benefits, and which the presiding politician is expected – by his electors – to redirect towards his constituency as far as possible.

Similar disgruntlement was voiced across the state. For instance, the NPF party unit of Kiphire District, none of whose democratic representatives was given an influential cabinet berth, publicly wondered how the party could so neglect them. They pleaded with the chief minister to reconsider (*Nagaland Post*, 08-03-2013). Further east, the Khiamniungan Tribal Council also felt 'deeply hurt' that a Khiamniungan politician, a three-time MLA, had not been given a cabinet position (*Morung Express*, 07-03-2013).

In a desperate attempt to defuse the situation, the NPF's leadership issued a statement, saying 'No portfolio should be tagged as small or big, lucrative or barren.' However, it then acknowledged voters' sensibilities by stressing that the extent to which an MLA could help his constituents was subject to his own 'creativity, influencing power, fund raising acumen and administrative ability' (*Morung Express*, 08-03-2013). But Naga villagers knew this was true only to an extent, and that those politicians who held a 'plump' portfolio were invariably better placed to provide. This resulted, in the post-statehood period, in an agitated politics of portfolios, aided by an effervescent politics of defection; by the 1970s, a 'politics of defection was the order of the day' (Zhimomi 2004: 124) and remained in 'full swing' during the 1980s, eventually including 'almost all Naga politicians' (Murry 2007: 65). The then Nagaland governor lamented:

> Those who are already Ministers wanted so-called better portfolios and those who were MLAs wanted to be ministers.... Why is it that the Government changes so frequently in

> Nagaland, that is, with average tenure of about two years and some with as little as few days? People elect MLAs on the basis of [a] party's ideologies, objectives and programmes, and the MLAs defect and re-defect for personal aggrandizement, how can stability be achieved in any government? (cited in Zhimomi 2004: 127)

Evaluated against home-grown Naga political theory, the governor's reasoning was evidently ill-informed because, for most Naga electors, 'party ideologies, objectives and programmes' were the near-obligatory humdrum behind which they knew actual politics operated. Despite the noted political scientist Kaviraj (1984: 239) asserting that political defection is 'morally execrable' because it 'undermines the reliance on the party system as a reliable register of political attitudes', for Naga politicians and electors alike, such defections – if they promise more access to state resources – were not judged as 'morally execrable' but as political and moral imperatives.

It was the perpetual political anxiety of politicians that they would not be able to provide that, in the aftermath of the 2013 elections, led to another political crisis. Not a single senior politician was willing to commit to becoming speaker, yet without a speaker it was impossible to form a new government. While honourable, the position of speaker was not lucrative because he had no direct access to government departments, thus preventing him from offering government employment or state benefits to his constituents, a potential draw-back upon his political life expectancy. Hectic consultations ensued, and the crisis was eventually defused – so it was understood and rumoured in and around Kohima – by the party leadership promising an annual lump sum to the speaker for him to spend on his constituents.

CONCLUSION

Whereas vote-buying, clientelism, and corruption are today popularly associated with the democratic habitats of (many) post-colonial societies, until the middle of the nineteenth century the exchange of cash, feasts, and services for votes was also integral to democratic politics in 'the West'. During elections in the 1830s in Liverpool in Britain, 'the bribery was wholesale...the average price of a vote was fifteen pounds' (Seymour 1915: 173). In Leicester, 'as soon as the canvass began, public houses were opened by each party in the various villages near the borough. The voters were collected as soon as possible, generally locked up until the polling, and, according to an election agent, "pretty well corned"' (ibid.: 173). Clientelism, too, was commonplace:

> At Coventry the use of Bablake Hospital was granted only to those electors who had voted in the interest of the Liberal Cooperation which controlled it. If an impecunious voter applied for assistance from a poor-law board, instead of retailing the size of his family and the misfortune which had fallen upon his work, he found it more worthwhile to begin his plea by stating the colour of his politics (ibid.: 179).

However, as the Victorian age drew to a close, various reforms acts and anti-corruption legislation, but also the larger sizes of constituencies, the expansion of the electoral franchise, the rising affluence of voters, and moral makeovers put an end to most instances of vote-buying and clientelism (Seymour 1915: 179).

Some Naga voices now call for similar reforms: '*Dzieyha ze mu khrü cuha kephouma zo*' ('Selling and buying of votes is a sin'), a banner in Phugwumi's church premises proclaimed. The banner was part of a statewide clean election campaign launched by the locally commanding Nagaland Baptist Church Council (NBCC). 'I have a dream', a Phugwumi ex-pastor told me. 'That one day a poor man from this village can contest an election and win'. For most villagers, however, as this essay illustrates, this dream amounts to an ontological nightmare as the idea of a 'poor leader' unable to dispense generosity contravenes the very essence of Naga conceptions of what makes it worthwhile to have political leaders in the first place.

If, at the end of this essay, Naga versions of democratic representation and politics seem dissolute and corrupt, they are, I hope, no longer primarily judged as immoral because they deviate from the norms of 'liberal democracy', but because contemporary politics and politicians have depreciated the Naga moral visions of a good and meaningful political life. Earlier, the accrual of wealth, and its generous communitarian distribution, translated into social ascendency and political voice, but more influence and power did not usually lead to more wealth because the moral obligations of recurrent feasting and generosity led to the continuous social redistribution of wealth. It was this closed cycle of power and wealth that was cracked open by the enactment of Nagaland state. In the post-statehood period, the political leaders' source of wealth and generosity changed from the hardship of agriculture to the 'easy money' available through the Nagaland specifics of politically-driven state largesse. However, it is not considered equally virtuous to reap riches without toil and sweat, and if earlier the dispensing of wealth generated virtue and wealth, many in Phugwumi today are not sure whether this cultural correlation applies equally to the wealth of politicians, which they understand is acquired instantly, not painstakingly.

Democratic representation in Nagaland fails too because the personal profits politicians accrue are held to greatly surpass their levels of generosity, thus subverting the earlier moral and material logic of humble and selfless leadership. This contemporary cultural dissonance is only exacerbated by the increasingly-partial and politically-motivated nature of politicians' generosity, which they direct no longer to the village community as a whole, but reserve for their supporters. By contrast, Fürer-Haimendorf (1939: 47) observed how, in the past, 'the wealth of the ambitious was employed to provide food and enjoyment for the less prosperous members of the community, for at a Feast of Merit there was meat, rice, and rice-beer, for every man, woman, and child in the village.' In displaying partiality in governance, Naga politicians now cause divisions and promote competitive self-advancement and individualism over communal welfare. It is in such discrepancies between the normative logic of villagers' understanding of political leadership, and the behaviour and motivations of post-statehood politicians, that the iniquities of democratic representation lie.

'Grand concepts of political science', Bayart (1989: 226) wrote, 'are misleading.' Democratic representation is one such grand concept, but it misleads because in its conventional, political-science usage, its forms and moral substance are assumed *a priori* and so embody the universalisation of a particular and provincial moral and political sense. Fortunately, anthropology is now taking steps to reclaim its earlier expertise in the study of politics to unsettle these universalistic projections. If two decades ago, Spencer diagnosed an 'excess of certainty' in political anthropology (Spencer 1997: 13), the recent 'vernacular turn' in the study of South Asian politics, including the idea of democratic representation, is now shaping a promising body of creative analysis that is paving the way for a much fuller and richer understanding of existing democratic life-worlds. This essay adds to this discussion by postulating and illustrating that the question 'what makes a good politician?' is as much a problem of ethnography and anthropology as it is of liberal political heuristics.

11

THE FIELDWORKER IMAGINED AMONG THE NAGAS

Autoethnography has come to mean many things. For its critics, its writings are near narcissistic reflections as they turn attention from the imperative 'other' to the self-gratifying 'self.' Geertz (1988:97) derides such ethnography as 'author saturated texts', unsolicited explorations of the 'self' through a 'detour of the other', even though he readily accepted that 'what we call our data are really our own construction of other people's construction of what they and their compatriots are up to' (Geertz cited in Spencer 1985: 148). For others autoethnography involves 'confessional tales' (Van Maanen 1988), of which examples include *Tristes Tropiques* (Levi-Strauss 1961), *The Savage and the Innocent* (Maybury-Lewis 1965), *Return to Laughter* (Bohannan 1954), *Reflections on Fieldwork in Morocco* (Rabinow 1977), *Tuhami: Portrait of a Moroccan* (Crapanzano 1980) and *The Headman and I* (Dumont 1991) and which is seen as a necessary response to – although some of these bio-confessional critiques well preceded – the so-called 'crisis of representation' (Clifford and Marcus 1986) that came to unsettle the anthropological world from the mid-eighties onward.

Gone, the fiercest of post-modernists say, are the days of 'scientific' and universalistic projections of *Elementary Structures of Kinship* (Levi-Strauss 1949), the double necessity of symbolism inherent to cultures everywhere as elucidated in Needham's (1978) methodological *Symbolic Classification*, or, disgracefully so, the ethnographic authority of Evans-Pritchard (Rosaldo 1986). Evans-Pritchard's writing, Rosaldo decries, lacks accountability to the British colonial political context in which he was working, while, worse still, his fieldwork was financed by the Anglo-Egyptian colonial government, making Evans-Pritchard an imperialist of sorts, or so Rosaldo (1986) conceives.

A view more balanced holds that autoethnography promotes the inclusion of subjectivity, emotionality, and reflexivity in ethnographic texts because they, in their final evaluation, can never be completely neutral, impersonal, or value free. 'The writing and reading of ethnography are overdetermined by forces ultimately beyond the control of either an author or an interpretive community. These contingencies – of language, rhetoric, power and history – must now be openly confronted in the process of writing', Clifford (1986: 25) insists. But if autoethnography is one of the responses to this critique, in another guise autoethnography is the outcome of a post-colonial trend in which more and more anthropologists opt to study their own communities, combining the roles of 'anthropologist' and 'native' (Marak 2015). If studying one's own culture may have become a feat of modern Indian anthropology and sociology, Srinivas went further still and towards the end of his career and life he argued for a 'sociology of the self':

> It is my plea that the movement from studying one's own culture or a niche in it, to studying oneself as an ethnographic field, is a natural one. In the west, anthropology started as a study of 'the other', generally a weaker, inferior and exploited 'other', but in India it has largely been a study of the self or the self in-the-other. And this should extend to include one's own life. 'Sociology of the Self' should be rich field given the diversities and unities which the members of Indian civilization are heir to (1998: xi)

However, as understood, and engaged with here, autoethnography is taken as a form of self-reflection that explores the ethnographer's personal experiences in the field to then analytically connect these not just to one's own positionality but also to the cultural, political, and historical contexts, meanings, and understandings in which one's fieldwork unfolds.

What follows, as a preliminary exercise, is a reflection on how some of the inhabitants of the Chakhesang and Chang Naga villages of Phugwumi and Noksen, located in the Naga uplands of India's Northeast, imagined me, the ethnographer residing among them. I will then link these assumptions and stereotypes to the historical experiences and circulating discourses the villagers had at their disposal to interpret the rather sudden arrival of a differently phenotyped 'foreigner.' Subjectivity rife of course, as what I am offering is my interpretation of the villagers' interpretation of who I was, and why I had come. That said, I hold that the ways villagers imagined my presence, at least initially, may tell us a thing or two about the historical and political context in which my ethnographic fieldwork unfolded.

Let's start with an opening vignette: fire in the village.

BUILDING RAPPORT: AN OPENING VIGNETTE

Skywards, upward curling, a broad column of smoke climbed from the middle of the village. Commotion flared at the church ground, located a little off the main village and where two newly-weds received handshakes and wishes, lavish pork, mithun and chicken dishes spread their aroma, and the local favorite wedding tune 'you're so beautiful in white' echoed from large sound-boxes. The church ground was filled with villagers, seated on colorful, plastic chairs or standing huddled in small groups; talking, laughing, eating. Weddings equated plenty of meat, enough reason for anyone to forgo their fields and chores for a few hours. I had arrived in the Chakhesang Naga village I call Phugwumi barely two weeks earlier and in good anthropological fashion I had crashed the wedding celebration, hoping to learn a thing or two about culture and kinship.

The previous week the village pastor had introduced me to his Baptist congregation – since most villagers were regular in attending Sunday service, the church, so the pastor reasoned, would be the best platform to announce my presence and intentions. From the pulpit, he told the villagers that I was an anthropologist, a depiction which mostly caused confused glances, raised eyebrows, and uncertain whispers. 'Anthropologists', the pastor then explained, 'study culture.' This made more sense to the villagers. 'You've come to the right place', I was told after the benediction had ended the service: 'We have lots of culture out here!' In spite of the pastor's friendly introduction, most villagers remained somewhat unsure about both my antecedents and intentions, a confusion probably only compounded by my manifold – and, to them, rather useless – inquiries into the minutia of their daily lives. 'This is not our culture', some objected when I tried venturing into the depths of kinship. 'You should study our shawls, dances, and especially our Sukrunyi festival. You will find our culture there.'

The column of smoke quickly thickened. The loud-speakers fell silent, as did, for a split-second, the wir-war of conversation and laughter. Then panic. Shouting, followed by villagers rushing back to the main village, the village youth running ahead. Phugwumi was compactly built, a labyrinth of houses, standing roof to roof. The perfect place for a fire to spread quickly. Over my shoulder, I glanced at the bridal-couple, their faces bewildered, shocked – an inauspicious collusion of events as an elderly woman concluded that evening. She had seen it all in her life. This marriage, she predicted, was going to be unfertile, unhappy, or both. I started running too, down the narrow jungle path and then up to the village, to the source of the smoke. A house had caught fire, right in the village's centre. The fire had already spread from the plaited bamboo walls of the kitchen to the roof and now threatened to jump over to nearby houses. Organised chaos. Buckets appearing in bulk, from everywhere, from nowhere. Screams and shouts. Water taps, near and far, switched open. Bodies rushing.

I discarded my notebook, caught hold of a grey, iron bucket, filled it at a tap hundred yards or so away and hurried with it to the burning house, joining the rush of all able-bodied men and women in the village. Fighting the fire was everybody's concern, collective action at its best. But water was ever scarce in the village and the pressure on the pipes low, as it was in most Naga hilltop villages. Mud was resorted to. Heap after heap thrown unto the fire. Half an hour later the fire was dead. The house had been beyond saving, but the fire had been successfully prevented from jumping over. My notebook was smeared with dirt, my clothes drenched, my face and hands dirtied with mud, as was everyone's.

Reflecting on the incident later, the fire in the village, my contribution (even if a very modest one) in helping to fight it came to denote my initial success in gaining local trust and building rapport; in its effect not dissimilar to the famous episode of the Geertz (1973) hiding in a Bali village – together with the villagers – from the police which had suddenly arrived to stop an illegal cock-fight. My soaked shirt, the dirt spread everywhere, it had perhaps communicated to the villagers that I was not a high-flying, self-absorbed 'outsider' who demanded to be treated differently, but that I was a simple student – like so many youths in the village were – who, his phenotypes apart, was perhaps not all that different.

While I was usually able to explain the purpose of my stay, throughout my two years residence in Nagaland, both among the Chakhesang and Chang Naga, and while crisscrossing the state, my presence often caused confusion and speculation at first, especially among elders in rural villages. In this essay, I will reflect on three different roles in which I was occasionally cast by villagers when we first met, and which carried narratives and explanations that made sense to them, even if they deviated widely from who I was, and from what I sought to achieve. The first ascribed role, but which admittedly occurred explicitly only in one instance, was that of a 'tax collector' and the resurgence of British rule. The interpretation most common, however, was that I had come as a missionary, another one in a long line of foreign evangelists who had spent long years, at times decades, introducing sin and salvation to Naga villagers. The third attributed identity was related to the protracted Indo-Naga conflict and portrayed me either as a spy – on part of a third country, or of one Naga faction or another – or, even more presumptuously, as an interlocutor sent by the British Government (While I am not, my face apparently can go for that of an Englishman) or the United Nations.

As we proceed, I will briefly contextualize these three assumptions about who I was, and why I had come. In terms of autoethnography, the framing by the villagers of my presence into different roles indicates how ethnographers are invariably cast into roles they have little influence on – and might need to mitigate to manage expectations – but which do tell us something about the history of a place, of past encounters between locals and (in my instance) with what often goes for the 'West' (as I will show, researchers on the Naga hailing from the Indian 'mainland' can be imagined rather differently). In the upshot, the villagers' imagination of the fieldworker reveals both some of the peoples' historical registers and present-day expectations, opinions, and concerns.

'I DON'T HAVE MONEY TO PAY TAXES!'

It was one of my first days in Phugwumi. The fire had not yet broken out. Haze was hanging low over the village when Neisalie, whom the Village Council had requested to show me around Phugwumi and who became a trusted friend, and I strolled into an open compound. Forked wooden posts rose from the roof of one of the houses, like the branched horns of a deer. It communicated, I was to learn, that this was the house of a feast-giver (or more likely of the progeny of a feast-giver as the advent of Christianity had led to the departure of feasts of merit);[1] the blessed abode of a man who had successfully transmuted his wealth into generosity, which had earned him status, standing, and, in a sense, eternity as feast-givers were fondly remembered in the village, even with the passing of generations. The doors were locked. 'Must be in the fields', Neisalie said. 'It is almost time to transplant paddy. Busy days.'

The house to the opposite was simpler; the walls a mixture of wood and bamboo, cut in long strings, painstakingly plaited, and capped by a tin-sheet roof, acquired through one of the countless and still counting development schemes directed to Nagaland. An elderly woman sat on her heels in front of the door, her back turned towards us, cleansing the day's rice from small stones and grains of sand. Neisalie greeted her in the distinctive local style of pointing out the activity a person is doing: 'Are you cleaning rice?' (Other frequently used greetings were 'are you eating?', 'are you sitting?', 'are you walking?'). She glanced over her shoulder and affirmed that she was indeed cleaning the rice. She smiled. That is, until she noticed me, upon which she unceremoniously discarded her work, muttered a few words to Neisalie and retreated into her house, not forgetting to bolt the door behind her.

Neisalie smiled.

'What happened?', I asked. 'Did I do something wrong?'

'No, no. Just some confusion', Neisalie responded. 'She thinks you are a British officer coming to collect taxes from her. She told me she is old and poor and doesn't have any money to give away.'

'She is illiterate and very old now', Neisalie continued. 'Maybe she has forgotten that the British left already many, many years ago.'

I had long been intrigued by the many semi-ethnographic accounts drawn up by colonial administrators-cum-anthropologists, and had recently published a critical re-reading of some of them (Wouters 2012). The last thing I had expected was to be mistaken for a colonial officer myself.

Among some village elders, memories of British days remained vivid. What was remembered was often idiosyncratic. Not necessarily the new policies introduced, the new laws enacted, or the courts installed. But instead the nose of Charles Pawsey (the last British District Commissioner of the then Naga Hills) which was compared to the size of a full-grown mango, the tinned fish colonial officers carried with them on tours and occasionally distributed ('nothing like the tinned fish our village shop sells today!', it was remarked), and they remembered that British officers always paid for the chickens they wanted for dinner when they stayed overnight in the 'British bungalow' built at the village's outskirts – 'much unlike the Japanese [referring to the Japanese invasion of the Naga Hills]. They stole our pigs, chickens, and rice, and ate it all right in front of us.' What was remembered, too, were British imposed taxes, in the form of an annual house-tax, and which the villagers had always resented, and had always tried evading.

While at the moment of initial contact, from the early decades of the 19th century onward, the British and Naga fought numerous battles – always unequal with British bullets perforating Naga shields, and always bloody – after the fall of the powerful Angami village of Khonoma in 1879, British presence was not just accepted as a *fait accompli* but came to be gradually appreciated by many, though certainly not all, Nagas. 'Our grandfather and fathers knew only the British', a retired *Dobashi* (interpreter) remarked on hearing about the impending British departure midway the 1940s. 'It is like losing a father. You cannot get used to a new one quickly... Hutton Sahib was our father. Mills Sahib was our father, Pawsey Sahib is our father.'[2]

When the British announced their upcoming withdrawal, many Nagas expressed confusion: 'Why are the British leaving? Are they afraid?', it was remarked. 'They defeated the Japs. The Hindus are mere women. Why are the British not driving them away? Under the British we were free and happy. We helped them all we could. Why are they deserting their friends? We will never listen to an Indian Raj.'[3] So accustomed had some Konyak Naga villages become to the presence of British officers that in the days after the 15th of August 1947 — when India had achieved her freedom — a group of Konyak leaders barged into the District Commissioner's bungalow in Mokokchung, then occupied by Bill Archer who was to remain the district's Sub-Divisional Officer for a few months into India's Independence. For six days, the Konyak delegation had marched, 'their matted hair pinned up in a bun.' 'Word had gone all round the Konyak Country', they said, 'that since August 15th the sahibs had ceased to exist.' This they did not desire, and they requested Bill Archer to stay. Although Bill Archer expressed his inability and regrets, the Konyaks had already thought of a solution of their own: '[they had] levied Rs 10 from each village "to buy a new sahib."'[4]

Far from romanticising British rule in the Naga Hills, or even from asserting that, in its final evaluation, they brought more good than harm, colonial officers had nevertheless gained a certain trust which most Nagas could not find in their 'Indian successors.' The officers posted to the Naga Hills after India's independence were met with suspicion, hostility even. Of Imdad Ali, who came to replace Pawsey, Rustomji (1971:79) was to write later:

> Imdad was a first class officer, but I am not sure whether he ever felt quite at home in the tense and unpredictable atmosphere of the Naga Hills... He told me of a Naga who made a point of brandishing a dagger at him every morning in his office and Imdad evidently apprehended that he would put it to more constructive use at night, as our house was surrounded after sunset by sentries sporting fixed bayonets, who shouted 'who goes there' if as much as a chicken crossed the road.

Even Jawaharlal Nehru knew about this, and with the British gone he remarked: 'fortunately or unfortunately the only administrative officers whom the Nagas trust are Anglo-Indians, and unfortunately we do not have enough Anglo-Indian administrative officers' (cited in Stracey 1968: 63).

Nagas refusal to 'listen to an Indian Raj' eventually culminated into the protracted Indo-Naga conflict, of which much has been written (e.g. Horam 1988; L. Ao 2002), and of which more in the next section. The Indo-Naga struggle posed a challenge for an 'Indian' anthropologist I once met in Kohima and who complained that most villagers refused to talk to him. They did not trust his antecedents, found his questions suspicious, and thought of him as a progeny of the Indian Armed Forces which, especially in the decades immediately following India's independence, had brought havoc and misery to the Naga Hills (Iralu 2002). While both he and I had nothing to do, or were even remotely connected, to past colonial officers or Indian soldiers, the Nagas' differential historical experiences of both influenced our positionality in the field in different ways, perceptions which, trying as we might, could not be mitigated easily.

'ANY UPDATES ON THE PEACE NEGOTIATIONS?'

Despite guesses that he was at least a centenarian, every time his weakening limps permitted Abi would passionately throw his hands in the air and move his body in worship during the weekly Sunday service held in the Noksen Town Baptist Church. Abi was an ardent Christian, knew chunks of the Bible and many hymns by heart, and never wavered to express his devotion out loud. Noksen village, of which Noksen town was an off-shoot, was the locale of my second fieldwork and during my stay I interacted several times with Abi. 'I knew about your coming', he told me when we first met. 'I saw you in my dreams.'

Abi's life-story was one fraught with hardship and experiences of brutal violence, both as its executor and recipient. For long years, he had served in the Naga Army, contributing to the Naga National Council's struggle for Naga independence. Long and arduous marches he had made. One of them had brought him to the border of (then) East-Pakistan where he and his comrades had to undergo months of guerrilla training. That is, if not they were attacked and scattered by a battalion of the Indian Army. Abi survived the encounter. Many of his compatriots did not. While his multiple, often fierce, often lethal, past encounters with Indian troops he now rationalized as part of his call to duty, what he regretted, in the autumn of his life, were the attacks on those Naga villages which defied the NNC and collaborated with the Indian Army. 'We meted out punishments. Heavy punishments. It was often bloody', he told me one day. 'It should not have happened. They were Nagas. Our own brothers.'

Even though Abi had resigned from the NNC decades ago, he remained a staunch Naga nationalist. He refused to vote, in what he called 'Indian Elections', and even though his body was weakening and he had grown nearly deaf, he remained convinced that he would live to see Nagaland achieve its independence. His dreams, in which he had reportedly seen me, were a reflection of this conviction. Like many Naga elders, especially retired NNC cadres, he felt at once betrayed by the British, who he accused of having left them in the hands of India, but also remained hopeful that sooner or later the British would realise their moral duty towards the welfare of the Nagas — after all, the Nagas had sided with them during the Japanese invasion, sacrificing lives and properties — and intervene in the continuing Indo-Naga conflict. Abi also occasionally mumbled about the United Nations and wondered why they were waiting so long to help mediate a settlement. Abi was convinced that I had been sent by either of them, and, much to my regret, came to perceive my presence as, in some way or another, foretelling the outside intervention he had so long prayed for.

Invariably our conversations ended by him inquiring about the status of the negotiations, as they were, and had been, taking place between the National Socialist Council of Nagalim (IM-Faction), arguably the strongest Naga powerhouse today, and the Central Government in Delhi since 1997. 'How are the talks progressing? When will we get our independence', he would ask, and ignored my polite returns that I was a simple PhD scholar whose only struggle in life seemed to be crafting a thesis out of Abi's and the other villagers' daily lives. My explanations were to no avail, and occasionally Abi, despite his faltering health, would walk from the town, where he lived, up to the village where I was residing only to ask me an update about the negotiations in Delhi. One day he gifted me a self-made, beautifully embellished *dao* (broad-shaped knife). 'As an appreciation', he said, only to quickly inquire about the chances of Naga independence. No matter my persistent explanations that I knew nothing about the negotiations, or at least not more than what the newspapers said, and which Abi too read, up until my departure from Noksen Abi remained convinced that I was not who I said I was, a mere research scholar.

A similar misreading of my person and purpose occurred in Phugwumi when, one day, an elderly man from a neighbouring village strolled into the compound I was living. He had heard about my presence, so he explained, and came to entrust me with an important task. It was a message he wanted me to convey. Or a plea rather, to be personally delivered to both the British Government and the offices of the United Nations. *Atsa* (a Chakhesang classificatory term for grandmother) offered him tea. After taking a sip, he explained himself:

> For many years we Nagas lived under the British. When the Japanese invaded we did not side with them even though their faces were similar to ours but helped the Britishers to defeat them. So many Nagas sacrificed their lives. But then, all of a sudden, they left us and told us to obey the Indians. We couldn't believe their treason; still I find it hard to believe they did this to us.

He continued:

> But we did not obey the Indians. We fought them. Suffering everywhere. Now we have our own state, but it is still within India and we deserve our independence. But India will never give it to us. Outside intervention is our only hope. When Phizo [then President and main ideologue of the NNC] left for Britain he appealed to the United Nations. We are still waiting for their response. You must remind them about Phizo's letter, and when you go home please also tell the Britishers about our fate.

Once again my plea that I had no such connections, that I was only there to carry out fieldwork fell on deaf ears. 'Please do your best', my visitor said before he left.

But if some Naga elders saw in me a connection to the outside intervention they still hoped for, intelligence agencies evaluated my presence rather differently, and despite the official permissions to carry out fieldwork I had on me, over the course of my fieldwork I — as well as the people who hosted me — had to repeatedly answer questions from intelligence officers about my doings and non-doings. Over the past decades, a handful 'western' activists had joined the ranks of the NNC, or publicly endorsed the stance for Naga independence in international fora and media, while the NSCN-IM had in recent years successfully aligned themselves with numerous international bodies, the Unrepresented Nations and Peoples Organisation (ENPO) among them, and which had catered them with levels of international sympathy. Despite my purely academic intentions, my resolute non-partisan attitude, and the least of desire to get mixed up in a complex and ever so contested struggle, this context nevertheless rendered my presence suspicious to the eyes of intelligence agencies, and which came to cause me measures of hardship and misery well transcending the PhD thesis I was writing, but which, alas, I should not detail here.

'WILL YOU PREACH THIS SUNDAY?'

'As I looked for the first time into the hard faces of these hill people, dubbed by the Assamese as head cutters', wrote Mary Clark in the 1870s, 'how little I thought that soon our commodious pleasant bungalow, with its garden and its flowers, situated at the bank of the artificial lake at Sibsagor [sic] (Sib's or Siva's ocean), would be left for a home in a small bamboo mat house in the mountain wilds' (Clark 1097: 1-2). Together with her zealous husband, Reverend Edwin Clark, Mary was to spend the next decades introducing Christianity to the Nagas. Today the Clarks are credited with bringing the Gospel to the Naga Hills — even though, during their life-time, they were criticised, by British officers, for working to destroy Naga culture[5] — and Reverend Clark's continuing veneration among Naga clergy first struck me while visiting the house of a well-known Dimapur based Reverend and finding Edwin Clark's face meticulously carved into a large wooden pillar. 'He brought us Nagas to our senses', the Reverend explained to me. 'Before his arrival, we were all heathens.' The Reverend then thanked God for bringing a 'scholar' to his kitchen, in the same way as he thanked Him for the delicious food his wife had prepared, and which he insisted we shared.

If initially missionary efforts proved futile — 'Christianity does not appear to have many attractions to them [Nagas]', a government report stated in 1880 (cited in Elwin 1969: 517) — things started to change with the shift of the missionary centre from Molung, where the Clarks had first established base, to Impur in 1894. Couched between two Naga villages, Impur translated as 'nobody's land' (Joshi 2012: 181) and was known locally to be haunted by malevolent spirits. The Clarks perceived the place otherwise and found it 'an ideal, picturesque location, a little over four thousand feet altitude, with pretty rolling lands, and a little eminence for each of three bungalows.' 'Our little mission oasis', Mary wrote, then continued: 'There was soon gathered at Impur quite a little community of Christian workers. A little church was organised, and the place became a real beehive of earnest, consecrated work' (Clark 1907: 146-7). Soon other missionaries announced their arrival in the hills, among them Reverend Perinne, and the couples Heggard and Dowd, and Naga conversions to Christianity accelerated. After a long residence, Edwin Clark reflected:

> Thirty years ago I took up residence in these Naga hills in a village where some work had been done by a native evangelist. Save at this place, over all these ranges of hills hung the black pall of heathen, barbaric darkness. Now from some twenty of the fifty or more villages crowning the mountain crests floats the glorious banner of Christ, held by his Naga disciples. The softening twilight of Christianity is here. Soon the broad daylight with its transforming power will reveal a Christianized people (ibid.: 148)

Cutting a long story short, in the span of less than a century nearly all Nagas converted to Christianity, forever changing their culture and philosophical outlooks, and also informing, to an extent, the later Naga Movement for independence, which some dub as an evangelistic struggle, sentiments roused further by the still popular slogan: 'Nagaland for Christ.' Today, in local parlance, Nagaland is termed as a Christian state with Christian discourse, rituals and symbols central to the minute texture of everyday life (see Joshi 2012). 'Even Gandhi loved Christian hymns', a big placard in the middle of Kohima reads.

Nowadays, Nagas are no longer the recipients of missionary attention but have become exporters of the Gospel as Naga missionaries, many of them young, zealous and bent on adventure, are dispatched to evangelise in places as close as Assam, Arunachal Pradesh, and just across the border in Myanmar or as far-away as Thailand and Sudan where they set up fellowships, churches, and congregations, carrying with them Bibles, hymnbooks, as well as prayers and tithes from their home-congregations. As for the foreign missionaries in the Naga Hills, they were expelled by the Central Government in the 1950s on the suspicion of them favouring the idea of Naga independence.

Yet, that I must be a missionary of sorts was the most readily available explanation for many Nagas when I first met them. Often I was asked which church had sent me, and when I explained that I was a student, not a missionary, it was quickly assumed that I must be a student of theology. 'Many Nagas also study theology these days', an elder remarked when I explained I was a student. In the end, to defuse confusion, I started to introduce myself as a student engaged in 'secular studies.' I was also regularly invited to speak in Sunday Schools and to share the Gospel from the pulpit, invitations I struggled hard to escape, stressing that I am not a missionary and citing my limited knowledge of the Bible. Yet, the ascribed identity of a missionary was not to fade, and throughout my stay, when making new acquaintances it was this stereotype – of foreigners as missionaries – which, in the first instance, explained my presence to many villagers.

CONCLUSION

If auto-ethnography advocates more of 'the self' into ethnographic texts, this essay, in a way, suggests the need for more on how 'the other' sees 'the self', that is of their interpretations of the ethnographer's presence and activities carried out among them. What the circulating discourses which projected me as a 'missionary', 'interlocutor or spy', or even as a 'colonial reincarnate' indicated, if anything, is that the ethnographer's positionality in the field is as much influenced by historical registers and particularistic experiences as it is the result of the personal characteristics, cultural attributes, and value-systems of the 'self.' Thence, if — as some do insist — 'the anthropologist projects his expectations on the result... [and] interpret data according to specific thought patterns, prejudices, conceits, and so on' (Nazaruk 2011: 74), ethnographic subjects similarly project their own particularistic 'thought patterns, prejudices, conceits, and so on' unto the ethnographer, casting him or her in roles the researcher has little influence on — and which may be far removed from the ethnographer's own perception of the Self — but which nevertheless may shape the ethnographer's positionality, or even explain successes and failures in the field. Of course the difference continues to be that the self-reflexive personality of the ethnographer may find its projection in more or less authoritative texts whereas the assumptions and interpretations of ethnographic subjects usually remain untold.

But there is more to a mere schematic exploration of how the ethnographically 'investigated' perceive their 'investigator.' As I tried to show for the Naga, the particularistic frames locally adopted to interpret the presence of the ethnographer may serve as windows into the historical constructions and contemporary experiences of a community vis-à-vis the wider, outside world. As suggested ethnographically, it may reveal anxieties and antagonisms, concerns, worldviews, and expectations, as well as stir up old memories — and into all of which the ethnographer and his fieldwork may, even if unknowingly, become absorbed.

ENDNOTES

Chapter 1

1. 'Telezüme' is a phatic expression, in the sense coined by Malinowski (1923), that serves to recognize bonds of sociality in the village, but which is not communicative in the sense of communicating relevant information.
2. On the still lingering Naga Movement, see Gundevia (1975), Horam (1988) and Franke (2009), among others.
3. For an account of the creation of Nagaland, see Sema (1986). On the relationship between political conflict and democracy in Nagaland, see Sen (1974), Singh (2004) and Kikon (2005).
4. This statement, however, is usually not attributed to Phizo, as Misra claims, but to T. Sakhrie, another early Naga nationalist leader (see Nuh 1986: 56).
5. In abridged form, I have discussed this predicament elsewhere (Wouters 2015).
6. For some comparative cases of consensus-making as a democratic form, see Wiredu (1995) and Snellinger (2009).
7. *Genna* connoted taboos, festivals and ritual observances, and generally meant traditional 'no work days' (see Joshi 2012: 84–85).
8. In line with this reverence for the village 'old', today inventories circulate in the village listing the twenty oldest villagers in descending order, starting with the oldest person alive.
9. To date, not a single woman has been elected into the Nagaland Assembly, and but a handful have tried to contest. This absence of women voices in Naga politics is now increasingly critiqued among Nagas, and condemned, by some, as evidence of a patriarchal cultural set-up (Kikon 2002, see also: Kuotsu and Walling 2018).
10. Members of Phugwumi's village council were – akin to the VDB – *selected* clan-wise with the added precondition that each member had to be over forty-five years of age (it is forty years for membership of the VDB) in continuation with the cultural conviction that wisdom and maturity come with age.

11. This number increased to twelve in 1969 and to twenty in 1974, the year voting was first introduced in Tuensang District, bringing the total number of Nagaland Assembly seats up to sixty.
12. The absence of opposition should not be equated with the absence of political debate. Murry (2007: 31) writes: 'Though it was a unique feature in a party system [to have a single party occupy all the assembly seats] of a parliamentary democracy, the House witnessed lively, heated, and intense debates and discussions on issues of public concern'.
13. In this case, too, this creation of a party-less government should not be read as the absence of divisions within. In fact, this 'coming together' of all parties was preceded by intense bickering and disagreements over positions of leadership and ministerial berths within the ruling government, and some accused the Chief Minister of engaging in 'power politics', of inviting other parties into his government to strengthen his own position, which some of his own party men had started to undermine.

Chapter 2

1. Phizo's letter was first published in Nuh (1986: 84–102)
2. Gandhi reportedly said to a Naga delegation which called on him in Delhi in 1947: 'Nagas have every right to be independent. We did not want to live under the British and they are now leaving us. I want you to feel that India is yours. I feel that the Naga Hills are mine just as much as they are yours. But if you say that they are mine, the matter must stop here... If you don't want to join the Union of India, nobody will force you to do that' (cited in Vashum 2000: 77).
3. Such divisions within – with today up to eight (albeit not all equally active) Naga underground groups operating – made Shimray argue that 'Nagas became the fatal enemy of themselves' (2005: 87), and Isak Swu, NSCN-IM's President, emphasise, in projecting the Naga future, that: 'Tribalism, communalism and factionalism are he weapons of the enemies of the people. The psychology of the Nagas today needs to be rebuilt' (cited in: Assam Tribune 23/03/2015).
4. 'Lim' translates as land, and the term Nagaland is often used as an expression to denote all Naga inhabited areas.
5. This does not mean that 'Burmese Nagas' are out of the struggle but that they are today primarily looked after by a Myanmar based faction of the NSCN; the NSCN-K, named after its chairperson S. Khaplang, who himself hails from the Hemi Naga tribe inside Myanmar. The NSCN-IM and the NSCN-K are at loggerheads. Until it recently unilaterally abrogated its ceasefire with the Indian Government, the NSCN-K found itself in the rather exceptional situation of being the signatory to ceasefires with both the Indian and Myanmar governments. According to Goswami, recent moves within the Naga

underground are posed towards 'pushing out and limiting the NSCN(K) to being a diminished Myanmar based outfit' (Goswami 2014: 2).

6. Referring here to the ideas of nation, nationalism and patriotism they were introduced to, and to the 'mind-stretching done by these "coolies"' [the Naga labour corps in France and Mesopotamia (Chasie 2005: 35). About the later Japanese invasion and the battle of Kohima, Horam (1992: 162) asserts that it 'provide[d] a definite break from the uninterrupted past and brought to their [the Naga] unaccustomed eyes the glare of a totally new world – new people, new weapons, new attire, new food and above all new ideas.' For a concise reconstruction of the construction of the Naga ethnie see Joshi (2013).

7. In a remarkable inverse of Baumann's (1996) ethnography on Southall, London, where official ethnic categories present groups as insulated and distinct in ways local cross-cutting relations and identification defy, among the Naga it is the demotic discourse that emphasises difference while the dominant narrative often, though not always, as will become clear below, presents a unified Naga category.

8. I thank Vibha Joshi for this reference.

9. In this plebiscite, organised by the NNC, Nagas were asked whether they wanted to join India or become part of a sovereign Nagaland. It is said that 99% of those Nagas consulted pressed their thumbs in favour of Naga Independence (Kikon 2005: 2833). Phizo's speech, spoken in 1951, can be found at: http://www.neuenhofer.de/guenter/nagaland/phizo.html

10. Based on Phizo's framing of 'sovereignty' some argue that India's Constitutional Provision of 371A gives the Naga (although only those residing in Nagaland) what they strive for. Article 371A of the Indian Constitution reads: 'Notwithstanding anything in this Constitution, (a) no Act of Parliament in respect of (i) religious or social practices of the Nagas, (ii) Naga customary law and procedure, (iii) administration of civil and criminal justice involving decisions according to Naga customary law, (iv) ownership and transfer of land and its resources, shall apply to the State of Nagaland unless the Legislative Assembly of Nagaland by a resolution so decides'

11. Given that the negotiations are taking place with India's Central Government, it is usually taken as implicit that integration in this instance implies the integration of Naga territories within India.

12. It might be qualified here that it is not always straightforward to denote which tribes in Manipur belong to the Naga fold as there have been historical instances in which certain communities initially belonged to another tribe but shifted their alliance to the Naga. 'The Naga identity has become such a force', Banerjee and Athparia (2004: 79) write, 'that many groups like Koirao, Loireng, Anal, Aimol, Chote, Lamkang, Mensang and Moyon who were formerly not known very much as "Naga" have, in recent years, claimed themselves as Naga.'

13. To illustrate some of the complexities in drawing the boundary, note the following entry of Colonel John Butler in his diary in the year 1873: 'Both colonel Thomson and I tried very hard to induce Major Roma Sing [a representative of the Manipur King] and the Manipuries to come out this morning and assist us in demarcating the boundary across the neck of land between the Sijjo and the Zullo dividing the villages forming the Sopoomah group on the one side from Kidimah [present-day Nagaland] on the other, but in vain.' They were then told that 'he was ready to do anything he could for us but that he begged we would not ask him to put up any pillars or otherwise mark out the boundary as he had the [Manipur] Rajah's orders not to recognize any boundary which did not include Kohimah [today's Nagaland's capital] until he had received her Majesty's Commands upon the memorial which he had already submitted... My first idea was that we should be able to make the boundary between Assam [of which the Naga Hills was then a district] and Manipur coincide with and run along the existing boundary between the villages of Kidimah and Sopoomah so that the boundary between the two villages would also form the boundary between the two Government, but in this we were disappointed for on enquiry, we found that the fields not only of Kidimah but of Viswemah and Khuzamah jutted out into uncultivated lands claimed by Sopoomah and vice versa. Besides which we discovered that all these villages were in the habit of buying and selling landed property among themselves so that any such boundary as there I had originally wished to adopt if laid down this year would in all probability have to be changed the next, and so on ad infinitum. And we therefore determined to adopt the present boundary between the several villages only so far as it might happen to fall in with the natural features of the country' (cited in Digital Himalaya. http://himalaya.socanth.cam.ac.uk/collections/naga/record/r87983.html)
14. The full text of this memorandum can be found at: http://www.satp.org/satporgtp/countries/india/states/manipur/documents/papers/mem2001_pm.htm (accessed on 27-06-2015).
15. In Nagaland 'forward' and 'backward' or 'advanced' tribes refer to legal categories with preferential treatment provided to 'backward tribes'. Except for the Chakhesang Naga, who reside in 'Western Nagaland', all of Nagaland's so scheduled 'backward tribes' reside in Eastern Nagaland.
16. After completing this article, the Centre and the NSCN-IM announced a framework agreement for the final settlement of the Indo-Naga conflict on the 3rd of August 2015. The details of which have not yet been divulged publicly, although they are intensely speculated over. While this agreement has led to new hopes, the agreement's legitimacy has simultaneously been contested by other Naga nationalists groups. At the time this article goes to press, it remains too early to comment on what the agreement might hold for the near future.

Chapter 3

1. No woman has ever been elected into the Nagaland Assembly, while village and municipal councils across the hills are, with a few exceptions, all male. This is to the consternation of the Naga Mothers Association (NMA), which has recently moved the Supreme Court for reservation of seats in certain local and customary bodies, a proposed change that is resisted by most Naga tribal councils and pan-Naga apex bodies.
2. See Wouters (2014: 62–63) for numerous instances in which Naga villages' apex bodies, in the wake of the 2013 elections, conferred and announced a village consensus candidate to whom all, or nearly all, votes were subsequently cast.
3. If such conditions of 'good democracy' do not exist, they must be fostered, or so many liberal theorists insist. Among them are Mark Tessler and Eleanor Gao who argue how successful democratization relies on citizens possessing 'norms and behaviour patterns that are conducive to democracy—in other words that they possess a democratic political culture orientation' (2009: 197). When such political orientations don't exist in a particular place, the argument implies that they must be taught or 'emerge in response to the experience of democratic transition,' as Tessler and Gao (2009: 197) try to put it less directly.
4. Given that at the brink of independence, India was ravaged, poor, and deeply divided, India's democratic surge and success is often seen as either a miracle or a great exception, as constituting 'an anomaly for academic political science, according to whose axioms cultural heterogeneity and poverty do not make a nation, still less a democratic one' (R. Guha 2008: xvi).
5. While this argument was framed in the context of Assembly elections in Nepal, a similar logic appears evident across the Subcontinent. But if Paul Brass (1990: 19) explains the existence of social relations and contestations, including caste-based and community-wise political mobilization, at the heart of India's democracy as 'an all-pervasive instrumentalism which washes away party manifestos, rhetoric, and effective implementation of policies in an unending competition for power, status, and profit,' I will stress, for the Naga, a deeper historical and cultural logic that informs the centrality of social relations to electoral politics and democracy.
6. In taking 'country' as his unit of analysis, Geertz however greatly understated the heterogeneity of understandings of politics and 'the political' that may exist within a country, certainly in a polity as large and diverse as India and where it makes more sense to think about Indian democracy in the plural, as *India's Democracies* (Heierstad and Ruud 2014).
7. See Piliavsky's (2014b) treatise on 'demotic democracy' for an insightful example of how applying the ethnographic *longue durée* can lead to better

understandings and critical appreciation of contemporary political practices, even if they appear to diverge from accepted democratic forms and norms.

8. The usage of the term 'vernacular" is deliberate. It suits better than, say, 'alternative democracy' (Nugent 2002) as the latter presupposes a derivation from an 'original' or 'pure' version of which there might exist 'alternatives.' Vernacular implies originality and creativity on its own 'wrought in an ongoing, situated engagement with the unfolding history of the present' (Comaroff and Comaroff 2012: 118). Let me stress that all democracies are of course vernacular, including the ones based on 'Western' history and thought. Recognizing this is precisely the point.

9. For massive Christian conversions among the Nagas from the end of the nineteenth century onward and today's Christian effervescence see Joshi (2012).

10. In response to the Naga uprising, the Centre passed the Armed Forces Special Powers Act in 1958, which commissioned soldiers posted in Nagaland (as well as in certain other so-called 'disturbed areas') to shoot at Nagas at mere suspicion, and while since the 1997 ceasefire major incidents have much diminished, the continuing presence of this draconian law raises questions about the nature and scope of Naga political space (see Kikon 2005; 2009). For more on the Naga Movement see, among many others, L. Ao (2002), Horam (1988), Franke (2009), and Joshi (2013).

11. Chasie (2001: 247) argued that Nagaland's democratic experience has been 'complex, difficult, an painful,' among others because of 'the unresolved Naga political issue with simultaneous 'insurgency' operating during the entire period [of post Nagaland statehood democracy].' While during the 2013 elections, akin to earlier elections, there were some accusations of 'underground groups' attempting to use their muscle power to influence election outcomes in some of the constituencies, in Phugwumi's constituency the 'undergrounds,' even if always a stakeholder politicians have to soothe, refrained from openly interfering in the political process.

12. The Chakhesang is a new tribe, in the sense that it is an amalgamation of different language groups that united themselves as 'Chakhesang' in 1946. In colonial annals Phugwumi was classed as Eastern Angami, thus part of the larger Angami tribe. Hence, any subsequent colonial reference to the Angami tribe in this article may be held as including Phugwumi.

13. In comparison, in India's larger states such as Bihar, the average size of a constituency is more than ten times the size of Nagaland's, while during Bihar's 2010 State Elections in 60 out of its 243 constituencies the voting margin of the winning candidate was higher than the total number of electors in the average Nagaland constituency.

14. Nagaland regularly pitches among those Indian states with the highest turnout of voters, and during the 2014 general elections even topped the country

with a turnout of 87.82 percent, which is over 20 percent higher than the national average (*Times of India* May 22, 2014). In the words of Amer, 'the causes and factors for such abnormal voter turnout could be understood by the fact that proxy voting is so rampant that it has become the rule rather than the exception' (Amer 2014: 9). It is here that Yadav (2009) seems ill-informed, or at least so in the context of Nagaland, when stating that 'if we assume spurious names of those dead, migrated or simply non-existent make up 10 per cent of our electoral rolls, the real turnout figures would be at five per cent higher [compared to what is given as the national average today].' With the dead, migrated, and nonexistent 'voted for,' Nagaland's voting turnout would decrease drastically as the electoral list matched the actual number of eligible voters. Even more misinformed are national newspaper reports that tend to interpret Nagaland's high turnout of votes as sufficient proof of Nagas having finally pledged their allegiance to the idea of India.

15. This play of money during Nagaland elections has been various noted (Misra 1987; Singh 2008; Dev 2006; Amer 2014). And yet, if the play of money is evident, money alone did not suffice for candidates to win as the richest or most generous candidates often did not win their constituencies, and for most voters 'monetary incentives' was only one consideration among others, and often not the decisive one.

16. Such genealogical evaluations were pervasive as the candidate himself was widely respected in the village and known and praised for his concern and commitment toward the villagers' welfare. In private, many villagers admitted that had they voted for him back then, the village would probably have been in a much better shape today.

17. If there is much talk about 'deepening democracy' (Heller 2009) in India and elsewhere, the case of Phugwumi shows a differential 'deepening' in which voting decisions are often vested in the deep social archeology of village life.

18. This is not to say that party differences were wholly absent or unimportant. They occasionally are discussed. Especially when it comes to the tension between regional and national political parties. I do, however, contend that party ideologies are often not a major determinant in explaining voting behavior in Nagaland.

19. Elsewhere I argued how among the Naga the throwing of lavish feasts, known in anthropological annals as the Naga Feast of Merit, was often crucial for an aspirant villager to climb the social ladder, to expand his sway in the village, and to have his voice heard more loudly (Wouters 2015).

20. Assam Administrative Report. Naga Videodisc. See The Naga Database, accessed September 9, 2015. http://himalaya.socanth.cam.ac.uk/collections/naga/record/r88456.html.

21. For an Ao Naga village, Temsula Ao reflects on her upbringing, 'Father belonged to a founding clan of our village Changki. ... Father's clan and particularly father

was always the target for his rivals, a clan which was constantly manoeuvring to distort village history and establish their superiority in the village hierarchy' (T. Ao 2013: 28).

22. In the light of Nagaland's politics of small numbers, and voting-results being declared ward and village wise, the political leaning (the majority of village votes) of each village was open knowledge; thus a village could be known, for instance, as a NPF (Naga People's Front), a Congress, or a BJP village, as a ruling or an opposition village (which, of course, could change from one election to the next).

23. There certainly also existed an instrumental hinge to bogus votes as its presence would increase the chances of a villager being elected into the assembly, so becoming in the position to 'help' his natal place by privileging it with state resources. This logic is provided, of course, that the village would vote in unison (more below).

24. This individualization is of course exactly what De Tocqueville long ago saw as intrinsic to democracy. For America he noticed a democracy-infused 'calm and considered feeling which disposes each citizen to isolate himself from the mass of his fellows and withdraw into the circle of family and friends; with this little society formed to his taste, he gladly leaves the greater society to look out after itself' (1969: 506). It is this individualism that Phugwumi elders lament as puncturing the more communitarian social and moral ethos of the prestate village polity.

25. Lamenting the social and political havoc intermittently caused by state elections, and in its self-assigned task to morally and spiritually guide the Nagaland populace, the NBCC—mostly made up of pastors and other church-workers—launched a state-wide Clean Election Campaign, which included, among many others, popularizing the principle of 'one man, one vote.' In its approach to elections, the NBCC, unlike most Nagas, guided itself by universalistic and normative projections of 'good democracy.' The NBCC had launched similar campaigns during earlier elections but to limited avail. Neither was their 2013 campaign to turn into a big success.

26. Such an obsession with caste goes deeper than mere electoral arithmetic; political rhetoric adopted by the 'ritually low' but politically powerful (by virtue of their preponderating numbers) Yadav caste, for instance 'portrays 'democracy' as a primordial phenomenon passed in the blood from the democratic ancestor-god Krishna to the contemporary Yadavs and describes Yadavs' political skills as innate' (Michelutti 2007: 643).

27. Situating caste in the historical *longue durée*, Sumit Guha (2013) emphasizes that, besides its religious and ritual associations, castes must also be seen as bounded, corporate lineages vying for territorial dominance and hegemony. Guha frames the caste-system as 'a highly involuted politicized form of ethnic ranking shaped by the constant exercise of socio-economic power' (2013: 2).

Seen thus, the workings of clans and castes may, at least in terms of political economy, not be altogether different, perhaps making the above clan versus caste argument not only a contrasting but also a comparable case.

28. To be sure, in 'the everyday' clan-relations were cordial in the village and in terms of kinship bonds, friendships and neighbours clan affiliations were everywhere transcended. 'Struggle' here refers to deeper, historical relations of dominance and subordination as they became invoked and expressed in the village's political rhetoric in the run up to Polling Day.

29. Social bonds of clan assume political significance not just among the Chakhesang but the Naga more widely. For the Lotha Naga, for instance, Ovung (2012: 122) writes, 'every serious treatment of Lotha politics finds clan as the most important determinant in patterns of political life.'

30. Kinship bonds could also cut across clans, and in one such case the daughter of a close aide of the sitting MLA happened to have one of the village politicians as her godfather, a social role obtained through a small ritual ceremony when a youth comes of age. Her father, as a result, separated her vote from the household-vote and made sure it went to her godfather.

31. Phugwumi had already earned a peculiar reputation in 'doing politics' because during two previous elections electronic voting machines in the village had been destroyed by angry party workers, leading to re-polling. It was because of this history, and the tension anticipated as the result of the presence of two village candidates, that the Nagaland Government, in the wake of Polling Day, declared Phugwumi as 'hypersensitive' resulting in the presence of well over a hundred soldiers to oversee polling.

32. On India's politics of patronage more widely see Chandra (2004). See Piliavsky's (2014a) edited volume on *Patronage as politics* for insightful explorations of the social and moral logic that reproduce long-standing patron-client relations inside India's democratic arena.

33. In Phugwumi, where everyone knew—and implored—everyone else's actions and loyalties, the principle of 'secret balloting' was plainly nonsensical.

34. In the somewhat romanticized description of Hokishe Sema (1986: 10), a former Nagaland Chief-Minister: 'the collective life took precedence over the individual life. A Naga's obligation and loyalty was to his family and village and this required a total submission to the village community.'

35. See Frederick Bailey [1969] 2001: 149) for a discussion on the normative rule of consensus in traditional Indian villages, and how this became gradually replaced by notions of competition and majority voting. Amanda Snellinger (2009) provides an account of the norm of consensus-making among politically powerful student organizations in Nepal with voting only coming in as a last resort. For a more generalized perspective of consensus-making in Ghana and other parts of Africa see Wiredu (1995).

36. Phugwumi's Razu Kuhu may be understood as a contemporary manifestation of such a council, although it is no longer 'informal' but made up of village leaders and intellectuals selected for a set period of time. In the Razu Kuhu, each clan in the village is equally represented.
37. This appears as a microencounter of what Paley (2008: 6) entreats more broadly as 'the ebb and flow of a [democracy] discourse,' or 'the outer edges of discourse, the shifting borderline between the instances in which [liberal] democracy discourse is picked up and used [as did the supporters of the sitting MLA] and those in which it is cast aside in favor of other possibilities,' such as the deliberating of a consensus-candidate preferred by the rest of the villagers.
38. For a critical reflection on Needham's polythetic classification, including its possible limitations, see Saler (1999).

Chapter 4

1. For an early critique of the application of 'tribe' and its portrayal as a discrete group, see Southall (1970), which was presaged by, among others, Leach's (1961) and Firth's (1957) important critiques of the concepts of 'lineage' and 'descent group' in response to Radcliffe-Brown's (1941) hard and fast distinction of lineages as distinct entities.
2. Speaking as the (then) Nagaland Home Minister, Imkong Imchen stated that 'the prevalence of tribalism was destroying the social fabric of the Naga society and obstructing Nagas to go ahead. Whether it is in the government, civil society or in the church, this monster of tribalism overshadow us and curb all minds' (see 'Root out tribalism' in *Nagaland Post*, 16 February 2010).
3. This changed with the arrival of colonial and post-colonial governmentality which operated to institutionalise 'tribe' as a prime axis of identity and governance. For some insights into colonial governmentality and its effects in India's Northeast, see Misra (2011), Robb (1997) and Zou and Satish Kumar (2011). For the production of colonial knowledge in India's Northeast, see Subba and Wouters (2013) and Wouters (2012).
4. This appears to be a bit of an overstatement, however. Consider, for instance, the tribus in ancient Rome and the 12 tribes of Israel whose existence well preceded the colonisation of Africa.
5. Captain Butler, cited in R.G. Woodthorpe, R.G., 'Report of the Survey Operations in the Naga Hills 1875-1876', published online by Digital Himalaya, 1876. Available at http://himalaya.socanth.cam.ac.uk/collections/naga/record/r87256.html. Accessed on 10 December 2013.
6. Some, of course, have criticised popular conjectures of perennial and historically constant tribes; among them, Xaxa (2005: 1363) who argues how the formation of tribal identities was initially a 'process from without', while

Beteille (1986) stresses that, as a category, 'tribe' was a colonial construct, one not always well-suited to the Indian scenario.

7. See Béteille (1998) and Roy Burman (2003) for a critique of the notion that Indian tribes should be understood as indigenous.
8. The spelling of these clans may vary between Chang villages and at times also between different persons within a single village. Alternative spellings include Ung, Kangcho, Hongang and Lomo, among others. By choosing the spelling in the main text, I have followed what I felt is the majority spelling in Noksen, but in doing so I levy no judgement on which spelling is more phonetically correct or historically adequate. It may also be mentioned that in certain Chang villages, there are other recognised Chang clans, that is, Chongpo, Khudumsi, Hinghousi and Haki Oungh (spelling again phonetically), which seem to exist as independent clans in some Chang villages and as incorporated in one of the four mentioned above in others. Their historical configurations remain subject to local debate as well as require further ethno-historical inquiry and in this analysis I concentrate on the four clans as they exist in Noksen.
9. In a broader light, the colonial administrator J.P. Mills emphasised the remarkable stability of language groups locally, to the extent (here referring mostly to the neighbouring Ao Naga) that 'a husband and a wife will at times converse together each in his or her own language'(1922: 1).
10. When citing colonial sources, I have retained the spelling of villages and clans as they appeared in those texts, even though, in many cases, village and clan names are today spelled differently.
11. The argument that Noksen villagers were Ao before Chang is also pursued, again based on linguistic evidence, by Alexander Coupe: 'The villages of Jakpa, Noksan [sic] and Litim for (sic) have a very high percentage of Chang-Ao bilingualism. Possibly they were former Ao villages that were annexed by the Chang...this might explain the high rate of bilingualism'(2007: 341).
12. Such historical episodes find confirmation, although less enthusiastically so, in the oral histories told by neighbouring villages.
13. A few elders turn this logic around and propound that the Chang took the initiative in re-establishing the village and thereafter allowed the Ya to join them.
14. A comparative historical sequence is reported about the clans of certain Kacha villages in relation to the historically powerful and expansionist Khonoma village, inhabited by Angami Nagas. Hutton wrote: 'In many Kacha Naga villages exogamous clans are found bearing the names of the Khonoma clans and probably adopted as a result of their subjection to Khonoma' (1921a: 16).
15. The Dikhu river constituted, broadly speaking, the dividing line between British administered and non-administered territories.

16. As far as I have been able to ascertain Ya segments are also present in the neighbouring villages of Longra and Yangpi, which seem to have a similar story of Chang invasion. The village of Yacham—which I could not visit—is also said to have a Ya element in its history. It would therefore be possible to posit that initially the Ya constituted a cluster of villages, even though oral history tells of frequent conflicts and raids between Noksei and those villages with Ya inhabitants.
17. This is, admittedly, somewhat of a simplification as classic studies on kinship also discussed concepts of moiety and phratry, which, while somewhat out of anthropological fashion, seem to resonate with some of my data here. In fact, a proposition may be coined that the various 'corresponding clans', discussed in more detail below, constituted a single phratry but which, over time, became fragmented with different sections moving away and coming to associate themselves with different tribes.
18. That said, Evans-Pritchard (1940), while devising his segmentary lineage system for the Nuer, was clearly aware of the, at times, complex relationship between 'clan' and 'tribe.' He wrote:

    'We speak of a clan which is dominant in a tribe as the aristocratic clan.... Not all members of the aristocratic clan live in the tribe where it is dominant, but many are also found in other tribes. Not all clans are associated with a tribe in this manner. A man is, only an aristocrat in the one tribe in which his clan is dominant. If he lives in another tribe, he is not an aristocrat there.' (1940: 287).
19. When it comes to marriage patterns, Mills writes:

    In cases where a Lhota marries a woman of another tribe he may, however, take a wife from a corresponding clan. For the clans being of different tribes they are regarded as being so widely separated, though corresponding, that there is no harm in intermarriage. But it is quite possible that intermarriage was once forbidden' (1922: 92).

    Mills however, makes an exception for the Chang tribe: 'Changs who keep old customs very strictly will not intermarry with a corresponding Ao clan' (ibid.: 93). While much has changed, in Noksen today villagers uphold the notion that marrying into a corresponding clan is prohibited.
20. In another work, however, Hutton somewhat retracted from this view, ascribing their existence to the 'considerable diffusion of common blood among the Naga tribes' (cited in Mills 1922: 92).
21. A radical constructivist reading would see such folktales too as nascent inventions. Scott, for instance, perceives oral histories as especially instrumental for they

    ...permit a certain 'drift' in content and emphasis over time–a strategic and interested readjustment of, say, a group history in which certain events are now omitted and others given stronger emphasis, and still others 'remembered'. Should a group with a common background split into two or more subgroups, each of which finds itself in a materially different setting, one imagines that their oral histories will diverge accordingly (2009: 230).

In our case, however, what ought to be explained is how despite such different material settings, similar oral histories persist.

22. With the help of colonial documents, we can however tentatively expand the number of corresponding clans from the Oungh clan's point of view, even though Noksen villagers could not confirm these. Mills noted that the 'Lhota muri clan correspond to Ao Pongrr and Sema Chishilimi' (Mills 1926: 92), with the Pongener, as we have seen, corresponding to the Chang Oungh clan.
23. While the Poumai is a state-recognised tribe in the neighbouring state of Manipur, it is not so in Nagaland.
24. To complicate matters more, the Khezha-speaking village of Jessami, situated just across the boundary with Manipur, did not join the Chakhesang and instead became associated with the Tangkhul Naga, a dominant and state-recognised tribe in Manipur. But while recognised as belonging to the Tangkhul tribe today, its villagers have retained their Khezha language.
25. In line with this reasoning, Krocha and Dukru write:

    Although many distinctive similarities extending to cultural activities, singing, style of cultivation, and other traditions are being shared both by the Chakhesang and the Angami tribe till date, the need for formation of a separate tribe and community was realized by the Chakhesang people party for political reasons and mostly to develop its own people socially, economically and educationally (2013: 1).
26. To be fair, there exists not just a single Chang folk sociology and during my fieldwork I came across a variety of Chang origin and migration stories. Some of them were highly essentialist in composition, others allowed for more flexibility. As a result, my conjectural reconstructions here might be more acceptable to some Chang than it would be to others.
27. Angfang remained a Konyak village, which still exists today, even though its population was nearly wiped out in the late 1940s by a joint attack of neighbouring villages (see Roy 2004). I must add that Hutton's reconstruction is not uniformly agreed upon by Chang elders today as some highlight that while a group came from Angfang to settle in Tuensang village, its members were not only Oungh but represented a number of clans.
28. For more on tribal conversions, see Ramirez (2014: 61–71).

Chapter 5

1. Clearly, Phizo's view as mirrored in his own Angami Naga background, a tribe which falls in the 'household model' of electoral politics, as discussed later, and the model which appears closest to modern principles of democracy.

2. It is important to assert that 'Naga' is a generic term that denotes a conglomeration of tribes, and although they all identify as Naga, they simultaneously emphasise their separate tribal identities, speak divergent languages and differ, at times radically so, in their traditional social and political organisation.
3. Elections in Nagaland are a relatively new phenomenon as the first three general elections in 1952 and 1957 were largely boycotted locally. While subsequent post-Nagaland statehood elections have been both regular and participatory, the Naga National Council (NNC) – as well as various factions of the National Socialist Council of Nagalim (NSCN), which later separated from the NNC – continue to oppose, at least so rhetorically, what they call are 'Indian elections imposed on Naga soil.'
4. This is not to argue that party differences are not marked. They are. Especially when it comes to the tension between regional and national political parties, the first insisting that only regional parties can understand the 'Naga mind' and the latter countering that only a strong national party, with strong connections to Delhi, can bring development and peace to the state. I do, however, contend that party ideologies are often not a major determinant in explaining voting behaviour in Nagaland.
5. The 'declarations of support' cited in this essay appeared in the *Morung Express*, *Nagaland Post* and the *Eastern Mirror*, the three main Nagaland dailies, during the months and weeks preceding the 2013 Nagaland assembly elections. As elections are invariably sensitive, I have omitted the names of both the supporters and candidates from the citations. I have not omitted the names of villages and clans, as it would be impossible to do so without affecting the accountability (and verifiability) of my data. My aforehand apologies if the inclusion of the names of certain villages or clans will incite discontentment among those who identify themselves with it.
6. As Gupta (1995: 385) puts it eloquently: 'Treated with benign neglect by students of contemporary life, they mysteriously metamorphize into invaluable 'field data' once they have yellowed around the edges and fallen apart at the creases'. And yet, it is not entirely clear by what alchemy time turns the 'secondary' data of the anthropologist into the 'primary' data of the historian.
7. While the Konyak territory is often referred to as 'the land of anghs', it ought to be qualified that the angh system does not exist in the entire Konyak area, and is most prominent among the so-called Thendu section of the tribe, not so among the Tenkoh division (Mills 1922: xxxiii).
8. The position of Gaonburas was introduced by the British who selected a number of persons in each village, whom they thought had considerable local influence, as intermediaries between the British administration and the village. They were bestowed with the responsibility to collect house-tax and to submit these to the government offices, upon which they received a commission. They were also empowered to settle local disputes, and to notify the government in

the event of any serious disturbances. Besides occasional commissions, they were also granted a red shawl to signal their allegiance to the British, and, in some instances, a gun. After the British departed from the Naga Hills, the position of Gaonbura was kept in place by the postcolonial government.

9. One reason explaining this high voter turnout is because in at least three of the four models discussed above votes are cast collectively, so including those who did not intend to vote or who are enrolled on the voting list but happened to be absent in their village on polling day.

Chapter 6

1. Examples include: Iralu (2000); Horam (1988); Anand (1980); Aram (1974); Sema (1986).
2. Examples of more detached exercises of Naga history writing include Franke (2009) and Thomas (2016)
3. On the role of the Indian Labour Corps, including Nagas and other hill tribes, see Singha (2015).
4. See, among several others, Rooney (1992); Campbell (1956) and Swinson (1956).
5. This assertion by Phizo is not corroborated by any other source I am aware of.
6. The Naga 'Control Area' here refers to the Naga uplands east of the Naga Hills District, and which were not formally administered by the British, but where colonial offices and officers nevertheless exerted considerable influence, mostly through military and punitive expeditions.
7. Administrators like Mills, Reid, and Adams variously envisaged this in the form of a Crown Colony or North-East protectorate, the creation of a separate province for the hill tracts within India, or through the inclusion of the Assam hills not in India but in Burma. These proposals were however resisted by Andrew Clow, the last British Governor of Assam, his successor Akbar Hydari, and the Congress Party, and in the course of 1946 were shelved. The Crown Colony was discussed in early NNC meetings with its members perceiving positively of a plan that 'would sever them from the administration of the plainsmen'; 'thus when the British abandoned the idea of a crown colony and withdrew from India, they left the Council with its expectations heightened by the discussions of a crown colony' (Franda 1961: 154).
8. Letters from Mills to Archer. Digital Himalaya, Naga Video-Disc. Url: http://himalaya.socanth.cam.ac.uk/collections/naga/record/r66612.html This is the first of a large number of references I make to the Naga videodisc (http://www.digitalhimalaya.com/collections/naga/), hosted by Digital Himalaya of the University of Cambridge, and which now offers a significant collection of letters, tour-diaries and memoires written mostly by colonial administrators. Rather than in-text referencing these sources, I will provide a link to each source I use from the Naga Videodisc in the endnotes that follow.

9. The tribal dimension emphasised here does of course not mean that all Ao Nagas were in favour of autonomy and all Angamis wishing independence, but that these views were popularly associated with NNC members of these tribes and became talked about as tribal political positions.
10. NNC, *Golden Jubilee: Naga Independence 1947–1997*, p. 28.
11. Mildred Archer Diaries, 18-07-1947. Digital Himalaya, Naga videodisc. Url: http://himalaya.socanth.cam.ac.uk/collections/naga/record/r67023.html
12. Notes by W.G. Archer, not dated. Digital Himalaya, Naga videodisc, Url: http://himalaya.socanth.cam.ac.uk/collections/naga/record/r66445.html
13. Mildred Archer Diaries, 18-07-1947. Url: http://himalaya.socanth.cam.ac.uk/collections/naga/record/r67024.html
14. Mildred Archer Diaries, 18-7-1947. Url: http://linux02.lib.cam.ac.uk/nagas/record/r67026.html
15. Mildred Archer diaries, 18-7-1947. Url: http://linux02.lib.cam.ac.uk/nagas/record/r67028.html
16. Mildred Archer diaries, 18-7-1947. Url: http://linux02.lib.cam.ac.uk/nagas/record/r67029.html
17. Mildred Archer Diaries, 18-7-1947. Url: http://linux02.lib.cam.ac.uk/nagas/record/r67031.html
18. Mildred Archer Diaries, 18-07-1947. Url: http://linux02.lib.cam.ac.uk/nagas/record/r67032.html
19. Ibid.
20. Ibid.
21. Mildred Archer Diaries, 21-07-1947. Url: http://linux02.lib.cam.ac.uk/nagas/record/r67033.html
22. Mildred Archer diaries, 24-07-1947. Url: http://linux02.lib.cam.ac.uk/nagas/record/r67036.html
23. Mildred Archer diaries, 29-07-1947. Url: http://linux02.lib.cam.ac.uk/nagas/record/r67039.html
24. Mildred Archer diaries, 06-08-1947. Url: http://linux02.lib.cam.ac.uk/nagas/record/r67053.html
25. Mildred Archer diaries, 12-08-1947. Url: http://linux02.lib.cam.ac.uk/nagas/record/r67074.html
26. Mildred Archer diaries, 19-08-1947. Url: http://linux02.lib.cam.ac.uk/nagas/record/r67087.html
27. Mildred Archer diaries, 19-08-1947. Url: http://linux02.lib.cam.ac.uk/nagas/record/r67088.html
28. Ibid.
29. Mildred Archer Diaries, 23-08-1947. Url: http://linux02.lib.cam.ac.uk/nagas/record/r67104.html
30. Mildred Archer Diaries, 23-08-1947. Url http://linux02.lib.cam.ac.uk/nagas/record/r67105.html

31. Letter from Pawsey to Archer, Digital Himalaya, Naga videodisc, not dated. Url: http://himalaya.socanth.cam.ac.uk/collections/naga/record/r66645.html
32. Manuscript notes W.G. Archer. Digital Himalaya, Naga videodisc, not dated. Url: http://himalaya.socanth.cam.ac.uk/collections/naga/record/r66666.html
33. Mildred Archer Diaries, 9-7-1947. Url: http://himalaya.socanth.cam.ac.uk/collections/naga/record/r67110.html
34. W.G. Archer notes, 13-01-1947: Url: http://himalaya.socanth.cam.ac.uk/collections/naga/record/r66662.html
35. Mildred Archer Diaries, 23-8-1947. Url: http://himalaya.socanth.cam.ac.uk/collections/naga/record/r67104.html
36. Mildred Archer Diaries, 30-08-1947. Url: http://himalaya.socanth.cam.ac.uk/collections/naga/record/r67121.html
37. Mildred Archer Diaries, 4-10-1947. Url: http://himalaya.socanth.cam.ac.uk/collections/naga/record/r67186.html
38. Mildred Archer Diaries, 31-8-1947, Url: http://linux02.lib.cam.ac.uk/nagas/record/r67125.html
39. Mildred Archer Diaries, 31-8-1947, Url: http://linux02.lib.cam.ac.uk/nagas/record/r67126.html
40. Mildred Archer Diaries, 18-09-1947, Url: http://himalaya.socanth.cam.ac.uk/collections/naga/record/r67164.html
41. Mildred Archer Diaries, 18-09-1947, Url: http://himalaya.socanth.cam.ac.uk/collections/naga/record/r67164.html
42. Mildred Archer Diaries, 21-9-1947, url: http://himalaya.socanth.cam.ac.uk/collections/naga/record/r67173.html
43. Mildred Archer Diaries, 15-10-1947, Url: http://himalaya.socanth.cam.ac.uk/collections/naga/record/r67201.html
44. Mildred Archer Diaries, 31-10-1947. Url: http://himalaya.socanth.cam.ac.uk/collections/naga/record/r67232.html
45. Mildred Archer Diaries, 2-12-1947. Url: http://himalaya.socanth.cam.ac.uk/collections/naga/record/r67331.html
46. *The Statesman*, 'Warrant Issued Against Phizo', (04-02-1956).
47. *The Statesmen*, 'Full Army Operations in Naga Hills' (31-03-1956).
48. *The Statesman*, 'Warrant issued against Phizo.'
49. *The Statesman*, 'Naga Leaders go Underground' (01-02-1956).
50. *Assam Tribune*, 'Nagas pledge to break with Phizo', (26-06-1956).
51. *The Statesmen*, 'Rebels behead four loyal Nagas' (05-04-1956).
52. Pawsey Papers, Letter from Stephen Laing, (13-08-1956).
53. Pawsey Papers, Letter from Stephen Laing, (05-02-1957).
54. *The Statesmen*, 'Police Accused of "Excesses" in Naga Hills' (27-03-1956)
55. Pawsey Papers, Newspaper clipping (name of newspaper not mentioned), 'Nehru told: try peace in your own land' (27-08-1956).
56. *The Telegraph*, 'Naga Tribes Hold Down 30.000 Men' (20-03-1957),

57. Pawsey Papers, Newspaper clipping (name newspaper not mentioned), 'Head-Hunters Strip Nehru's Soldiers' (05-08-1957).
58. *Assam Tribune*, 'Dissolution of NNC', 23-05-1956.
59. *India News*, 'Prime Minister meets Naga delegation', 22-09-1956.
60. Yonuo (1974: 222) speaks of '1765 traditional representatives of the different Naga tribes particularly from the Naga Hills and Tuensang Area of NEFA and about 2.000 observers from the other Naga areas.'

Chapter 8

1. Through a special Constitutional provision Naga tribes, as well as other resident tribes in parts of the region, are exempted from paying income-tax.
2. While crimes against women are, on the whole, comparatively low in Nagaland, it must be qualified that cases of crime against women, when they occur, are regularly dealt with by customary bodies, and are therefore not always officially reported.

Chapter 9

1. In local parlance Nagaland is dubbed a Christian state as well over 90% of its populace professes Christianity and because Christian discourse, rituals and symbols often permeate the minute texture of everyday life (see Joshi 2012).
2. The term 'moral economy' is one heavily loaded and my usage of it here builds upon its initial theorizing by Thompson (1971) and Scott (1976) and their assertion – positioned against conventional rational choice and overtly utilitarian perspectives – that economic and political action – of which throwing feasts is one – is governed by patterns of social and moral norms, values and expectations that exist within a historically situated 'moral universe.'
3. According to Lanunungsang Ao (2002: 49): 'When the first Indian Parliamentary General Election was extended to Nagaland, they [the NNC and the Naga more widely] resorted to civil disobedience and completely boycotted the election on 25, January 1951 [sic]... when the second parliamentary election took place in 1957, the Naga people once again boycotted the election. Not a single Naga candidate fought for election nor voted in that election.'
4. No account on contemporary democracy in Nagaland may be considered complete without a discussion on what is locally referred to as the 'underground factor', but this will not figure in our discussion, and in any case has little bearing on the wining and dining elements of Nagaland's elections.
5. For reasons I will not delve into here, one of the constituency's four candidates had been proscribed by Phugwumi's Village Council from campaigning within the village, and hence no camps and election feasts were organized by him

or his aides. Two of the four candidates belonged to Phugwumi itself. Both Phugwumi candidates established two camps, while the sitting MLA nourished the remaining one.
6. It might be qualified that, among certain Naga tribes, certain clans were traditionally associated with specific ritual functions. However, such ritual acts were first and foremost symbolic and performed sporadically, and not part of an elaborate ritual division of everyday labour.
7. Compared to surrounding villages Christianity came late to Phugwumi. The first villager converted in 1947 but it was to take several years before Christianity became the dominant, and later only, religion in the village.
8. Pointing to the money play during Nagaland Elections, Ezung (2012: 2) writes: 'A person who is elected through the use of money will always try to cover up the expenses he/she made during the election and will also try to retain some extra money for the next election.' See also Nuh (1986), Dev (1988), Misra (1987; 2000), and Kiewhuo (2002).
9. The politician 'eating', in local idiom, referred to him trying to recover his electoral expenses and more by appropriating state resources
10. Such campaign inducements hardly only concern election feasts, but involved a wider assortment of inducements, including monetary ones.
11. Of course, the very occurrence of such explicit demands is another subversion of past feasts of merits, in which the act of 'providing' was seen as self-evident, to be offered by a wealthy villager, not demanded by ordinary villagers.
12. The NBCC election guidelines included a great deal more than a prohibition on feasting and the intake of liquor. Among others they warned against vote-buying, proxy-voting, double entries in the electoral role, and the use of intimidation and undue pressure to win votes.
13. Although these do play a role, especially when it comes to the tension between regional and national political parties, these often remain of little help to understand local voting behaviour.

Chapter 10

1. Theoretical traditions associated with 'liberal democracy' are undoubtedly diverse, but they are a historically contingent product of 'Western' history and thought, and therefore come with limitations when applied to explaining democratic representation, and 'the political' more widely, in South Asia. On this, see: Dipesh Chakrabarty (2000).
2. Witsoe (2011: 621) argues that 'positive' in this context must be understood 'in the sense of not being reduced to the frameworks of analysis that have emerged from, and formed part of, liberal democratic models of governance or even that derive from critiques of liberal democracy'.

3. On a historical scale, and in terms of political representation more broadly, Spencer (1997: 12) postulates the 'semantic and cultural "emptiness"' of political representation, explaining: 'We all know there is a link between representative and represented, but we cannot necessarily specify what form this link may take'.
4. While Holmberg's argument is focused on the Tamangs in Nepal, his observation certainly carries a much wider application within South Asia.
5. On the 'Eastern Angami' turning themselves into 'Chakhesangs', see Wouters (2017a).
6. Tanabe (2007: 560) captures 'moral society' as that vernacular public space 'in which morally desirable human relationships rather than individual rights or political gains are at issue'..
7. 'Age among Nagas has both prestige and power', Horam (1988: 18) writes.
8. In comparison, the population of Uttar Pradesh, India's most populous state, exceeds Nagaland's population 100 times over but has only four times more Legislative Assembly seats, making its constituencies much larger. To illustrate further, during the 2010 state elections in Bihar, in 60 out of its 243 constituencies the voting margins of the victorious candidates were larger than the total tally of an average constituency in Nagaland.
9. Diagnosing the corruption and malvoernance all across Nagaland, the state's then development commissioner ascribed them to a 'lack of sense of belonging in the government by the people', lamenting the 'very debilitating' effect this had on development' (Jamir 2002: 3-4).
10. Within India, this politics of feeding and eating is not confined to Nagaland. In Rajasthan, Piliavsky (2014b: 163) notes how, besides actually offering meals, 'the language of feeding is the key moral idiom in which people evaluate politicians and conceive of the ways in which politicians relate, or ought to relate, to their constituents.'

Chapter 11

1. In Phugwumi, and in many – though not all – Naga villages, feasts of merit constituted the basis of social life and communitarian ethics. Through performing a feast of merit, or rather a series of feasts, a wealthy man absolved his material wealth – which was proof of his own fertility – but accumulated material symbols which indicated his social standing and prestige (See Wouters 2015).
2. Mildred Archer's diaries: http://himalaya.socanth.cam.ac.uk/collections/naga/
3. Mildred Archer's diaries: http://himalaya.socanth.cam.ac.uk/collections/naga/
4. Mildred Archer's diaries: http://himalaya.socanth.cam.ac.uk/collections/naga/

5. 'It is a pity', wrote Fürer-Haimendorf, 'that the American Baptist Mission had little sympathy with the aims of the Government and even less appreciation of the valuable elements of Naga culture.' He declared the cultural destruction he witnessed all around him as rather unnecessary given that 'many of its aspects conflict in no way with the principles of Christianity, and I believe that even some of the old feasts and ceremonies – certainly agricultural festivals – could have been adapted to the new faith, given a new meaning and retained by Christian communities.' (1939: 57).

REFERENCES

Abeles, Marc. 1988. 'Modern Political Ritual: Ethnography of an Inauguration and a Pilgrimage by President Mitterrand.' *Current Anthropology* 29 (3): 391–404.

Abrams, Philip. 1988. 'Notes on the Difficulty of Studying the State.' *Journal of Historical Sociology* 8 (1): 58–89.

Agrawal, Ankush & Vikas Kumar. 2013. 'Nagaland's Demographic Somersault.' *Economic and Political Weekly* 48 (39): 69–74.

Almond, Gabriel & Sidney Verba. 1963. *The Civic Culture: Political Attitudes and Democracy in Five Nations*. London: Sage Publications.

Amer, Maomenla. 2013. 'Political Status of Women in Nagaland.' *Journal of Business Management & Social Science Research* 2 (4): 91–95.

Amer, Maomenla. 2014. 'Electoral Dynamics in India: A Study of Nagaland.' *Journal of Business Management & Social Science Research* 3 (4): 6–11.

Anand, V.K. 1980. *Conflict in Nagaland: A Study of Insurgency and Counter-Insurgency*. Delhi: Chanakya Publications.

Anderson, Benedict, R. 1996. 'Elections and Participation in Three Southeast Asian Countries.' In *The Politics of Elections in Southeast Asia*, edited by R. H. Taylor, 12–33. Cambridge: Cambridge University Press.

Ao, Lanunungsang. 1993. *Rural Development in Nagaland*. New Delhi: Har-Anand Publications.

Ao, Lanunungsang. 2002. *From Phizo to Muivah: the Naga National Question in North-East India*. New Delhi: Mittal Publications.

Ao, Temsula. 2004. 'Ao-Naga Myths in Perspective.' In *Between Ethnography and Fiction: Verrier Elwin and the Tribal Question in India*, edited by T.B. Subba and S. Som, 157–72. New Delhi: Orient Longman.

Ao, Temsula. 2014. *Once upon a life: A memoir*. New Delhi: Zubaan.

Aram, M. 1974. *Peace in Nagaland: Eight year story, 1964–1972*. New Delhi: Arnold-Heinemann

Asian Tribune. 2015. 'Nagaland Heading for Opposition-Less Government; Not Healthy in democratic government. then followed by 21 March.

Atal, Yogesh. 2009. 'Inaugural Address.' In *Tribal Development since Independence*, edited by S.N. Chaudhary, 13-27. New Delhi: Concept Publishing Company.

Badiou, Alain. 2010. 'The Democratic Emblem.' In *Democracy in What State?*, edited by Giorgio Agamben et al., 6-15. New York: Columbia University Press.

Bailey, Frederick G. 2001 [1969]. *Stratagems and Spoils: A Social Anthropology of Politics*. Boulder, CO: Westview Press.

Banerjee, M. & R.P. Athparia. 2004. 'Emergent Ethnic Crisis: A study of Naga-Kuki Conflict in Manipur.' *The Journal of the Anthropological Survey of India* 53(1): 77-90.

Banerjee, Mukulika. 2007. 'Sacred Elections.' *Economic and Political Weekly* 42 (17): 1556-62.

Banerjee, Mukulika. 2008. 'Democracy, Sacred and Everyday: An ethnographic Case from India.' In *Democracy: Anthropological Approaches*, edited by Julia Paley, 63-96. Santa Fe, NM: School for Advanced Research Press.

Banerjee, Mukulika. 2011. 'Elections as Communitas.' *Social Research*, 78(1): 75-98.

Banerjee, Mukulika. 2014. *Why India Votes*. New Delhi: Routledge.

Bareh, Hamlet M. (ed). 2001. *Encyclopaedia of North-East India*. Volume 6. New Delhi: Mittal

Barth, Frederik. 1969. 'Introduction.' In *Ethnic Groups and Boundaries: The Social Organization of Cultural Differences*, edited by F. Barth, 9-37. London: Allen and Unwin.

Baruah, G.C. 1980 [1935]. *Ahom Buranji: From the Earliest Time to the End of Ahom Rule*. Guwahati: Spectrum Publications.

Baruah, Sanjib. 2003. 'Confronting Constructionism. Ending India's Naga war.' *Journal of Peace Research* 40 (3): 321-338.

Baruah, Sanjib. 2003. 'Nationalizing Space: Cosmetic Federalism and the Politics of Development in North-East India.' *Development and Change* 34 (5): 915-939.

Baumann, Gerd. 1996. *Contesting Culture: Discourses of Identity in Multi-Ethnic London*. Cambridge: Cambridge University Press.

Bayart, Jean-François 1993. *The State in Africa: The Politics of the Belly*. London: Longman.

Bendangjungshi. 2012. *Confessing Christ in the Naga Context: Towards a Liberating Ecclesiology*. Berlin: Lit Verlag.

Berenschot, Ward. 2011. 'On the Usefulness of Goondas in Indian politics.' *Modern Asian Studies* 34 (2): 255-275.

Berger, Peter. and Frank. Heidemann. 2014. 'Introduction: The Many Indias: The Whole and its Parts.' In *The Modern Anthropology of India: Ethnography, Themes and Theory*, edited by Peter Berger and Frank Heidemann, 1-11. London: Routledge.

Béteille, Andre. 1965. *Caste, Class and Power in a Tanjore Village: Changing Patterns of Stratification in a Tanjore Village*. Berkeley: University of California Press.

Béteille, Andre. 1986. 'The Concept of Tribe with Special Reference to India.' *European Journal of Sociology* 27 (2): 296-318.

Béteille, Andre. 1998. 'The Idea of Indigenous People.' *Current Anthropology* 39 (2): 187-91.

Béteille, Andre. 2017 [2012]. *Democracy and its Institutions*. New Delhi: Oxford University Press.

Bhaumik, Subir. 2009. *Troubled Periphery: Crisis of India's Northeast*. New Delhi: SAGE Publications.

Biolsi, Thomas. 2005. 'Imagined Geographies: Sovereignty, Indigenous space, and American Indian Struggle. *American Ethnologist* 32 (2): 239-259.

Birch, Sarah. 2011. *Electoral Malpractice*. Oxford: Oxford University Press.

Biswas, Prasenjit, & Chandan Suklabaidya. 2008. *Ethnic Life-Worlds in Northeast India: An Analysis*. Delhi: Sage Publications

Björkman, Lisa. 2013. '"You Can't Buy a Vote": Meanings of Money in a Mumbai Election.' *American Ethnologist* 41 (4): 617-634.

Bohannan, Laura. 1964. *Return to Laughter: an Anthropological Novel*. New York: Garden City.

Bose, Sumantra. 2013. *Transforming India. Challenges to the World's Largest Democracy*. Cambridge, MA: Harvard University Press.

Bower, Ursula 1950. *Naga Path* London: John Murray.

Brass, Paul. 1990. *The Politics of India Since Independence*. Cambridge: Cambridge University

Butler, John. 1855. *Travels and Adventures in the Province of Assam During a Residence of Fourteen Years*. London: Smith, Elder and Co.

Campbell, A. 1956. *The Siege – A Story From Kohima*. London: George Allen

Carrithers, Michael, Steven Collins & Steven Lukes. (eds.). 1985. *The Category of the Person: Anthropology, Philosophy, History*. Cambridge: Cambridge University Press.

Chakhesang Student Union. 1997. *Commemorating Golden Jubilee*. Kohima: Chakhesang Student Union.

Chakrabarty, Bidyut. 2008. *Indian Politics and Society since Independence: Events, Processes and Ideology*. London: Routledge.

Chakrabarty, Dipesh. 2000. *Provincializing Europe: Postcolonial Thought and Historical Difference*. Princeton: Princeton University Press.

Chandra, Kanchan. 2004. *Why Ethnic Parties Succeed: Patronage and Ethnic Headcounts in India*. Cambridge: Cambridge University Press.

Chasie, Charles. 2001. 'Nagaland – Land and People' Url: http://www.ide.go.jp/English/Publish/Download/Jrp/pdf/133_9.pdf (accessed on 16-09-2014)

Chasie, Charles. 2005. *The Nagai imbroglio (a personal perspective)*. Kohima: City Press.

Chasie. Charles. 2017. 'Naga society lies wounded again.' *Morung Express*, 5th February

Chatterjee, Indrani. 2014. *Forgotten Friends: Monks, Marriages, and Memories of Northeast India*. New Delhi: Oxford University Press.

Chatterjee, Partha. 1986. *Nationalist Thought and the Colonial World: A Derivative Discourse?* London: Zed Books.
Chaube, S.C. 1999. *Hill Polities in Northeast India* Noida: Orient Longman
Clark, Mary. 1907. *A Corner in India*. Boston: American Baptist Publication Society.
Clastres, Pierre. 1977. *Society Against the State: The leader as Servant and the Humane Uses of Power Among the Indians of the Americas*. Oxford: Basil Blackwell.
Clifford, James. & George, .E. Marcus. 1986. *Writing Culture: The Poetics and Politics of Ethnography*. London, University of California Press.
Cohn, Bernard S. 1996. *Colonialism and its Forms of Knowledge: The British in India*. Princeton: Princeton University Press.
Coles, Kimberley A. 2004. 'Election Day: The Construction of Democracy Through Technique.' *Cultural Anthropology* 19 (4): 551-80.
Collins, Kathleen. 2009. *Clan Politics and Regime Transition in Central Asia*. Cambridge: Cambridge University Press.
Colvin, John. 1994. *Not Ordinary Men*. London: Leo Cooper.
Comaroff, Jean & John L Comaroff. 2012. 'Theory from the South: Or, how Euro-America is evolving toward Africa.' *Anthropological Forum: A Journal of Social Anthropology and Comparative Sociology* 22 (2): 113-131.
Comaroff, Jean. & John L Comaroff. 1997. 'Postcolonial Politics and Discourses of Democracy in Southern Africa: An Anthropological Reflection on African Political Modernities'. *Journal of Anthropological Research* 53 (2): 123-146.
Coupe, Alexander R. 2007. 'Converging Patterns of Cause Linkage in Nagaland.' In *Trends in Linguistics: New Challenges in Typology*, edited by Matti Miestamo and Bernard Wälchi, 339-62. Berlin: Mouton De Gruyter.
Davis, A. W. 1969 [1891]. 'The Aos in 1891'. In *Nagas in the nineteenth century*, edited by Verrier Elwin, 323-329. Oxford: Oxford University Press.
De Tocqueville, Alexis. 1969 [1840]. *Democracy in America*. Translated by George Lawrence. New York: Doubleday Anchor.
Dev, Rajesh. 2006. 'Ethnic Self-Determination and Electoral Politics in Nagaland.' In *Ethnic Identities and Democracy: Electoral Politics North East India*, edited by Apurba Baruah and Rajesh Dev, 68-92. New Delhi: Regency Publications.
Dev, S. C. 1988. *Nagaland: The Untold Story*. Calcutta: Regent Publications.
Devi, Lakshmi. 1968. *Ahom-Tribal Relations: A political study*. Gauhati: Cotton College.
Dickey, S. 1993. 'The Politics of Adulation: Cinema and the Production of Politicians in South India.' *The Journal of Asian Studies* 52 (2): 340-372.
Directorate of Arts and Culture. 1976. *Proceedings of the Seminar on Naga Customary Laws, Kohima, 21-23*. Kohima: Nagaland Government.
Dirks, N. 2001. *Castes of Mind: Colonialism and the Making of Modern India*. Princeton: Princeton University Press.
Dumont, Jean-Paul. 1991. *The Headman and I: Ambiguity and Ambivalence in the Fieldworking Experience*. Long Grove: Waveland Press.

Dumont, Louis. 2004 [1970]. *Homo Hierarchicus: The Caste System and its Implications.* Chicago: Chicago University Press.

Dunn, J. 2014. *Breaking Democracy's Spell.* New Haven, CT: Yale University.

Elwin, Verrier. 1957. *A Philosophy for NEFA.* Shillong: North-East Frontier Agency.

Elwin, Verrier. 1961. *Nagaland.* Shillong: The Research Department Secretariat.

Elwin, Verrier. (ed). 1969. *Nagas in the Nineteenth Century.* London: Oxford University Press.

Evans-Pritchard, Edward, Evan. 1940. 'The Nuer of the Southern Sudan.', In *African Political Systems,* edited by Meyer Fortes and Edward Evans Evans-Pritchard, 272–96. London: Oxford University Press.

Ezung, Zarenthung. 2012. 'Corruption and its Impact on Nagaland: A Case Study of Nagaland.' *International Journal of Rural Studies* 19 (1): 1–7.

Firth, Raymond. 1957. 'A Note on Descent Groups in Polynesia.' *Royal Anthropological Institute of Great Britain and Ireland* 57 (January): 4–8.

Fortes, Meyer. 1949. *The Web of Kinship among the Tallensi.* London: Oxford University Press.

Foucault, Michel. 2003. *Society must be Defended: Lectures at the Collège de France, 1975–1976.* New York: Macmillan.

Franda, M.F. 1961 'The Naga National Council: Origins of a Separatist Movement', *Economic and Political Weekly*, February 4.

Franke, Marcus. 2009. *War and Nationalism in South Asia: The Indian State and Nagas.* London: Routledge.

Fürer-Haimendorf, Von. Christoph. 1936. 'The Sacred Founder's Kin among the Eastern Angami Nagas.' *Anthropos* 31 (5/6): 922–933.

Fürer-Haimendorf, Von, Christoph. 1939. *The Naked Nagas.* London: Methuen & Company.

Fürer-Haimendorf, Von, C. 1973. 'Social and Cultural Change among the Konyak Naga.' *Highlander* 1 (1): 3–12.

Fürer-Haimendorf, Von, Christoph. 1976. *Return to the Naked Nagas.* London: Methuen & Co Ltd.

Fürer-Haimendorf, Von, Christoph. 1982. *Tribes of India: The Struggle for Survival.* Berkeley: University of California Press.

Geertz, Clifford. 1973. *The Interpretation of Cultures – Selected essays.* New York: Basic Books.

Geertz, Clifford. 1980. *Negara: The theatre State in Nineteenth Century Bali.* Princeton: Princeton University Press.

Geertz, Clifford. 1988. *Works and Lives – the Anthropologist as Author.* Cambridge: Polity Press.

Geertz, Clifford. 1998. *After the Fact: Two Countries, Four Decades, One Anthropologist.* Cambridge, MA: Harvard University Press.

Gellner, David. 2009. 'The Awkward Social Science? Anthropology on Schools, Elections, and Revolution in Nepal.' *Journal of the Anthropological Society of Oxford* (n.s.) 1 (2): 115-140.

Gellner, David. (ed). 2013. *Borderland Lives in Northern South Asia*. London: Duke University Press.

Gellner, Ernest. 1977. *Patrons and Clients in Mediterranean Societies*. London: Duckworth.

Gellner, Ernest. 1983. *Nation and Nationalism*. Ithica: Cornell University Press.

George, Jacob & Khrietuo Yhome. 2008. 'Community Forest Management: A Case Study of Nagaland, India.' Paper presented at 12th *Biennial Conference of the International Association for the Study of Commons*: 1-13.

Gilmartin, David. 2007. Election Law and the 'People' in Colonial and Postcolonial India. Oxford: Oxford University Press.

Gilmartin, David. 2012. 'Towards a Global History of Voting: Sovereignty, the Diffusion of Ideas, and the Enchanted Individual.' *Religions* 3: 407-423.

Gluckman, Max. 1954. *Ritual of Tebellion in South-east Africa*. Manchester: Manchester University Press.

Gorringe, Hugo. 2011. 'Party Political Panthers: Hegemonic Tamil Politics and the Dalit challenge.' *South Asia Multidisciplinary Academic Journal*..http://samaj.revues.org/3224 (Accessed May 1, 2015)

Goswami, Namrata. 2014. 'Naga identity – Ideals, Parallels and Reality.' *The Hindu*, 14th June.

Graeber, David. 2009. *Direct Action: An Ethnography*. Oakland: AK Press.

Guha, Ramachandra. 2008. *India after Gandhi. The History of the World's Largest Democracy*. London: Picador.

Guha, Sumit. 2013. *Beyond Caste: Identity and Power in South Asia, Past and Present*. Leiden: Brill.

Gundevia, Y. D. 1975. *War and Peace in Nagaland*. New Delhi: Palit & Palit Publishers.

Gupta, Dipankar. 2005. 'Caste and Politics: Identity over System.' *Annual Review of Anthropology* 34: 409-27.

Guttman, Matthew, C. 2002. *The romance of democracy: Compliant Defiance in Contemporary Mexico*. Berkeley: University of California Press.

Guyot-Réchard, Bérénice 2017. 'When the Legions Thunder Past: the Second World War and India's Northeastern Frontier', *War in History*, Doi: 10.1177/0968344516679041.

Habermas, Jürgen. 1996. *Between Facts and Norms: Contributions to a Discourse Theory of Law and Democracy* (tr. By W. Rehg). Cambridge, Massachusetts: MIT Press.

Harvey, David. 2009. *Cosmopolitanism and the Geographies of Freedom*. New York: Colombia University Press.

Hauser, Walter. & Wendy Singer. 1986. 'The Democratic Rite: Celebration and Participation in the Indian elections.' *Asian Survey* 26 (9): 941-58.

Hazarika, Sanjoy. 2011 [1994]. *Strangers of the Mist: Tales of War and Peace from India's Northeast.* New Delhi: Penguin.

Heierstad, Geir. & Arild E. Ruud. (eds). 2014. *India's democracies: Diversity, Co-Optation, Resistance.* New Delhi: Primus.

Heller, Patrick. 2009. 'Democratic Deepening in India and South Africa.' *Journal of Asian and African Studies* 44: 123-149.

Herzfeld, Michael. 2004. *Cultural Intimacy: Social Poetics in the Nation-State.* London: Routlege.

Herzog, Hannah. 1987. 'The Election Campaign as a Liminal Stage-Negotiations over Meanings.' *Sociological Review* 35: 559-74.

Hickel, Jason. 2015. *Democracy as Death: The Moral Order of Anti-Liberal Politics in South Africa.* Berkeley: University of California Press.

Horam, Mashangthei. 1988. *The Naga Insurgency: The Last Thirty Years.* Delhi: Cosmo Publications.

Horam, Mashangthei. 1992. *Naga Polity.* Delhi: D K Fine Art Press

Hoshi, K. 2014. 'Election malpractices in Nagaland.' *Eastern Mirror* 25-04-2014.

Huntington, Samuel. 2000. 'Foreword: Cultures Count'. In *Culture Matters: How Values Shape Human Progress*, edited by Lawrence. E. Harrison and Samuel. Huntington, 12-16. New Delhi: Gian Publishing House.

Hutton, John. H. 1921a. *The Angami Nagas: With Some Notes on Neighbouring Tribes.* London: Macmillan.

Hutton, John. H. 1921b. *The Sema Nagas.* London: Macmillan.

Hutton, John. H. 1928. 'The Significance of Head-Hunting in Assam.' *The Journal of the Royal Anthropological Institute of Great Britain and Ireland* 58: 339-408.

Hutton, John. H. 1965. 'The Mixed Culture of the Naga tribes.' *The Journal of the Royal Anthropological Institute of Great Britain and Ireland* 95 (1): 16-43.

Hutton, John Henry. 1987. *Chang Language: Grammar and Vocabulary of the Language of the Chang Naga.* New Delhi: Gian Publishing House.

Imkongmeren. 2015. 'Land Resources and Indigenous Identity in the North East India: Constitutional Provisions Towards Tribal Communities as Colonial Legacy.' In *Challenges of Land Development in Nagaland*, edited by Takatemjen, 50-71. Mokokchung: Clark Centre for Peace Research and Action.

Imsong, M. 2011. *God-Land-People: An Ethnic Naga Identity.* Dimapur: Heritage Publishing house.

Inden, Ronald. 1990. *Imagining India.* Oxford: Blackwell Publishers.

Indian Election Commission. 2013. 'Instructions on Election Expenditure Monitoring.' Url: http://eci.nic.in/eci_main/CurrentElections/ECI_Instructions/Election ExpeditureMonitoring05042013.pdf (accessed, 25-11-2014).

Iralu, K. 2000. *The Naga Saga: A Historical Account of the Sixty Two Years Indo-Naga War and the Story of Those Who Were Never Allowed to Tell it.* Kohima: K. Iralu.

Jacobs, Julian, Alan Macfarlane, Sarah Harrison and Anita Herle. 1990. *The Nagas: Hill Peoples in North-East India.* London: Thames and Hudson.

Jaffrelot, Christophe. 2002. *The Silent Revolution*. New York: Columbia University Press.
Jamir, Alemtemshi. 2002. 'Keynote Address.' In *Dimensions of Development in Nagaland*, edited by C. J. Thomas and G. Das, 1-8. New Delhi: Regency Publications.
Jamir, S.C. 2016. *A Naga's Quest for Fulfillment* Bhubaneswar: Apurba.
Jamir, T. 2015. 'Women, Land and Identity in Naga society: A Sociological Viewpoint.' In *Challenges of Land Development in Nagaland*, 106-115. Mokokchung: Clark centre for Peace Research and Action.
Jimomi, V.H. 2009. *Political Parties in Nagaland*. Kohima: Graphic Printers.
Johnstone, James. 1971. *My Experience in Manipur and Naga Hills*. New Delhi: Vivek Publishing House.
Joseph, Richard, A. 1987. *Democracy and prebendal politics in Nigeria: The Rise and Fall of the Second Republic*. Cambridge: Cambridge University Press.
Joshi, Vibha. 2012. *A Matter of Belief: Christian Conversion and Healing in North-East India*. Oxford: Berghahn Books.
Joshi, Vibha 2013. 'The Micropolitics of Borders: The Issue of Greater Nagaland (or Nagalim). In *Borderland Lives in Northern South Asia*, edited by David Gellner, 163-93. Durham, NC: Duke University Press.
Kaba. 2014. 'Ethnicity and Nationalism: The Emergence of Class Consciousness of Pan-Naga Ethnic Community and Nationality Question as an Ethnic Boundary Marker in North-East India.' *The International Journal of Humanities and Social Studies* 2 (3): 68-77).
Kangla Online. 03-04-2011. 'Dr Shurhozelie on NPF expansion, says ENPO demand weakens peace-process', URL; http://kanglaonline.com/2011/04/dr-shurhozelie-on-npf-expansion-says-enpo- demand-weakens-peace-process/ (accessed,07-04-2015).
Karlsson, Bengt.G. 2011. *Unruly Hills: A Political Ecology of India's Northeast*. New York: Berghahn Books.
Karlsson, Bengt G. 2003. 'Anthropology and the "Indigenous Slot": Claims to and Debates about Indigenous Peoples' Status in India.' *Critique of Anthropology* 23 (4): 403-23.
Kaviraj, Sudipta. 1984. 'On the Crisis of Political Institutions in India.' *Contributions to Indian Sociology* 18: 223-43.
Khiamnuingan, Longkoi, T. 'Inequality in Nagaland: A Case Study of 'Advanced' and 'Backward' Tribes.' *International Journal of Sustainable Development* 7 (2): 71-78.
Khilnani, Sunil. 1997. *The Idea of India*. London: Penguin Books.
Khilnani, Sunil. 2009. 'Arguing Democracy: Intellectuals and Politics in Modern India'. *CASA Working Paper Series* 9 (2): 1-34.

Kiewhuo, Keviletuo. 2002. 'Constructive Political Agreement and Development.' In *Dimensions of Development in Nagaland*, edited by C. Joshua Thomas and Gurudas Das, 59-65. New Delhi: Regency Publications.

Kikon, Dolly. 2002. 'Political Mobilization of Women in Nagaland: A sociological background'. In *Changing Women's Status in India: Focus on the* Northeast, edited by Walter Fernandes and Sanjay Barbora, 174-182. Guwahati: North-Eastern Social Research Centre.

Kikon, Dolly. 2005 . 'Engaging Naga Nationalism. Can Democracy Function in Militarised Societies?' *Economic and Political Weekly* XL (26): 2833-2837.

Kohli, Atul. 2001. *The Success of India's Democracy*. Cambridge: Cambridge University Press.

Konyak, Chingwang. 2012. *Why There is a Demand for a Separate Frontier State? Why has it become a Subject of Debate Today*. Distributed letter. Unpublished.

Kothari, Rajni. 2009. *The Writings of Rajni Kothari: Politics in India, Caste in Indian politics, Rethinking Democracy*. New Delhi: Oxford University Press.

Krishna, Sankaran. 1994. 'Cartographic Anxiety: Mapping the Body Politic in India.' *Alternatives* 19(4): 507-521.

Krocha, Vishü Ritu and Rekha Rose Dukru. 2013. *Chakhesang: A Window to Phek District*.

Kumar, B. B. 2005. *Naga Identity*. New Delhi: Concept Publishing.

Kuotsu, Renchumi K. & A. Wati Walling 2018. 'Democratic Values and Traditional Practices: Gendering Electoral Politics in Nagaland.' In *Democracy in Nagaland: Tribes, Traditions and* Tension, edited by Jelle J.P. Wouters and Zhoto Tunyi, 101-122. Kohima: Highlander Press.

Kuper, Adam. 2003. 'The Return of the Native.' *Current Anthropology* 44 (3): 389-402.

Leach, E.R. 1960. 'The Frontiers of "Burma."' *Comparative Studies in Society and History*, vol. 3 (1): 49-68.

Leach, Edmund. 1961. *Rethinking Anthropology*. London: Athlone Press.

Levi-Strauss, Claude. 1949. *The Elementary Structures of Kinship*. Boston: Beacon Press.

Levi-Strauss, Claude. 1961. *Tristes Tropiques*, translated by J. Rusell. New York: Criterion Books.

Levitsky, Steven & James Loxton. 2013. 'Populism and Competitive Authoritarianism in the Andes.' *Democratization* 20 (1): 107-136.

Liénard, Pierre. & Pascal Boyer. 2006. 'Whence Collective Rituals? A Cultural Selection Model of Ritualized Behavior.' *American Anthropologist* 108 (4): 814-27.

Lindgren, Björn. 2004. 'The Internal Dynamics of Ethnicity: Clan Names, Origins and Castes in Southern Zimbabwe.' *Journal of the International African Institute* 74 (2): 173-93.

Lisam, K.S. 2011. *Encyclopedia of Manipur, Vol. 2* New Delhi: Kalpaz Publications.

Longchar, Wati. 1996. 'Dancing with the Land: Significance of Land for Doing Tribal Theology.' *Indian Journal of Theology* 38 (3): 16-28.

Longkumer, Arkotong. 2010. *Reform, Identity and Narratives of Belonging: The Heraka Movement in Northeast India*. London: Continuum International Publishing Group.

Lukes, Stephan. 1975. 'Political Ritual and Social Integration.' *Sociology* 9: 289-308.

Lyons, Harriet D. 2007. 'Genital Cutting: The Past and Present of a Polythetic Category.' *Africa Today* 53 (4): 3-17.

Maitra, Kiranshankar. 2011. *Nagaland: The Land of Sunshine*. New Delhi: Anjali Publishers.

Malinowski, Branislaw. 1923. 'The Problem of Meaning in Primitive Languages'. In *The Meaning of Meaning: A Study of the Influence of Language Upon Thought and the Science of Symbolism*, edited by C. K. Ogden and I. A. Richards, 296-336. London: Kegan Paul.

Malkki, Liisa. 1992. 'National Geographic: The Rooting of Peoples and the Territorialisation of National Identity among Scholars and Refugees.' *Cultural Anthropology* 7 (1): 24-44.

Marak, Queenbala. 2015. 'A "Native" and an Anthropologist: Dilemmas and Ethics of Doing Fieldwork'. *Man in India* 95(1): 133-143.

Mauss, M. 1966. *The Gift: Forms and Functions of Exchange in Archaic Societies* (translated by I. Cunnison). London: Cohen and West

Mauss, Marcel. 1985 [1938]. 'A Category of the Human Mind: The Notion of the Person, The Notion of the Self.' In *The Category of the Person*, edited by Michael Carrithers, Steven Collins and Steven Lukes, 1-45. Cambridge: Cambridge University Press.

Maybury-Lewis, David. 1965. *The Savage and the Innocent*. London: Evans-Brothers limited.

McDuie-Ra, Duncan. 2009. 'The Predicament of Justice: 50 Years of Armed Forces Special Powers Act.' *Contemporary South Asia Journal* 17 (3): 271-82.

McLeod, James R. 1999. 'The Socio-Drama of Presidential Politics: Rhetoric, Ritual, and Power in the Era of Teledemocracy.' *American Anthropologist* 101 (2): 359-73.

Michelutti, Lucia. 2004. 'We (Yadav) are a caste of politicians: Caste and modern politics in a North Indian town.' *Contributions to Indian Sociology* 38: 43-71.

Michelutti, Lucia. 2007. 'The Vernacularisation of Democracy: Popular Politics and Political Participation in North India'. *Journal of the Royal Anthropological Institute*, New Series, 13: 639-656.

Michelutti, Lucia. 2008. *The Vernacularisation of Democracy: Politics, Caste and Religion in India*. London: Routledge.

Mills, James Philip. 1922. *The Lhota Nagas*. London: Macmillan

Mills, James Philip 1926. *The Ao Nagas*. London: Macmillan.

Mills, James Philip. 1935. 'The Effect of Ritual Upon Industries and Arts in the Naga Hills.' *Man* 35: 132–135.

Mishra, J. P. 2004. 'A.Z. Phizo: As I knew him. http://nagaland.faithweb.com/articles/phizo.html (accessed, 10 April 2015).

Misra, Sanghamitra. 2011. *Becoming a Borderland: The Politics of Space and Identity in Colonial Northeast India*. New Delhi: Routledge.

Misra, Udayon. 1978. 'The Naga National Question.' *Economic and Political Weekly* 13 (14): 618–624.

Misra, Udayon. 1987. 'Nagaland Elections.' *Economic and Political Weekly* 22(51): 2193–2195.

Misra, Udayon. 2000. *The Periphery Strikes Back: Challenges to the Nation-State in Assam and Nagaland*. Shimla: Indian Institute for Advanced Studies.

Moffatt-Mills, A. J. 1980 [1854]. *Report on Assam*. New Delhi: Gian Publications.

Morphy, Howard, & Morgan Perkins. 2006. 'The Anthropology of Art: A Reflection on its History and Contemporary Practice.' In *The Anthropology of Art: A Reader*, edited by Howard Morphy and Morgan Perkins, 1–32. Oxford: Blackwell Publishing.

Morung Express. 2013. 'CPO Statement on Clean Elections.' 19th January.

Morung Express. 2013. 'Inflow liquor restricted in Phek.' 13th February.

Morung Express. 2013. 'Office of the Diphupar Village Council: public information.' 18th February.

Morung Express. 2013. 'Khiamniungan people "deeply hurt" without a cabinet berth.' 7th March.

Morung Express. 2013. 'NPF plea for restraint and patience.' 8th March.

Morung Express. 2013. 'Resentment continues over cabinet choice, portfolio allocation.' 8th March.

Mukherjee, Sumit. 2013. 'Conceptualisation and Classification of Tribe by the Census of India.' *Journal of the Anthropological Survey of India* 62 (2): 805–20.

Murry, Khochamo, Chonzamo. 2007. *Nagaland legislative assembly and its speakers*. New Delhi: Mittal Publication.

Nader, Laura. 1990. *Harmony Ideology: Justice and Control in a Mountain Zapotec Town*. Stanford, CA: Stanford University Press.

Nag, Sajal. 2013. 'Expanding Imaginations: Theory and Praxis of Naga Nation Making in Post- Colonial India', *South Asian History and Culture* 30(2): 177–196.

Nagaland Baptist Church Council. 2012. *Clean election campaign. Engaging the powers: Elections – A spiritual issue for Christians*. Kohima: Nagaland Baptist Church Council.

Nagaland Post. 2010. 'Root out Tribalism: Imchen.' 16th February.

Nagaland Post. 2016. 'Patton asks NCS Officers to Rededicate Themselves.' 22nd April

Nagaland Pradesh Congress Committee, '*Bedrock of Naga Society*', URL: http://www.nenanews.com/ng10.htm (accessed,15-04-2014).

Nandy, Ashis. 2002. *Time Warps: The Insistent Politics of Silent and Evasive Pasts*. Oxford: Permanent Black.

Narahari, N.S. 2002. *Security Threats to North-East India: The Socio-ethnic Tensions*. New Delhi: Manas Publications.

Nash, Kate. 2004. *Contemporary Political Sociology: Globalisation, Politics, and Power*. Oxford: Wiley-Blackwell.

Nazaruk, Maja. 2011. 'Reflexivity in Anthropological Discourse Analysis.' *Anthropological Notebooks* 17(1): 73-83.

Needham, Rodney. 1971. 'Remarks on the Analysis of Kinship and Marriage.' In *Rethinking Kinship and Marriage*, edited by Rodney Needham, 8-13. London: Tavistock.

Needham, Rodney. 1975. 'Polythetic Classification: Convergence and Consequences.' *Man* (n.s.) 10(3): 349-69.

Needham, Rodney. 1978. *Symbolic Classification*. Santa Monica: Goodyear Publishing Company

Newmai News Network. 2012. 'Scarcity of Pigs Worry Tribal Politicians.' 8th September.

Neyazi, Taberez A., Akio Tanabe, & Shinya Ishizaka. (eds.). 2014. *Democratic Transformation and the Vernacular Public Arena in India*. London: Routledge.

Nibedon, Nirmal. 1978. *North-East India: the Ethnic Explosion*. New Delhi: Lancers Publishing. Nimmo, Dan. 1985. 'Elections as Ritual Drama.' *Society* 22 (4): 31-38.

Nugent, David. 2008. Democracy Otherwise: Struggles over Popular Rule in the Northern Peruvian Andes. In *Democracy: Anthropological Approaches*, edited by Julia Paley, 21-62. Santa Fe: School for Advanced Research Press.

Nugent, David. 2002. 'Alternative Democracies: The Evolution of the Public Sphere in 20th Century Peru.' *Political and Legal Anthropology Review* 25 (1): 151-63.

Nuh, V. K. 1986. *Nagaland Church and Politics*. Kohima: V. K. Nuh.

Nuh, V. K. 2002. *My Native Country: The Land of the Nagas*. Guwahati: Spectrum.

Nuh, V.K. 2002. *The Naga Chronicle*. New Delhi: Regency.

Ovung, Athungo. 2012. *Social Stratification in Naga Society*. Delhi: Mittal Publications.

Paley, Julia. 2002. 'Towards an Anthropology of Democracy.' *Annual Reviews of Anthropology* 31: 469-96.

Paley, Julia. 2004. Accountable Democracy: Citizens' Impact on Public Decision Making in Post- Dictatorship Chile. *American Ethnologist* 31(4): 497-513.

Pandey, Raghav S. 2010. *Communitisation: Third Way of Governance*. New Delhi: Concept Publishing House.

Panwar, Namrata. 2017. 'From Nationalism to Factionalism: Faultlines in the Naga insurgency.' *Small Wars and Insurgencies* 28(1): 233-258.

Pemberton, R.B. 1835. *Report on the Eastern Frontier of British India*. Calcutta: Government of India.

Phizo, A.Z. 1951. Plebiscite speech. Url: http://www.npmhr.org. (Accessed, 13-07-2013)

Phizo, A.Z. (1960) 'The Fate of the Naga People: An Appeal to the World' (London, 1960). Url: http://naganationalcouncil.org/the%20Fate%20of%20the%20Naga%20People.html.

Piliavsky, Anastasia. (ed). 2014. *Patronage as Politics*. Cambridge: Cambridge University Press.

Piliavsky, Anastasia. 2013. 'Where is the Public Sphere? Political Communications and the Morality of Disclosure in Rural Rajasthan.' *Cambridge Anthropology* 31 (2): 104–22.

Piliavsky, A. 2014a. 'Introduction.' In *Patronage as politics*, edited by Anastasia Piliavsky, 1–38. Cambridge: Cambridge University Press, 1–38.

Piliavsky, Anastasia. 2014a. 'Introduction.' In *Patronage as politics in South Asia*, edited by Anastasia Piliavsky, 1–35. Cambridge: Cambridge University Press.

Piliavsky, Anastasia. 2014b. 'India's Demotic Democracy and its "depravities" in the Ethnographic *Longue Durée*.' In *Politics as patronage*, edited by Anastasia Piliavsky, 154–175. Cambridge: Cambridge University Press.

Piliavsky, A. 2015. 'India's Human Democracy.' *Anthropology Today* 31 (4): 22–25.

Prasad, Madhav, M. 2010. 'Fun with Democracy: Election Coverage and the Elusive Subject of Indian politics'. In *Elections as Popular Culture in Asia*, edited by Chua Beng Huat, 139–154. London: Routledge.

Price, Pamela. 1989. 'Kingly Models in Indian Political Behaviour: Culture as a Medium of History.' *Asian Survey* 29(6): 559–572.

Rabinow, Paul. 1977. *Reflections on Fieldwork in Morocco*. Berkeley: University of California Press.

Radcliffe-Brown, Alfred Reginald. 1941. 'The Study of Kinship Systems.' *Journal of the Royal Anthropological Institute* 71(1/2): 1–18.

Rajkumar, Faiguni. 2010. *Rainbow People: Reinventing Northeast India*. New Delhi: Manas Publications.

Ramirez, Philippe. 2007. 'Politico-Ritual Variations on the Assamese Fringes: Do Social Systems Exist?' In *Social Dynamics in the Highlands of Southeast Asia: Reconsidering Political Systems of Highland Burma*, edited by François Robinne and Mandy Sadan, 91–108. Leiden: Brill.

Ramirez, Philippe. 2011. 'Belonging to the Borders: Uncertain Identities in Northeast India.' In *The Politics of Belonging in the Himalayas: Local Attachments and Boundary Dynamics*, edited by Joanna Pfaff-Czarnecka and Gerard Toffin, 77–97. New Delhi: SAGE Publications.

Ramirez, Philippe. 2014. *Peoples of the Margins: Across Ethnic Boundaries in North-East India*. Guwahati and Delhi: Spectrum Publications (in association with CNRS, France).

Ramunny, M. 1993. *The World of Nagas.* New Delhi: Northern Book Centre.
Robb, Peter. 1997. 'The Colonial State and Constructions of Indian Identity: An Example on the Northeast Frontier in the 1880s.' *Modern Asian Studies* 31 (2): 245-83.
Robinne, François. 2007. 'Transethnic Social Space of Clans and Lineages: A Discussion of Leach's Concept of Common Ritual Language.' In *Social Dynamics in the Highlands of Southeast Asia: Reconsidering Political Systems of Highland Burma*, edited by F François Robinne and Mandy Sadan, 283-98. Leiden: Brill.
Rooney, D. 1992. *Burma Victory: Imphal, Kohima, and the Chindits – March 1944 to May 1945.* Oxford: Osprey Publishing.
Rosaldo, Renato. 1986. 'From the Door of his Tent: the Fieldworker and the Inquisitor.' In *Writing Culture; The Poetics and Politics of Ethnography*, edited by J. Clifford and G.E. Marcus, 77-99. London: University of California Press.
Ross, Anamaria I. 2012. *The Anthropology of Alternative Medicine.* London: Bloomsbury.
Roy, Ashim. 2004. *The Konyak Nagas: A Socio-cultural profile.* Leicestershire: Upfront Publishing Ltd.
Roy-Burman, Bikram Keshari. 2003. 'Indigenous and Tribal Peoples in World System Perspective'. *Studies of Tribes and Tribals* 1 (1): 7-27.
Rustomji, Nari. 1971. *Enchanted frontiers: Sikkim, Bhutan, and India's Northeastern borderlands.* New Delhi: Oxford University Press.
Ruud, Arild E. 2003. *Poetics of Village Politics: The Making of West-Bengal's Rural Communism.* Delhi: Oxford University Press.
Saha, R.K. 2005 'Where civilizations meet to differ: The hill – Valley Ethnic Cleavage in Manipur.' In *Between Ethnography and Fiction: Verrier Elwin and the Tribal Question in India*, edited by Tanka B. Subba & S. Som, 227-241. New Delhi: Orient Longman.
Sahlins, Marshall. 1963. Poor Man, Rich Man, Big-Man, Chief: Political Types in Melanesia and Polynesia. *Comparative Studies in Society and History* 5 (3): 285-303.
Sahlins, Marshall. 1999. 'What is Anthropological Enlightenment? Some Lessons of the Twentieth Century'. *Annual Reviews* 28: i–xxiii.
Saler, Benson. 1999. *Conceptualizing Religion: Immanent Anthropologists, Transcendent Natives, and Unbounded Categories.* Oxford: Berghahn.
Samaddar, Ranabir. 2009. *Emergence of the Political Subject.* New Delhi: Sage.
Sashimatsung 2015. 'Workforce Participation Rate in Nagaland: A Female Situation.' *Journal of Research in Humanities and Social Science* 3 (5): 28-37.
Schlee, Günther. 1985. 'Interethnic Clan Identities among Cushitic-speaking Pastoralists.' *Journal of the International African Institute* 55 (1): 17-38.
Schulte-Nordholt, Henk. 2005. 'Decentralisation in Indonesia: Less State, More Democracy?' In *Politicizing Democracy: The New Local Politics of Democratisation*,

edited by John Harris, Kristian Stokke, and Olle Törnquis, 29-47. New York: Palgrave.

Scott, James, C. 1969. 'Corruption, Machine Politics, and Political Change.' *The American Political Science Review* 63 (4): 1142-1158.

Scott, James, C. 1976. *The Moral Economy of the Peasant: Rebellion and Subsistence in Southeast Asia.* New Haven: Yale University Press.

Scott, James, C. 1998. *Seeing Like a State: How Certain Schemes to Improve the Human Condition have Failed.* New Haven: Yale University Press.

Scott, James, C. 2009. *The Art of Not Being Governed: An Anarchist History of Upland Southeast Asia.* New Haven: Yale University Press.

Sema, Hokishe. 1986. *Emergence of Nagaland.* New Delhi: Vikas Publishing House.

Sema, Khekiye. 2016. *Encountering Life: Antics of a Government Servant.* Dimapur: Heritage Publishers.

Sen, Amartya. 1999. 'Democracy as a Universal Value.' *Journal of Democracy* 10(3): 3-17.

Sen, A. N. 1974. 'Operation Election.' *Economic and Political Weekly* 9(11): 424.

Seymour, Charles. 1915. *Electoral Reform in England and Wales: The Development and Operation of the Parliamentary Franchise: 1832-1885.* New Haven: Yale University Press.

Shah, Alpha. 2010. *In the Shadows of the State: Indigenous Politics, Environmentalism, and Insurgency in Jharkhand India.* Durham, NC: Duke University Press.

Sakhrie, A. 2006. *The Vision of T. Sakhrie for a Naga Nation.* Kohima; published by author.

Sharma, H.S. 2011. *Self-Determination Movement in Manipur.* Unpublished PhD thesis. Mumbai: Tata Institute of Social Sciences (Url: http://shodhganga.inflibnet.ac.in/bitstream/10603/2710/13/13_chapter%205.pdf (accessed,20-06-2015).

Shimray, Atai, S. 2005. *Let Freedom Ring: Story of Naga Nationalism.* New Delhi: Promilla.

Shimray, Gam, A. 2011. 'Foreword: Legal Pluralism in Southeast Asia – Insights from Nagaland.' In *Diverse Paths to Justice: Legal Pluralism and the Rights of Indigenous Peoples in Southeast Asia*, edited by Marcus Colchester and Sophie Chao, 8-16. Chiang Mai: S.T. Film & Plate.

Shimray, R.R. 1985. *Origin and Culture of Naga.* New Delhi: Somsok Publication.

Shimray, U. A. 2007. *Naga Population and Integration Movement.* New Delhi: Mittal Publication.

Shonreiphy, Lonvah. 2014. 'Territorial Dimension in the Naga Peace Process.' *International Research Journal of Social Sciences* 3 (5): 41-45.

Singh, Chandrika. 2004. *Naga Politics: A Critical Account.* New Delhi: Mittal Publications.

Singh, Chandrika. 2008. *The Naga Society.* New Delhi: Manas Publications.

Singh, R. P. 1986. 'Electoral politics in Nagaland.' In *Electoral politics in North East India*, edited by P. S. Dutta, 179-91. New Delhi: Omsons Publications.

Singha, Radhika 2015. 'The Short Career of the Indian Labour Corps in France, 1917-1919', *International Labor and Working-Class History*, 87: 27-62.

Slim, William 1956. *Defeat into Victory*. London: Cassell and Company.

Snellinger, Amanda. 2009. 'Democratic Form: Conceptions and Practices in the Making of "new Nepal."' *Sociological Bulletin* 58 (1): 43-70.

Solo, Thepfulhouvi. 2011. *From Violence to Peace and Prosperity: Nagaland*. Kohima: N. V. Press.

Southall, Aidan W. 1970. 'The Illusion of Tribe.' In *The Passing of Tribal Man in Africa*, edited by Peter. Gutkind, 28-50. Leiden: Brill.

Southwold, Martin. 1978. 'Buddhism and the Definition of Religion.' *Man* (n.s.) 13(3): 362-79.

Spencer, Jonathan. 1989. 'Anthropology as a Kind of Writing.' *Man (New Series)* 24(1): 145-164.

Spencer, Jonathan. 1997. 'Post-colonialism and the Political Imagination.' *The Journal of the Royal Anthropological Institute* 3 (1): 1-19.

Spencer, Jonathan. 2007. *Anthropology, Politics, and the State: Democracy and Violence in South Asia*. Cambridge: Cambridge University Press.

Srikanth, H and C.J. Thomas. 2005. 'Naga Resistance Movement and the Peace Process in Northeast India.' *Peace and Democracy in South Asia* 1(2): 57-87.

Srinivas, M.N. 1955. 'The Social Structure of Life in a Mysore Village.' In *Village India: Studies in the Little Community*, edited by McKim Marriot, 1-35. Chicago: Chicago University Press.

Srinivas, M.N. 1998. *Indian Society through Personal Writings*. Delhi: Oxford University Press.

Staveley, E.S. 1972. *Greek and Roman Voting and Elections*. London: Thames and Hudson.

Steyn, Peter 2002. *Zaphu Phizo: The Voice of the Nagas*. London: Kegan Paul.

Stracey, P.D. 1968. *Nagaland Nightmare*. Bombay: Allied Publishers.

Subba, Tanka B. 1988. 'Interethnic Relationship in Northeast India and the "Negative Solidarity Thesis".' *Human Science* 37: 153-63.

Subba, Tanka B. and Jelle J.P. Wouters. 2013. 'North-East India: Ethnography and the Politics of Identity.' In *The Modern Anthropology of India: Ethnography, Themes and Theory*, edited by P. Berger and F. Heidemann, 193-207. London: Routledge.

Swinson, A. 1956. *Kohima*. London: Arrow Books.

Swu, I 2015. 'Naga Psychology needs to be rebuild.' *Assam Tribune* 23-03-2015.

Takam, S. 1988. *Imlong Chang O.B.E. 1899-1987*. New Delhi: Print Connection.

Tambiah, Stanley, J. 1977. 'The Galactic Polity: The Structure of Traditional Kingdoms in Southeast Asia.' *Annals of the New York Academy of Sciences* 293: 69-97.

Tanabe, Akio. 2007. 'Towards Vernacular Democracy: Moral Society and Post-Postcolonial Transformation in rural Orissa, India.' *American Ethnologist* 34 (3): 558–574.

Tessler, Mark, and Eleanor Gao. 2009. Democracy and the Political Culture Orientations of Ordinary Citizens: A Typology for the Arab World and Beyond. *UNESCO*. Oxford: Blackwell publishing.

The Hindu. 2015. 'Women are Safest in Nagaland.' 22nd August.

The Telegraph. 2012. 'Wanted: A Chief Guest with a Fat Purse.' 30th January.

Thomas, John. 2016. *Evangelizing the Nation: Religions and the Formation of Naga Political Identity*. New Delhi: Routledge.

Thompson, E.P. 1971. 'The Moral Economy of the English Crowd in the eighteenth century.' *Past & Present* 50: 76–136.

Thong, Tezenlo 2016. *Colonization, Proselytization, and Identity: the Nagas and Westernization in Northeast India*. London: Palgrave.

Thong, Tezenlo. 2014. *Progress and its Impact on the Naga: A Clash of Worldviews*. New York: Ashgate.

Times of India. 2014. 'Nagaland Tops in Lok Sabha Voter Turnout.' 22nd May.

Tinyi, Venusa. 2017. 'The Headhunting Culture among the Nagas: Reinterpreting the self.' *The South Asianist* 5(1): 83–98.

Turner, Victor. 1969. *The Ritual Process: Structure and Anti-Structure*. Chicago: Aldine Publishers.

Vamuzo, Meneno. 2012. 'Narratives of Peace: Naga Women in the Self-Determination Struggle.' *Tensions Journal* 6: 1–23.

Van Maanen, John. 1988. *Tales of the Field: on Writing Ethnography*. Chicago: Chicago University Press.

Van Schendel, Willem. 2002. 'Geographies of Knowing, Geographies of Ignorance: Jumping Scale in Southeast Asia.' *Environment and Planning D: Society and Space* 20: 647–68.

Van Schendel, Willem. 2005. *The Bengal Borderland: Beyond State and Nation in South Asia*. London: Anthem Press.

Van Schendel, Willem. 2011. 'The Dangers of Belonging: Tribes, Indigenous Peoples and Homelands in South Asia.' In *The Politics of Belonging in India: Becoming Adivasi*, edited by Daniel, J. Rycroft and Sangeeta Dasgupta, 19–43. London: Routledge.

Van Schendel, Willem. 2013. 'Afterword: Making the Most of Sensitive Borders.' In *Borderland Lives in Northern South Asia*, edited by David Gellner, 266–271. Durham and London: Duke University Press.

Van Schendel, Willem 2016. 'A War Within a War: Mizo Rebels and the Bangladesh Liberation Struggle', *Modern Asian Studies* 50(1): 75–117.

Varah, Franky. 2013. 'Situating the Human's Relationship with Nature in the Tangkhul Naga's Lifeworld.' *Journal of Human Ecology* 41 (3): 247–254.

Vashum, Reisang. 2000. *Nagas' Right to Self-Determination: An Anthropological – Historical Perspective.* New Delhi: Mittal Publications.

Venuh, Neivetso. 2005. *British Colonization and Restructuring of Naga polity.* New Delhi: Mittal Publications.

Verma, A. 2005. *The Indian Police: A Critical Evaluation.* New Delhi: Regency Publications.

Vitso, Adino. 2003. *Customary Law and Women: The Chakhesang Nagas.* New Delhi: Regency Publications.

Wade, Robert. 1985. 'The Market for Public Office: Why the Indian state is Not Better at Development.' *World Development* 13 (4): 467–97.

Wang, Guohui. 2014. *Tamed Village 'Democracy': Elections, Governance and Clientelism in a Contemporary Chinese village.'* New York: Springer.

Weber, Max. 1978 [1922]. *Economy and Society: An Outline of Interpretive Sociology.* Berkeley: University of California Press.

Wettstein, Marion. 2012. 'Origin and Migration Myths in the Rhetoric of Naga Independence and Collective Identity.' In *Origins and Migrations in the Extended Eastern Himalayas,* edited by Tony Huber and Stuart Blackburn, 213–238. Leiden: Brill.

Wiredu, Kwasi. 1995. 'Democracy and Consensus in African Traditional Politics: A Plea for a Non-Party Polity.' *The Centennial Review* 39 (1): 53–63.

Witsoe, Jeffrey. 2009. 'Territorial Democracy: Caste, Dominance and Electoral Practice in Postcolonial India'. *POLAR* 32 (1): 64–83.

Witsoe, Jeffrey. 2011. 'Rethinking Postcolonial Democracy: An Examination of the Politics of Lower-Caste Empowerment in North India.' *American Ethnologist* 113 (4): 619–31.

Witsoe, Jeffrey. 2013. *Democracy Against Development: Lower-caste Politics and Political Modernity in Postcolonial India.* Chicago: Chicago University Press.

Woodthorpe, R.G. 1881. 'Notes on the Wild Tribes Inhabiting the So-Called Naga Hills on Our North-East Frontier of India.' In *Nagas in the Nineteenth Century,* edited by Verrier Elwin, 46–82. London: Oxford University Press.

Wouters, J.J.P. 2011. 'Keeping the Hill tribes at Bay: A Critique from India's Northeast of James C. Scott's Paradigm of State Evasion.' *European Bulletin of Himalayan Research* 39: 41–65.

Wouters, Jelle, J. P., and Tanka, B. Subba. 2013. 'The "Indian face," India's Northeast, and the "Idea of India."' *Asian Anthropology* 12(2): 126–40.

Wouters, Jelle, J.P. 2014. 'Performing Democracy in Nagaland: Past Polities and Present Politics.' *Economic and Political Weekly* 49 (16): 59–66.

Wouters, Jelle, J. P. 2015. 'Polythetic Democracy: Tribal elections, Bogus Votes, and the Political Imagination in the Naga uplands of Northeast India.' *Hau: Journal of Ethnographic Theory* 5 (2): 121–151.

Wouters, Jelle, J.P. 2015. 'Feasts of Merit, Election Feasts, or No Feasts? On the Politics of Wining and Dining in Nagaland, Northeast India.' *The South Asianist* 3 (2): 5-23.

Wouters, Jelle, J.P. 2016. 'Sovereignty, Integration or Bifurcation? Troubled Histories, Contentious Territories and the Political Horizons of the Long Lingering Naga Movement.' *Studies in History* 32(1): 97-116.

Wouters, Jelle, J. P. 2017a. 'Who Is a Naga village? The Naga Village Republic Through the Ages.' *The South Asianist* 5 (1): 99-120.

Wouters, Jelle, J. P. 2017b. 'The Making of Tribes: The Chang and Chakhesang Nagas in India's Northeast'. *Contributions to Indian Sociology* 51 (1): 79-104.

Xaxa, Virginius. 2005. 'Politics of Language, Religions and Identity: Tribes in India.' *Economic and Political Weekly*, 40(13): 1363-70.

Yadav, Yogendra. 2009. 'The Truth about Theories on Turnout.' *The Hindu*. 13th April.

Yapp, Malcolm E. 1983. 'Tribes and States in the Khyber, 1838-42.' In *The Conflict of Tribe and State in Iran and Afghanistan*, edited by R. Tapper, 150-87. New York: St. Martins.

Zhimomi, K.K. 2004. *Politics and Militancy in Nagaland*. New Delhi: Deep and Deep Publications.

Zou, David. & M. Satish Kumar 2011. 'Mapping a Colonial Borderland: Objectifying the Geo- Body of India's Northeast.' *The Journal of Asian Studies* 70 (1): 141-170.

INDEX

A
accounts x, xi, 11, 53, 72, 179, 202
Advisory Committee 111, 112
affective realities of clan 7
Ahom Buranjis 137
Allied Forces 105, 107
ancestors 50, 73
Angami Naga 11, 26, 31, 50, 53, 60, 62, 75, 76, 81, 85, 94, 95, 104, 108, 109, 110, 111, 112, 113, 114, 116, 118, 121, 126, 140, 141, 142, 145, 165, 181, 202
antagonism 53
anthropology ix, x, xi, 44, 48, 52, 61, 66, 81, 139, 190, 195, 198
Ao, Lanunungsang 22, 47, 59
Ao, Longri 114
Ao Naga 26, 69, 70, 71, 72, 73, 74, 81, 89, 90, 91, 108, 109, 110 111, 112, 113, 114, 118, 121, 122, 126, 140, 141, 142, 145, 217, 221, 222, 223, 226.
Ao, Temsula 176, 217, 218
arcadian space 6
Archer, Mildred 108, 109, 110, 113, 114, 115, 116, 117, 118, 119, 203
Archer, William 100, 109, 110, 116, 117, 118, 119
armed conflict 102, 103, 125, 183
Armed Forces 9, 85, 126, 127
Armed Forces Special Power Act 216
Article 371A 149, 150
Arunachal Pradesh xi, 36, 208
Assam xi, 21, 24, 29, 35, 38, 52, 53, 68, 75, 105, 107, 109, 110, 111, 112, 113, 114, 119, 121, 122, 123, 124, 126, 127, 128, 129, 138, 162, 169, 175, 183, 206, 208
attachments and loyalties 179, 185
Autoethnography 197
autonomy xii, 3, 4, 5, 17, 109, 111, 112, 113, 114, 118, 119, 121, 122, 128, 134, 143, 154, 178, 179

B
backward(ness) 145, 184
Badiou, Alan 45, 62, 180
Baruah, Sanjib 25, 29, 30, 138, 184
Béteille, André 134, 135, 179
Bharatiya Janata Party (BJP) 145
Bifurcation xii, 21, 34
Biolsi, Thomas 28, 30, 38
bogus or proxy votes xii, 42
Bordoloi, Gopinath 111, 122
Bose, Subhas 106, 109
British India 23, 29, 66, 104, 137
Burma 21, 22, 24, 27, 29, 35, 105, 106, 107, 111, 127, 136
Burma/Myanmar 75, 78, 208
Butler, John 3, 12, 47, 53, 67, 80, 95, 116, 181

C
campaign 4, 42, 93, 169, 170, 176, 177, 194
caste 5, 31, 46, 57, 67, 134, 135, 136, 138, 139
ceasefire xi, 26, 47, 102, 162, 183
Chakhesang Baptist Church Council

(CBCC) 171, 172
Chakhesang Naga tribe x, xiii, 1, 2, 5, 11, 27, 43, 46, 47, 62, 65, 75, 76, 77, 78, 86, 94, 95, 151, 159, 162, 163, 165, 171, 176, 181, 186, 198, 199, 200, 205
Chakhesang Public Organisation (CPO) 2
Chang, Imlong 142
Chang Naga tribe x, 34, 35, 37, 68, 69, 70, 71, 72, 73, 74, 78, 80, 90, 91, 113, 119, 140, 141, 142, 198, 200
Chang Tribal Committee/Council 79, 80, 142
Chasie, Charles 12, 15, 22, 33, 34, 104, 150, 162
Chief Guest 191
chief minister 23, 59, 84, 111, 122, 128, 145, 182, 191, 192
China 21, 78, 136, 137, 179
Christian/Christianity 46, 53, 57, 69, 103, 110, 115, 116, 125, 161, 166, 204, 207, 208
church 2, 8, 49, 53, 56, 80, 142, 144, 159, 161, 167, 171, 172, 194, 199, 204, 207, 208
clan rivalries 62, 85
clan(s) 7, 9, 12, 14, 25, 37, 46, 47, 49, 50, 51, 53, 54, 57, 58, 60, 61, 62, 63, 69, 70, 72, 73, 74, 75, 78, 79, 81, 85, 92, 93, 94, 95, 96, 97, 103, 104, 115, 122, 125, 145, 185, 187
clan-wise selection system 7
class 5, 37, 44, 184, 203
Clean Election Campaign 160
collective vote 8, 87, 89, 90, 91, 92, 186
colonial/colonialism ix, x, xi, 2, 10, 21, 22, 23, 24, 26, 27, 28, 29, 30, 31, 32, 35, 37, 38, 47, 50, 51, 52, 60, 67, 75, 76, 77, 80, 81, 87, 89, 92, 98, 102, 103, 104, 105, 108, 115, 118, 125, 136, 137, 138, 139, 140, 141, 142, 143, 144, 146, 155, 156, 157, 166, 181, 183, 193, 197, 198, 202, 203, 204, 208
colonial monographs, of Naga 141
commensality 2, 178
Commission 8, 23, 28, 55, 56, 104, 160, 161, 169, 172, 185

communal harmony xii, 2, 16
communitarian 2, 3, 5, 6, 12, 18, 28, 59, 61, 151, 182, 185, 187, 194
communities x, xi, 3, 10, 30, 53, 65, 68, 76, 80, 85, 96, 97, 134, 135, 136, 137, 138, 149, 153, 160, 198
Communitisation 10, 54
competitive 3, 4, 5, 6, 9, 16, 17, 136, 163, 180, 187, 195
complimentary co-existence 2
Congress Party 34, 145, 163
consensus-building xii, 2, 6, 7, 10, 12, 13, 14, 17
consensus-candidate 8, 9, 58, 60, 61
consensus-making 6, 13, 14, 15, 16, 46, 53, 59, 60, 61
constituency 6, 8, 42, 47, 54, 55, 56, 60, 86, 88, 97, 163, 175, 185, 186, 189, 190, 191, 192
Constitution 8, 113, 115, 119, 149, 150
corruption 10, 85, 146, 177, 178, 184, 188, 190, 191, 193, 194
counter-insurgency 183
culturalist critique xii, 6, 15, 16, 17, 59, 98
culturally modulated 6
culturally modulated democracy 6
Culture 191
customary bodies 154
customary law/procedures xiii, 13, 16, 17, 55, 59, 71, 87, 89, 93, 149, 150, 151, 152, 153, 154, 155, 156, 157, 160

D

Daulatram, Jairamdas 121, 122
debating society 11, 12, 60, 95
decidedly 3
decidedly democratic 3
deepening 172
deep-seated 62
deep-seated clan 62
Delhi/New Delhi xi, xiii, 47, 49, 109, 111, 113, 114, 115, 123, 127, 128, 150, 183, 205
deliberation 7, 8, 14, 60, 94, 98, 135
democracy 2, 3, 4, 5, 6, 12, 13, 15, 16, 17, 18, 41, 42, 43, 44, 45, 46, 47, 48, 51,

55, 56, 60, 61, 62, 84, 85, 86, 95, 96, 97, 98, 133, 134, 135, 136, 144, 145, 146, 162, 170, 172, 173, 176, 177, 179, 180, 181, 183, 184, 188, 194
democratic xii, 3, 4, 5, 6, 8, 13, 17, 18, 43, 44, 45, 46, 47, 48, 49, 51, 52, 54, 55, 56, 57, 61, 62, 84, 85, 86, 91, 93, 94, 95, 97, 98, 133, 134, 135, 136, 144, 145, 161, 162, 175, 176, 177, 178, 179, 180, 183, 185, 186, 187, 189, 191, 192, 193, 194, 195
democratic communities 3
democratic heritage 5
democratic ideals xii, 17, 98
democratic politics 8, 45, 46, 49, 62, 91, 97, 133, 134, 135, 145, 161, 177, 183, 193
destruction 7, 102, 107
De Tocqueville, Alexis 134, 178
development 7, 15, 34, 37, 38, 66, 77, 131, 142, 143, 144, 150, 152, 154, 175, 186, 187, 189, 192, 201
Dimapur 96, 97, 143, 175, 207
disputes 11, 37, 49, 50, 51, 60, 95, 155
District Commissioner 56, 57, 67, 107, 111, 125, 202, 203
divides xii, 6, 35, 73
Dobashi 142, 202

E

Eastern Naga/Nagaland x, 22, 35, 36
Eastern Naga People's Organisation (ENPO) x, 23, 34, 36, 37, 206
Eastern Naga Revolutionary Council(ENRC) x
East Pakistan 21, 126
economy 51, 161, 166, 167, 170, 172, 183, 186
election-as-ritual approach 48
Election Campaign 160
Election Commission 8, 55, 56, 160, 161, 169, 172, 185
election feasts xiii, 159, 160, 161, 164, 167, 168, 169, 170, 171, 172, 173, 185
election(s) xiii, 1, 2, 4, 6, 7, 8, 9, 15, 16, 42, 48, 49, 54, 55, 58, 59, 60, 63, 83, 86, 87, 89, 91, 92, 93, 97, 121, 122, 123, 159, 160, 161, 163, 164, 167, 168, 169, 170, 171, 172, 173, 176, 185, 188, 189, 190, 194
electoral effervescence 5, 44, 49, 51
electoral politics 2, 3, 6, 50, 51, 71, 84, 85, 86, 88, 90, 92, 93, 94, 96, 135, 163, 169, 173, 176, 184, 186, 189
Elwin, Verrier 12, 31, 36, 75, 76, 107, 108, 140, 149, 153, 207
emancipatory performance 4
employment 37, 77, 145, 177, 184, 185, 186, 189, 193
Escape votes 56
ethnic 25, 30, 57, 65, 66, 68, 72, 81, 152, 177
ethnic affinities 30
ethnic boundaries 72
ethnic groups 57, 65, 81
ethnic homelands 30
ethnic identity 72, 152
ethnicity 180
ethnic labels 68
ethnic politics 25
ethno-genetic 140
ethnographic ix, x, xi, 6, 26, 43, 45, 46, 48, 49, 52, 61, 73, 80, 83, 138, 140, 161, 162, 163, 172, 175, 179, 197, 198, 199, 202, 208, 209
ethnographic accounts x, 202
ethnographic field xi, 198
ethnographic longue durée 6, 45, 46, 48, 163, 172
ethnography ix, x, 5, 51, 57, 65, 86, 162, 175, 177, 178, 195, 197, 198, 208
excluded 2, 154
exogamy 72

F

factional feuds 22
faction/factionalism/factional 22, 201
feast-giver 161, 164, 165, 166, 167, 169, 170, 172, 181, 182, 201
Feast of Merit (zhotho müza in Phugwumi) 161, 164, 165, 166, 167, 169, 171, 181, 192
Feasts 159, 165, 166, 181

Federal Government of Nagaland (FGN) 126, 128, 129, 130, 131
feuds xi, 22, 24, 79, 116, 145
fields 11, 12, 47, 49, 70, 126, 142, 154, 163, 170, 199, 201
fieldwork x, xi, xii, 37, 50, 86, 146, 176, 197, 198, 199, 204, 206, 209
folktales 73, 137
formal x, 2, 3, 12, 45, 69, 133, 134, 185, 187
formal democracy 2
Frontier Nagaland 23, 34, 35, 37
Fürer-Haimendorf, Christoph von 11, 50, 51, 53, 68, 74, 85, 87, 107, 164, 165, 181, 195

G

Geertz, Clifford x, 45, 197, 198
Gellner, David 6, 30, 45, 127, 142, 179, 180
Gellner, Ernest 25
gender 5, 150, 152, 153
Genealogies xiii, 133
generosity 11, 164, 167, 177, 181, 182, 185, 186, 187, 189, 190, 194, 195, 201
gifts 186, 189
Global democratic theories 43
good governance 146, 188, 191
governance 10, 11, 37, 45, 54, 59, 66, 133, 134, 137, 143, 144, 146, 152, 177, 178, 179, 180, 181, 182, 184, 185, 188, 189, 190, 191, 195
government xi, 3, 4, 5, 6, 9, 10, 13, 14, 15, 16, 34, 49, 54, 55, 56, 59, 68, 77, 81, 104, 107, 110, 111, 112, 115, 118, 120, 122, 123, 124, 126, 128, 140, 142, 143, 144, 145, 146, 150, 152, 153, 155, 156, 163, 167, 170, 175, 177, 183, 184, 185, 186, 187, 189, 192, 193, 197, 207
guerrilla 26, 124, 125, 126, 128, 129, 204

H

headhunting 53, 116, 127, 142, 145
heritage 5
historical experiences ix, xi, 109, 198, 204
historical intimacy 25
homegrown democratic theory 61
home votes 58
Horam, Mashangthei 10, 11, 13, 22, 25, 33, 52, 53, 54, 105, 121, 131, 145, 146, 203
Houngang clan 69, 74
household 42, 43, 61, 85, 86, 94, 95, 96, 168, 186, 187, 188
house-tax 118, 119, 155, 202
Hutton, J.H. 3, 11, 12, 24, 29, 35, 52, 53, 60, 62, 63, 67, 70, 71, 73, 75, 76, 78, 79, 81, 85, 87, 88, 89, 90, 95, 115, 137, 138, 139, 140, 141, 152, 156, 181, 182, 202
Hydari Agreement 112, 113, 115, 117, 118, 119
Hydari, Akbar 112, 117, 118, 119, 120, 121

I

ideal(s) 2, 5, 17, 55, 86, 93, 95, 97, 98, 135, 207
identity ix, 24, 25, 26, 46, 54, 65, 66, 68, 69, 71, 72, 73, 76, 78, 103, 104, 140, 144, 152, 180, 200, 208
ideology 6, 12, 15, 25, 45, 97, 134, 145, 146, 173, 176, 179, 181, 186, 187, 191
idiom 47, 48, 51, 66, 80, 81, 137, 163, 164, 173
Imkongliba 128, 130
Imphal 32, 105, 123
Imti, Aliba 109, 112, 113, 118, 119
Indian x, xi, xiii, 5, 13, 14, 22, 25, 27, 28, 29, 37, 45, 46, 47, 49, 95, 97, 98, 102, 105, 106, 109, 110, 111, 112, 113, 114, 115, 116, 119, 120, 121, 122, 124, 125, 126, 127, 128, 129, 130, 131, 133, 134, 135, 138, 139, 143, 149, 151, 155, 160, 162, 173, 177, 183, 184, 198, 201, 203, 204
Indian Army 124, 125, 126, 129, 204
Indian democracy 5, 45, 46, 47, 133, 135, 183
Indian elections imposed on Naga soil 47, 162
Indian National Army (INA) 105, 106, 109
indigenous 27, 28, 29, 30, 68, 98, 107, 137
individual autonomy xii, 3, 4, 5, 17, 134, 179
individualism 7, 9, 61, 195

individual voting 4, 6, 94
Indo-Burma border(land) 22
Indo-Naga ceasefire xi, 26, 102
Indo-Naga conflict ix, 22, 25, 38, 102, 131, 154, 201, 203, 205
inflated electoral list 54, 55
insurgency 162, 177, 183, 184
Integration xii, 21, 30
inter-clan tensions 122
Interim Body 129, 130
intra 7, 25, 116, 118, 136, 145

J
Jamir, S.C. 23, 24, 25, 128, 130, 152, 184
Japanese Army 105, 106

K
Kangshou clan 69, 74
Kevichusa 110, 112, 116, 120, 128, 129, 131
Kezo clan 47
khel 53, 69, 78, 93, 103, 115, 116, 125, 188
Khiamniungan Naga tribe 34, 74, 96, 192
Khilnani, Sunil 17, 97, 134, 172
Khonoma 112, 113, 114, 115, 116, 117, 118, 120, 122, 123, 124, 125, 127, 129, 202
Kikon, Dolly 23, 93, 154
Kinship ix, 197
Kiphire 192
kitchen politics 180
Kohima 76, 77, 102, 104, 105, 107, 108, 109, 110, 111, 112, 113, 114, 116, 119, 120, 123, 124, 127, 130, 143, 162, 187, 193, 203, 208
Konyak, Chingwang 35, 36
Konyak Naga tribe 34, 38, 71, 72, 73, 74, 78, 79, 85, 86, 87, 88, 89, 141, 181, 182, 203
Kuki tribe 29, 97

L
Land Tax 149
Leach, Edmund 27, 44
liberal democracy xii, 3, 5, 16, 43, 45, 177, 194
lived experiences x, xi, 7

Lomou clan 69, 74
Longkumer, Arkotong xiii, 9, 25
Longtrok 69
longue durée 6, 45, 46, 48, 161, 163, 172
Lotha tribe 26, 73, 81, 92, 93, 94, 109, 110, 140, 142

M
Mahatma Gandhi 22, 116
manifesto 13
Manipur xi, 29, 30, 31, 32, 33, 34, 123, 126, 168
Manipur Nagas 31, 33
Mayangnokcha 109, 111, 112, 113, 114, 118, 119
Medhi, Bishnuram 122
Michelutti, Lucia 5, 45, 46, 52, 57, 133, 135, 178, 179
Mills, J.P. 3, 10, 50, 51, 52, 53, 69, 70, 71, 73, 74, 79, 80, 81, 85, 89, 90, 92, 108, 140, 141, 156, 166, 181, 202
MLA Handbook xiii, 175
Mokokchung 108, 109, 110, 113, 114, 118, 121, 126, 129, 203
moral commensality 178
moral destruction 7
moral economy 161, 166, 167, 170, 172
moral idiom 163
moral logic 161, 177
moral/morality xii, 2, 3, 6, 7, 10, 11, 12, 14, 16, 17, 18, 44, 56, 155, 156, 161, 163, 164, 166, 167, 169, 170, 172, 173, 177, 178, 179, 181, 182, 185, 191, 193, 194, 195, 205
moral obligation 169
moral sense 17
moral society 2, 3, 10, 12, 16, 18, 181, 185
moral values 155, 173
moral vision xii, 14
Myanmar x, xi, 75, 78, 208

N
Naga ix, x, xi, xii, xiii, 1, 2, 3, 6, 8, 9, 10, 11, 12, 13, 14, 15, 16, 18, 21, 22, 23, 24, 25, 26, 27, 28, 29, 30, 31, 32, 33, 34, 35, 36, 37, 38, 41, 43, 46, 47, 50, 51,

52, 53, 54, 57, 59, 60, 61, 62, 67, 68, 69, 70, 71, 73, 74, 75, 76, 78, 80, 81, 83, 84, 85, 86, 87, 88, 89, 90, 91, 92, 94, 95, 96, 97, 98, 101, 102, 103, 104, 105, 106, 107, 108, 109, 110, 111, 112, 113, 114, 115, 116, 117, 118, 119, 120, 121, 122, 123, 124, 125, 126, 127, 128, 129, 130, 131, 136, 137, 138, 139, 140, 141, 142, 143, 144, 145, 146, 149, 150, 151, 152, 153, 154, 155, 156, 157, 159, 161, 162, 163, 164, 165, 166, 167, 168, 172, 173, 176, 177, 178, 180, 181, 182, 183, 184, 185, 188, 189, 190, 192, 193, 194, 195, 198, 199, 200, 201, 202, 203, 204, 205, 206, 207, 208, 209
Naga Army 127, 130, 204
Naga club 23
Naga democracy 3, 18
Naga Hills District x, 2, 31, 35, 36, 106, 107, 108, 113, 126, 127, 128, 138, 164
Naga Hills District Tribal Council (NHDTC) 107
Naga Hoho 33
Naga independence 3, 24, 47, 83, 106, 108, 109, 110, 113, 114, 115, 116, 119, 120, 124, 125, 128, 143, 162, 184, 204, 205, 206, 208
Naga Labour Corps 104
Nagaland ix, x, xi, xii, xiii, 1, 2, 3, 7, 9, 10, 13, 14, 15, 16, 23, 24, 27, 29, 30, 32, 33, 34, 35, 36, 37, 41, 42, 43, 46, 47, 48, 49, 52, 54, 56, 58, 59, 65, 66, 68, 71, 75, 76, 83, 84, 85, 86, 87, 96, 97, 102, 104, 106, 111, 120, 122, 126, 128, 129, 130, 131, 133, 136, 140, 143, 144, 145, 146, 149, 150, 151, 152, 153, 154, 156, 159, 160, 161, 162, 163, 164, 167, 170, 171, 172, 173, 175, 176, 177, 180, 182, 183, 184, 185, 186, 189, 190, 191, 192, 193, 194, 195, 200, 201, 204, 208
Nagaland Baptist Church Council (NBCC) 2, 56, 159, 160, 161, 169, 171, 172, 194
Nagaland state x, xi, xii, 2, 23, 34, 47, 86, 97, 102, 129, 136, 149, 177, 180, 182, 183, 184, 186, 194
Nagaland Village Council Act 54

Nagalim 22, 47, 162, 183, 205
Naga National Council (NNC) 2, 3, 13, 14, 22, 26, 28, 33, 34, 38, 47, 59, 83, 102, 104, 105, 107, 108, 109, 110, 111, 112, 113, 114, 116, 117, 118, 119, 120, 121, 122, 123, 124, 125, 126, 127, 128, 129, 130, 131, 151, 162, 182, 183, 204, 206
Naga Nationalism 103
Naga Nationalist Organisation (NNO) 14
Naga People's Convention (NPC) 14, 36, 127, 128, 129
Naga People's Front (NPF) 6, 33, 34, 87, 88, 93, 95, 96, 97, 163, 188, 192
Naga Raj 109, 110, 115
Naga Students' Federation (NSF) 24
Nandy, Ashis 43, 62, 139
nationalism 23, 24, 25, 38, 104, 151, 180
National Movement 143
National Socialist Council of Nagalim (Isak-Muivah)(NSCN-IM) xi, 29, 30, 47, 206
National Socialist Council of Nagalim (Khaplang)(NSCN-K) 33, 34
Needham, Rodney 44, 61, 62, 197
Nehru, Jawaharlal 22, 110, 111, 114, 116, 119, 123, 124, 126, 127, 128, 129, 149, 162, 203
Noksen x, xi, xiii, 68, 69, 70, 71, 72, 74, 80, 198, 204, 205
Normative theory 3, 17, 37, 43, 46, 59, 61, 135, 161, 176, 179, 182, 191, 195
North-Eastern Frontier Agency 36, 128, 149
North-Eastern Frontier Agency (NEFA) 36, 128, 149
Nuh, V.K. 2, 14, 16, 22, 28, 52, 59, 112, 115, 121, 123, 137, 153

O

Oungh clan 69, 72, 74, 78, 79
Oungh Clan 69, 72, 74, 78, 79
ownership 28, 136, 149, 151, 152, 186

P

Paley, Julia 43, 44, 61
Pandey, R.S. 10, 54
party-based xii, 5, 17

patronage 58, 108, 164, 177
Pawsey, Charles 107, 111, 115, 116, 119, 120, 126, 202, 203
People's Independence League (PIL) 112, 115, 116, 120, 122
Phizo, A.Z. 3, 13, 14, 21, 22, 25, 26, 27, 28, 35, 36, 38, 47, 59, 83, 84, 104, 105, 106, 111, 112, 116, 119, 120, 121, 122, 123, 124, 125, 126, 127, 128, 129, 130, 151, 152, 153, 162, 182, 206
Phom Naga tribe 34, 71, 73, 80, 130, 141
Phugwumi x, xi, xiii, 1, 2, 3, 6, 7, 8, 9, 10, 11, 12, 13, 16, 17, 27, 41, 42, 43, 45, 46, 47, 48, 49, 50, 51, 52, 53, 54, 55, 56, 57, 58, 59, 60, 61, 62, 63, 76, 77, 159, 160, 161, 163, 165, 166, 167, 168, 169, 170, 171, 172, 173, 176, 178, 180, 181, 185, 186, 187, 188, 189, 190, 191, 194, 198, 199, 201, 205
Piliavsky, Anastasia 8, 44, 46, 133, 134, 160, 163, 164, 173, 177, 178, 179, 190
Plebiscite 27
Pochury Naga tribe 77, 95
political imagination xiii, 30, 45, 62
political sociality 3, 10, 17, 25, 178
political subjectivity 26
politician(s) xiii, 8, 35, 49, 50, 54, 55, 56, 88, 93, 167, 168, 169, 170, 171, 172, 173, 175, 176, 177, 178, 179, 184, 186, 187, 188, 189, 190, 191, 192, 193, 195
politics ix, 2, 3, 5, 6, 8, 9, 10, 12, 13, 15, 21, 25, 26, 33, 43, 45, 46, 49, 50, 51, 52, 57, 58, 61, 62, 71, 83, 84, 85, 86, 88, 90, 91, 92, 93, 94, 96, 97, 113, 116, 133, 134, 135, 137, 143, 145, 154, 161, 163, 164, 169, 173, 176, 177, 178, 179, 180, 183, 184, 185, 186, 189, 190, 191, 192, 193, 194, 195
Polling Day 41, 42, 43, 46, 49, 54, 63, 159, 161, 168, 170, 171, 188
polythetic xii, 44, 61, 62, 178
Polythetic Democracy 41
portfolio 175, 188, 192
postcolonial 2, 10, 16, 44, 50, 134, 136, 137, 138, 139, 140, 141, 143
procedural democracy 43, 48, 51, 55, 162

Puro clan xiii, 47

R

raids 25, 35, 52, 53, 70, 115, 116, 124, 137
Ramirez, Philippe xiii, 65, 68, 72, 75, 81, 139
rebels 126, 127, 128, 129
reconciliation xii, 156
Rengma Naga tribe 76, 81, 110, 113
representative 2, 4, 14, 114, 129, 144, 175, 179
representative democracy 2, 179
reservation for women / women reservation xiii, 149, 150, 155
reservation system 143, 150
ritual 5, 11, 16, 32, 44, 48, 51, 61, 71, 73, 74, 160, 164, 180, 182, 186
rivalling 7, 8, 143, 159, 169
rivalries 7, 13, 22, 46, 49, 50, 53, 58, 62, 85, 116, 138, 162, 169
Rustomji, Nari 120, 203

S

Sakhrie, T. 110, 112, 122, 123, 124, 125, 127, 129
Samaddar, Ranabir 28, 29, 30
Sangtam tribes 34, 72, 76, 77, 79, 80, 113, 119
Scott, James 27, 77, 80, 140, 177
secret ballot 4
self-determination 26, 28
Sema/Sumi Naga tribe 3, 26, 73, 76, 81, 86, 87, 88, 89, 113, 121, 126, 140, 141, 142, 181
Sema, Hokishe 14, 15, 36, 59, 123, 167, 182
Sen, Amartya 4
Shah, Alpa 6, 98, 185
Shillong 108, 109, 112, 113, 119, 120, 121
Simon Commission 23, 28, 104
Sixth Schedule 113, 119, 123
socialism 28, 151, 166
social landscape 49, 65, 81, 185
society against voting xii, 6, 16, 18
South Asia ix, xiii, 26, 177, 179
sovereignty 23, 26, 27, 28, 29, 30, 32, 34, 37, 38, 43, 102, 122, 151

special federal relationship 29
specifics ix, 194
Spencer, Jonathan 45, 51, 195, 197
Srinivas, M.N. xii, 46, 198
State Assembly 83, 86, 87, 97
statehood 2, 8, 14, 34, 37, 71, 84, 87, 129, 130, 131, 136, 139, 143, 144, 145, 152, 154, 157, 162, 177, 180, 183, 184, 185, 189, 192, 194, 195
Subba, Tanka xiii, 49, 54, 76, 81, 140

T

talk 6, 9, 16, 68, 116, 117, 119, 203, 185
Tangkhul Naga tribe 31, 33, 126
tax(es)/taxation xiii, 149
territory/territoriality 21, 22, 28, 29, 32, 38, 50, 67, 68, 69, 136, 182
Thira clan 47
time-immemorial 24, 28, 81, 137, 151, 155
tradition/traditional 71, 83, 127, 155, 162
tribal council(s) 107, 192
Tribal/tribalism xii, xiii, 14, 41, 107, 133, 142, 192
tribes xiii, 8, 10, 14, 17, 24, 25, 27, 29, 31, 32, 33, 34, 35, 36, 37, 38, 66, 67, 68, 71, 72, 73, 74, 75, 77, 79, 81, 84, 86, 87, 89, 92, 94, 96, 97, 104, 108, 110, 111, 117, 119, 121, 127, 135, 136, 137, 138, 139, 140, 141, 142, 143, 144, 145, 146, 156, 161, 162, 163, 181, 185
Tuensang 14, 22, 36, 68, 70, 71, 78, 79, 102, 124, 127, 128, 140
Tunyi clan xiii, 47

U

underground xii, 22, 24, 47, 103, 125, 128, 129, 130
Ungma Convention 128
United Nations 115, 201, 205, 206

V

Vero clan 47
Village Chairperson 47
village council 13, 88, 89, 90, 93, 94
Village Development Board (VDB) 7

village electoral list 46, 54
village republic 6, 10, 53, 56, 57, 61, 137
violence 23, 25, 37, 57, 85, 124, 125, 126, 127, 128, 150, 151, 154, 171, 204
voter turnout 97
voting xii, 2, 3, 4, 5, 6, 7, 8, 9, 10, 13, 14, 16, 17, 18, 41, 42, 43, 48, 49, 50, 54, 55, 59, 60, 61, 84, 86, 89, 91, 92, 94, 96, 134, 178, 184, 189, 190
voting rights xii, 3, 5, 9, 10, 17
voting slips 2, 17, 41

W

Witsoe, Jeffrey 5, 44, 45, 46, 62, 134, 144, 177, 189
Wokha 110, 111
World War(s) 104, 105, 107, 109

Y

Yimchunger Naga tribe 34
Yhobu 47, 181

www.ingramcontent.com/pod-product-compliance
Lightning Source LLC
Chambersburg PA
CBHW051612030426
42334CB00035B/3497